The Compleat Astrologer's
Love Signs

The Compleat Astrologer's

Love Signs

Derek & Julia Parker

Grosset & Dunlap Publishers New York

The Compleat Astrologer's Love Signs
was edited and designed by Mitchell Beazley Publishers Limited,
14-15 Manette Street, London W1V 5LB

Editor: Glorya Hale
Assistant editor: Marsha Lloyd
Designer: Gail Howell-Jones

Published in the United States in 1974 and simultaneously in Canada
by Grosset & Dunlap, 51 Madison Avenue, New York, N.Y.10010
ISBN: 0-448-11798-3
Library of Congress Catalog Card Number: 74-2738
Printed in the United States of America

Contents

Introduction

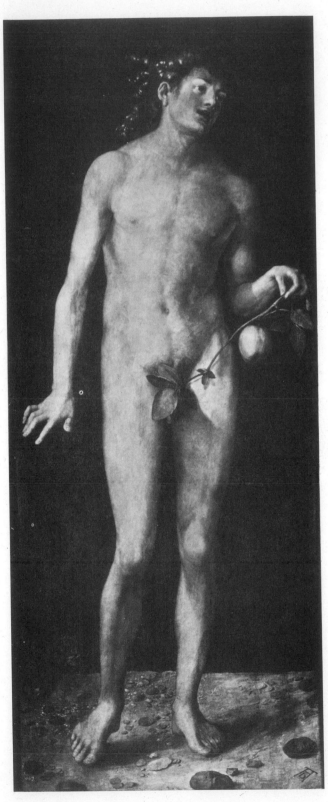

A person with only a vague general knowledge of astrology will often say to an astrologer, "Of course, I'm Pisces, so I must not date an Aquarius." To such a statement the simple answer is, "Nonsense!" No reputable astrologer would ever tell anyone not to date, much less not to marry, on the basis of Sun signs alone.

Everyone has all the Zodiac signs and all the planets working to affect their personality, their actions and reactions. So if an astrologer is asked whether two people are really suited to each other, he will calculate the positions of all the planets at the time when each of them was born, and draw up their birth charts, which will be carefully compared. It is true, of course, that there are signs of the Zodiac whose characteristics are so opposed that a partnership between them might seem to be asking for trouble. Yet such relationships are often highly successful and the full birth charts will almost always show mitigating factors.

This book, the only one of its kind, takes readers further than the Sun sign. At the back, diagrams and tables provide additional information which would normally have to be specially calculated. Using them, you can discover your rising sign (the sign which was rising over the eastern horizon at the moment you were born), which is as important as your Sun sign. You can also discover what sign Venus, Mars, Uranus and Neptune were in when you were born. These, too, have an effect on your personality and on your behaviour in love. You can also find the rising sign of your beloved and the positions of these four planets when he or she was born.

So first find your rising sign and the positions of these four planets for you and your partner. Then compare them. Suppose, for example, that your Sun sign is Leo and your rising sign Sagittarius, and your partner's Sun sign is Gemini and rising sign is Pisces. In addition, you will each have the four planets in certain signs—sometimes, fortunately, in the same signs.

To get the most out of this book, you should follow up all the possible permutations—reading not only *The Gemini Man in Love* and *The Way to the Gemini Heart,* but *The Piscean Man in Love* and *The Way to the Piscean Heart,* for he will have elements of both signs in his nature. In the

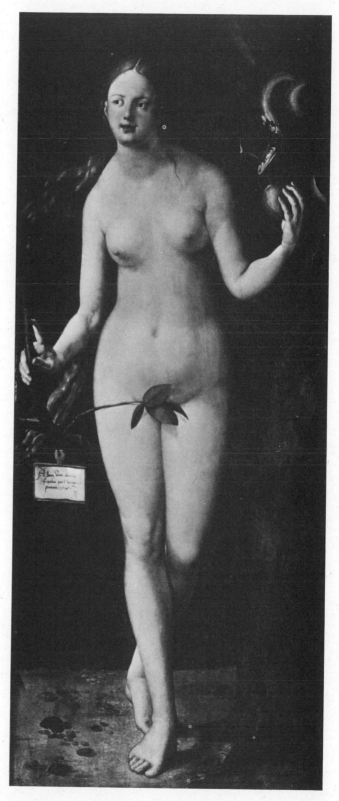

same way, to learn more about yourself and your own reactions to love and partnerships, read *The Leo Woman in Love* and *The Sagittarian Woman in Love* as well as *The Way to the Leo Heart* and *The Way to the Sagittarian Heart*. Then turn to the relevant pages and discover how the Leo woman and the Sagittarian woman react to both the Geminian man and the Piscean man. Next read the interpretations of the planetary positions. Finally, try to reconcile and balance all the information you have obtained.

But remember that all a book like this can do is give you, mainly for amusement, hints which you will have fun checking. We know many happy partnerships between people whose birth charts are not obviously compatible, for in love what matters is what you make of the relationship, and it is as true in this area of life as in any others that "The stars incline—they do not compel".

So good luck in love, and enjoy many cosy evenings proving, with the help of this book, that you were made for each other.

Derek and Julia Parker
Foxton
Cambridgeshire
England

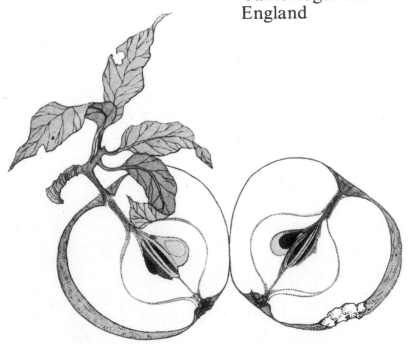

Astrology and You

A Brief History of Astrology

No one knows precisely how astrology originated. Certainly before the invention of the Zodiac, which was possibly as early as 750 BC, there could have been no horoscopes as they are understood today, but simply a system whereby the planets and stars were seen as omens.

Gradually, however, names, shapes and personalities were attached to the patterns in the night sky. The Mesopotamians, for example, saw Venus as a luminous lion roaming the heavens, put to death at dawn and cast into the underworld. Eventually, the Zodiac was evolved and the astrological signs became the permanent backcloth against which the planets moved. Horoscopes, as they are now known, came into being sometime before the fifth century BC and for the first time the astrologer's art—which earlier had been used to foretell the actions of kings and princes, or the fate of countries—was turned to use for the individual.

At first horoscopes were interpreted very simply. In 235 BC, for example, a father was told, "If the child is born when the Moon has come forth, his life will be bright, excellent, regular and long; if when Saturn has come forth, dark, obscure,

sick and constrained." By this time the characters of the planets were well defined, and during the next three hundred years the techniques of astrology were explored and rationalized by a system of trial and error.

In about AD 150 Claudius Ptolemy, the great astronomer and geographer, wrote the first real astrological textbook, the *Tetrabiblos*. He was careful to note that he presented no new material, but simply organized and set out facts already known. For, by Ptolemy's time, astrologers in Babylonia, Egypt and Greece had all contributed to the main body of knowledge which he gathered together, and it had long before been decided that astrology could not predict events. Ptolemy himself wrote, "We can understand only a general idea of an event, and not its particular form." This did not, however, prevent some astrologers from pretending to be able to foretell the future.

The Romans took astrology very seriously indeed. Julius Caesar wrote a book about various systems of divination. Cleopatra gave Mark Antony one of her astrologers and most Roman emperors either em-

ployed astrologers or dabbled in the subject themselves. Vespasian expelled all astrologers except his own, and for some time the death penalty was imposed on anyone found in possession of the imperial horoscope, since it was believed that they could only be plotting insurrection. Severus had the roof-top of his palace made into a observatory for his wife, Julia, who had been selected for him by astrology and was herself an adept practitioner. Few aspects of life in Rome were not affected by astrology, from the farmers' desire to know whether the harvest would be good or bad, to the emperor's fear of rebellion and assassination.

The Druids probably brought astrology to Britain. Certainly it was in use in Western Europe by the fifth century AD. *The Anglo-Saxon Chronicle* mentions astrological data, and figures of the Zodiac are found in many pre-medieval church buildings. From the time of William the

The creatures chosen to represent the twelve constellations within the Zodiac belt were taken from the everyday world of early civilizations in the Mediterranean region, and notably those of Babylonia, including Chaldea, and Assyria. There are seven bestial signs—Aries the Ram, Taurus the Bull, Cancer the Crab, Leo the Lion, Scorpio the Scorpion, Capricorn the Goat and

Conqueror until the end of the seventeenth century, astrology was used at every level of civilized life, from the Court and international politics to the individual and his financial, psychological and amatory affairs. In tracing the history of astrology many allusions to it are found in general, as well as in astrological, literature. St Thomas Aquinas, for example, approved of the subject, and Petrarch disapproved. Dante and Chaucer used astrological symbolism widely, and Shakespeare reveals in his plays the extent to which the Elizabethan Englishman quite naturally accepted the proposition that the position of the planets affected his character and behaviour. As Sir Walter Raleigh wrote, "If we cannot deny God hath given virtues to springs and fountains, to cold earth, to plants and stones . . . why should he rob the beautiful stars of their working powers?"

Queen Elizabeth herself relied on the advice of one of the most remarkable men of her time, Dr John Dee. He had befriended her when she was a lonely, imprisoned princess—for her horoscope told him that she would eventually succeed to the throne. He advised her throughout her reign on such personal matters as her proposed marriage to Philip of Spain, as well as on the significance of comets and eclipses.

During the seventeenth century the middle-class man for the first time had money in his pocket—and spent it freely on astrology, consulting such men as Simon Forman (one of whose clients was Emilia Lanier, identified as the Dark Lady of Shakespeare's sonnets), or, a generation later, the herbalist astrologer Nicholas Culpepper. Doctors, incidentally, invariably had a working knowledge of astrology, which they used to assess an individual's predilection to or immunity from disease or illness. In some European countries, a man was not allowed to practise as a doctor unless he had studied astrology.

During the eighteenth century astrological quacks proliferated. It became too easy to trick the public into accepting fortune-telling as "real" astrology. This, together with the spread of new astronomical discoveries, led to a diminution of belief in astrology as a scientific subject.

After the turn of the nineteenth century, the revival began, first with the Theosophists and Helena Blavatsky, and then with such popular astrologers of the 1920s and 1930s as the American Evangeline Adams and the English R. H. Naylor, the first newspaper astrologer.

Although a serious interest in the subject was beginning to grow, it has only been during the last twenty-five years that serious scientific astrology has begun to gain ground. The work of such statisticians as Michel Gauquelin in France has shown a correlation between planetary positions and psychological characteristics. In the United States investigations have begun on the effects of planetary positions on certain organisms, terrestrial weather and the growth of some plants, as well as on the prediction of a predisposition to certain illnesses and on the prediction of the sex of children before birth.

Meanwhile eminent men in England, Germany and the United States have been extending astrological technique in a variety of ways. With fifty centuries of history behind it, and with the new weapons of modern science at its disposal, astrology has perhaps still its most exciting years ahead.

Pisces the Fishes. Four signs are "human"— Gemini the Twins, Virgo the Virgin, Sagittarius the Archer and Aquarius the Water Carrier. Although half-horse, Sagittarius is judged to be human because of the human activity—firing a bow— with which he is associated. Libra the Scales is neither bestial nor human but is considered to be a "humane" sign, concerned with justice.

The Birth Chart

The art or science of astrology involves the study of the positions of the planets in the sky at the precise moment of a person's birth, and from the place of birth. The relationship between the planets and the angles they make to each other and to the Earth, reveal to the astrologer their influence on the human character.

To study these planetary relationships easily, the astrologer first calculates the precise position of each of the planets, and then sets them out in the form of a map of the sky as seen from the place of birth. Although the Sun, and not the Earth, is at the centre of the solar system, astrologers nevertheless adopt the convention of placing the home planet, the Earth, at the centre of the birth chart or horoscope. This has no effect upon the planetary positions, but simply makes the chart easier to read.

Because of the revolution of the earth, if two children are born in the same hospital, but even as much as four minutes apart in time, their birth charts will show a significant difference. The same, of course, is true of distance over the Earth's surface. Two babies born at the same moment of time, one in New York and the other in San Francisco, or one in London and the other in Cape Town, will have different birth charts.

The birth chart as it is known today, although in a simplified form, seems to date from about 500 BC. Until about the middle of the nineteenth century, however, it was set out within a square. The modern circular chart was developed as a matter of convenience.

When you look at the birth chart on this page, imagine Earth to be at the centre of the chart. It is encircled by the Zodiac, a band divided into twelve equal signs, each of 30 degrees. The signs, the Heavenly Twins, or Gemini, the Centaur, or Sagittarius, and so on, were originally named for the star patterns which were observed within them. The planets, moving around the Earth, are seen against this band. When, for example, the Sun is seen against the star pattern of

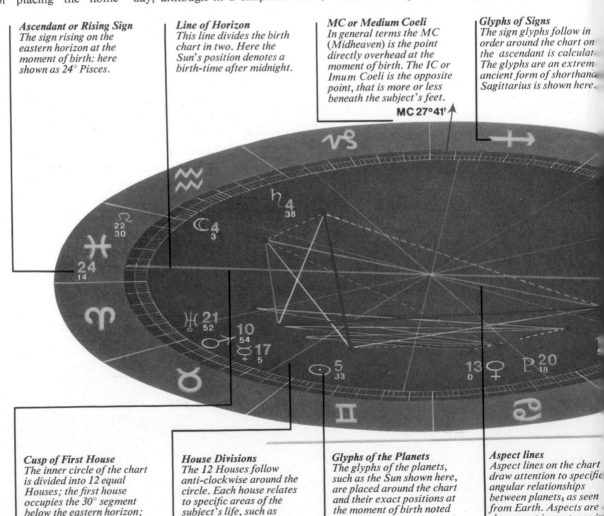

Ascendant or Rising Sign
The sign rising on the eastern horizon at the moment of birth: here shown as 24° Pisces.

Line of Horizon
This line divides the birth chart in two. Here the Sun's position denotes a birth-time after midnight.

MC or Medium Coeli
In general terms the MC (Midheaven) is the point directly overhead at the moment of birth. The IC or Imum Coeli is the opposite point, that is more or less beneath the subject's feet.

MC 27°41'

Glyphs of Signs
The sign glyphs follow in order around the chart on the ascendant is calculat. The glyphs are an extrem ancient form of shorthand Sagittarius is shown here.

Cusp of First House
The inner circle of the chart is divided into 12 equal Houses; the first house occupies the 30° segment below the eastern horizon; the cusp marks its starting point.

House Divisions
The 12 Houses follow anti-clockwise around the circle. Each house relates to specific areas of the subject's life, such as possessions, career and family.

Glyphs of the Planets
The glyphs of the planets, such as the Sun shown here, are placed around the chart and their exact positions at the moment of birth noted in figures.

Aspect lines
Aspect lines on the chart draw attention to specific angular relationships between planets, as seen from Earth. Aspects are the utmost importance in interpretation.

Gemini, as it is in this chart, it is said to be "in" Gemini, and the subject would call himself a Geminian.

It is important to note that because of the astronomical phenomenon which is known as the precession of the equinoxes, the star patterns no longer fit into their signs with complete accuracy. This, however, does not invalidate the astrological theory, for the names given to the signs are only for convenience. It is the planetary positions around the Earth that matter, rather than ancient references to Crabs or Bulls or Fish.

Everyone has all the planets in his or her birth chart. In this birth chart, for example, Uranus is in Aries, Mercury and Mars are in

Cusp of Sign
The cusp of a sign marks the point at which a new sign begins. A planet appearing precisely on the cusp in the illustration would be placed on 0° Scorpio (not 30° Libra).

Descendant
The opposite end of the horizon line to the ascendant.

Taurus, the Sun is in Gemini, Venus and Pluto are in Cancer, Jupiter is in Leo, Neptune is in Virgo, and Saturn and the Moon are in Aquarius. When working on the birth chart the astrologer will take all this into consideration, as well as the houses. These important astrological elements are the twelve segments of the centre of the chart which radiate from Earth, but are not identical in position to the zodiacal signs. Each astrological house symbolizes an aspect of life. The first house (which is always at the left-hand, or east, side of the chart, immediately below the line of the horizon) represents personal affairs; the second, possessions; the third, family; the fourth, the home; the fifth, creativity; the sixth work and health; the seventh, close relationships; the eighth, money; the ninth, intellectual pursuits and travel; the tenth, career; the eleventh, social pleasures; and the twelfth, the unconscious.

The calculation and drawing of the birth chart is a basically simple astronomical and mathematical task, which anyone should be able to master after a few weeks' work. Obviously, the greatest care is necessary, for if the basic birth chart is even the slightest bit wrong, all the inferences drawn from it will also be wrong. It is in the interpretation of the chart, the weighing of influence with influence, the dredging for every possible piece of useful evidence, that real skill and experience are required.

There are a great number of factors to be considered. It has been mathematically calculated that the number of possible astrological combinations in one chart is in excess of 539,370,750 plus thirty 0's. An astrologer will not have to deal with all these, but the position of every planet in every sign and house must be considered, as well as its relationship to

every other planet in its sign and house.

The *aspects*, the angles made by the planets to each other and to Earth, must also be calculated. These are described by traditional terms which refer to the number of degrees involved. A square aspect means that two planets are 90 degrees apart, measuring around the ecliptic or zodiacal band. A trine is of 120 degrees. Planets in opposition are 180 degrees apart. A sextile is of 60 degrees, a semi-square 45 degrees, a sesquiquadrate 135 degrees, and so on. Aspects reveal stresses and strains within the individual's character, or those areas where a person's characteristics can attain best realization. A sesquiquadrate, for example, indicates strain between the characteristics represented by two important planets 135 degrees apart.

The planets act and react on each other according to their own astrological nature, and the nature of the sign they are in. They are also affected by the astrological nature of the aspects they make to each other, which are deeply traditional. These are only some of the important factors in the birth chart which must also be considered.

Having carefully weighed all the factors in the chart before him, the astrologer reaches his conclusions and is ready to point them out to a client. To look ahead at the trends in the client's future life, the chart must be "progressed" so that it is no longer a map of the sky for the moment of birth, but for a time in the future when the client's life will be influenced by new planetary configurations.

The birth chart is an extraordinary pictorial record of the character of its subject. Provided it is accurately calculated and drawn, and skilfully interpreted, it could be called an accurate X-ray of the psyche.

Synastry

This book is based on the astrological art of synastry, which is the comparison of the astrological natures of two people to reveal the areas in which they are likely to agree, to get on well together and where there may be disagreement or strain.

A consultant astrologer, asked to advise a couple who are considering a permanent relationship, would calculate both birth charts and work with all the astrological data that these would provide. This requires training, experience and skill. The layman can, however, with the help of the charts and tables in this book, compare the Sun signs, the rising signs and the positions of certain planets.

Synastry is an important part of any astrologer's work, involving not only the comparison of the birth charts of a couple considering marriage, but also embracing other situations. In the case, for example, of a marriage in difficulty because one of the partners is having an affair, the astrologer can compare three charts —man and wife, and the third man or woman—and will be able to judge whether the new relationship is a serious and lasting one, or simply a passing infatuation. Other branches of synastry include the relationship between children and their par-

ents and between business partners.

Technically, synastry is a complex and sensitive area of astrological work. The more complete the astrological data available, the more helpful an astrologer can be, so the provision of the exact time, as well as the date and place of birth, is even more important here than usual. If only the date of birth is available, the all-important ascendant, or rising sign, may be missing, and the sign on the Midheaven certainly will be. Only the positions of the planets, except for the Moon, which moves too quickly, can be taken into account, and the astrologer cannot be nearly as helpful as when all the evidence is before him.

In this book, the diagrams on pages 172-191 will allow most readers to discover their rising sign, as well as the positions of Mars, Venus, Uranus and Neptune at the time of their birth. However, only calculation from the precise time of birth can reveal the rising sign with complete accuracy. Anyone looking at the diagram and finding that his rising sign is, say, Taurus, may think that the characteristics of that sign do not fit him at all. If this is so, he should read the accounts of the personality traits of the neighbouring signs—in this case, Gemini and Aries. He will certainly

recognize one of these as fitting him more accurately, and if this is so, it will probably be his true rising sign. He should then evaluate the characteristics of the rising sign with those of the Sun sign and of the planetary positions. Now he will have a fairly adequate sketch of his reactions in love.

To evaluate a couple's compatibility, the professional astrologer looks at the two birth charts, compares them and asks a number of questions, taking into account various relationships between the Sun sign and the rising sign. The reader can do this in the same way.

The first major point an astrologer will consider is whether A's Sun sign is the same as B's rising sign, or if B's Sun sign is the same as A's rising sign. If the relationship is present, there will be considerable similarity in personal behaviour and psychology—an influence strong enough to help offset any other less happy planetary relationships between the charts. This is a clear indication that the partnership will probably be a happy one.

Next compare the two charts and see if A's Sun sign and B's rising sign are "in opposition", that is, exactly 180 degrees apart (say, Sun sign Cancer and rising sign Capricorn). This, too, is positive, and there will be rapport between the two.

Is A's Sun "in square aspect" with B's Sun sign? That is, are they divided by 90 degrees, like Scorpio and Leo? If so, the relationship can be somewhat tense, but, on the other hand, there will be enormous drive and push. You should consider the other planetary circumstances carefully, for the relationship will be much easier if there are moderating factors elsewhere in the charts.

A trine or sextile aspect between A's Sun and B's rising sign will also be significant, that is, if they are 120 degrees or 60 degrees apart—like Taurus and Virgo, or Leo and Libra. This will indicate a pleasant, easygoing, but perhaps slightly dull partnership. It is almost the opposite of what is generally indicated by a square aspect. This can be excellent or irritating, depending on the

personalities of the people involved.

The aspect known as a semi-sextile—when two planets are 30 degrees apart, and therefore are zodiacal neighbours, since each sign occupies 30 degrees of the zodiacal circle—can be rather negative. Signs next to each other are different in almost every way, and common ground between them is lacking. In such a case it is not always easy even to have a constructive argument. If this aspect is present, then the other planetary relationships must be carefully considered, for there may be some mitigating circumstance—especially, perhaps, through Venus, which is always "near" the Sun in a birth chart, and so is particularly helpful when one is using simple Sun-sign astrology. On the whole, however, it is unfortunately true that those linked by neighbouring signs are most likely to get on each other's nerves and to be fairly incompatible. It is fair to warn them that there will be difficulties if they embark on a permanent relationship. However,

there are certainly many happy marriages between people of neighbouring signs in whose birth charts the planetary positions have militated against the strains.

There is one notable exception to the semi-sextile, or "neighbouring sign" rule, and this is in the case of Capricorn and Aquarius. Saturn rules Capricorn and is the old traditional ruler of Aquarius, and this may pull them together slightly. There may be coldness in some areas of the relationship, for Capricorn is extremely conventional and could be upset or even scandalized by the

Synastry

ultra-modern, radical attitudes of Aquarius. But these two have enough strength of character to fight their battles forthrightly.

The final relationship between two signs to be considered is when A's Sun sign and B's rising sign are in quincunx aspect—150 degrees apart, like Taurus and Virgo. This can be in general a difficult, negative factor, but again there are important exceptions. Aries and Scorpio could make an exciting partnership, with Aries ruled by Mars, the old traditional ruler of Scorpio. Storms, high emotions and an active and gratifying sex life will certainly play a part. The Venus signs, Taurus and Libra, will encourage a relationship which is peaceful, with a mutual love of good food and comfort and a pleasant environment. And, finally, there are Leo and Pisces, who have on the surface extremely opposing characters, but are both creative and often artistic. Leo can encourage Pisces's creativity and give some shape and drive to what can be a rather carefree, nebulous character. The combination is often a marvellous one.

It is important to emphasize that synastry is a meticulous and detailed art which can only be accurately practised by a professional astrologer. While you will find it fun to compare Sun signs and rising signs in two charts and will find that the planetary tables, too, can provide some interesting hints, do not take the results too seriously.

After calculating the birth charts in detail the consultant astrologer looks at the planets, each of which has its own significance in the area of love and personal relationships. The Sun shows self-expression; the Moon, habits and moods; Mercury, intellectual ties and personal opinions; Venus, true affection, the degree to which a partner's feelings will be truly considered; Mars shows the attitude to sex, but also reactions in quarrels or minor disagreements; Jupiter reveals a sense of humour and fun; Saturn can show frustration, unhappiness and frigidity and also, under certain circumstances, constructive progress; Uranus is concerned with the unexpected in a relationship, perhaps with the general tension of life together; Neptune shows a tendency to romance, idealism, but, perhaps, also deception and underhandedness; and Pluto can indicate helpful new beginnings, putting the past behind.

The astrologer will consider all these in their exact positions in each chart, allowing them to vary only a few degrees in exactitude in making aspects to other planets. To discover how a marriage is likely to go in the future, he will, of course, "progress" both charts, and again consider the aspects made by the planets in their new positions.

To show how an astrologer goes to work in synastry cases, we can look in detail at two examples, one happy, the other less so.

H.R.H. Princess Anne, who married Lieutenant Mark Phillips on November 14, 1973, was born in London on August 15, 1950, at 11.50 am, B.S.T. Her husband was born in Gloucestershire on September 22, 1948, at 2 am B.S.T. All the astrological signs indicate a lasting and happy relationship: Anne (like the Queen Mother and Princess Margaret) has Leo as her Sun sign, and Leo is also Mark's rising sign—a primary indication of psychological compatibility. Mark's Sun sign is Virgo, and the Moon was in Virgo when Anne was born: another basic link.

Both have Mars in Scorpio—a passionate planet in an intense, highly emotional sign—so they will share a happy outward expression of themselves, not only sexually, but also in other areas. The emphasis in Virgo will enable them to look at any problems which may arise in a detached and unemotional way. Anne's rising sign is Libra, a little indecisive, but she is given nerve and strength by Mars, Jupiter and Uranus. Moon, Mercury and Saturn, all close together, could bring moments of deep depression, but Mark's leonine Sun can help her over them.

Their companionship in competition riding is well known, and astrologically accounted for by Jupiter, the planet of sport and particularly of horsemanship, which is in that part of both their charts which rules, among other things, sport and games. It is difficult not to believe that the Princess and her husband selected each other on an astrological basis. It does often happen that these kinds of strong astrological ties appear in the charts of married couples—otherwise, of course, they would not have felt so strongly attracted.

Strong attraction, too, existed between John White and Alice Black. He had Aquarius rising with the Sun in Gemini and the Moon in Libra. She had Saturn rising in Pisces and a Scorpio Sun. The positions of Venus and Uranus in their charts indicated a dynamic sexual attraction, and it was evident that they could get a great deal of pleasure from each other's company. Emotionally he was basically a lightweight because of the prominence of Aquarius and Gemini, although, with the Moon in Libra, he was a romantic. His Gemini Sun made him flirtatious and susceptible and likely to have more than one affair at a time. Again, with Aquarius rising, his natural tendency was not to get deeply involved, emotionally.

The most powerful Scorpio fault is jealousy, and Alice was unable to cope with John's constant flirtations. Her strong emotional intensity was too powerful for him and too demanding. The position of Saturn exacerbated the situation; in Pisces in her chart, it made a conjunction to his ascendant, tending to cast a pall over the whole relationship. While there were many indications in their birth charts to bring them together, when these eased Alice became clinging and suspicious and simply unable to understand John.

An astrologer, had they consulted one earlier, could, of course, have interpreted one to the other. The relationship could possibly have worked well if they had both made an effort to compromise, but, as it happened, with their respective Mars opposing each other across the Zodiac, they had endless quarrels, with deep, smouldering resentment and passion on her side, and an outpouring of words, explanations and justifications on his. It was for the best that they finally parted.

In the past, there have been different attitudes to synastry, and there is still a radical difference between the way Eastern and Western astrologers use the art. The first step in an arranged marriage in India, for example, will often be the exchange of birth charts. But in the West it is usually the case that a couple meet in the way boy generally meets girl, and only after the relationship is under way do they, perhaps, approach an astrologer to confirm their instincts, or to suggest areas in which they may disagree once the first ecstatic rapture has worn off.

In any case, Western astrologers would consider it indefensible to tell a couple that they should or should not marry. They are happy to point out that, in the cases quoted above, Princess Anne and Lieutenant Phillips are likely to have an extremely sound and happy marriage; it would equally be their duty to tell John White and Alice Black that, should they marry, there would be certain difficulties within the relationship.

But in the courts of love, as in every other area of life, the old saying that "the stars incline, they do not compel" must be remembered. Astrology has patched up some partnerships, perhaps even made a few. But it must never be used as a prop. Your soul is your own, and so is your heart.

The Planets and You

All the planets in the solar system have an effect on human life. At the time of your birth, they were in a particular position in the heavens, as determined by precise factors. If you consult an ephemeris, or table of planetary positions, for the year of your birth, you will be able to see which signs of the Zodiac were occupied by each of the planets.

Planets are held by gravity to a fairly regular course around the Sun. By tradition, each one rules at least one sign of the Zodiac and has its own attributes. Astrologically, the Sun and the Moon are considered planets, although neither is according to the strict definition of the word. In ancient times, the Sun, Moon, Mercury, Venus, Mars, Jupiter and Saturn were known, and each gradually acquired a set of fixed characteristics. Mercury, for example, became associated with a shrewd kind of wisdom; Mars was the ruler of violence and war; Jupiter was known as a king-ruler of men; Saturn, a somewhat cruel, morose god. Since the eighteenth century, Uranus, Neptune and Pluto

have been discovered, and thus are regarded as relatively modern planets. These move very slowly through the Zodiac because of their remoteness.

In this book, only a few of the planets are of importance, for the others are not directly concerned with relationships or the way in which people react when they are in love. There are, for example, many references to the positions of Venus and Mars. Venus has a significant influence on your capacity to give and receive love and affection. It is strongest when it is in Taurus or in Libra. Mars has a definite effect on a man's and woman's sexual response. It is strongest in Aries or in Scorpio. You can easily find the positions of both of these planets at the time of your birth by consulting the tables on pp. 186–189.

Whenever Uranus and Neptune are mentioned, it is primarily in connection with Aquarius, which is ruled by Uranus, and with Pisces, which is ruled by Neptune. People who have either Aquarius or Pisces as their Sun sign or rising sign will be more powerfully influenced by the positions of those planets than

anyone else. These two planets stay in one sign of the Zodiac for many years—approximately seven for Uranus and up to fourteen for Neptune. Consequently, a vast number of people had these planets in the same sign when they were born. Unless the sign containing one of the planets also contains the Sun, or was rising at the time of birth, their effects must be considered generally. Uranus can bring about sudden, disruptive changes; Neptune is known for its receptivity and diffuseness.

Although the remaining planets do not positively relate to your love relationships, it is important that you be aware of the astrological significance of the Sun, Moon, Mercury, Jupiter, Saturn and Pluto since all the planets in all the signs are working for you.

In addition, there is information about what planet rules what sign, and in which sign they are "exalted". This is an ancient astrological tradition which means that a planet always works particularly well and positively when it falls in its "sign of exaltation".

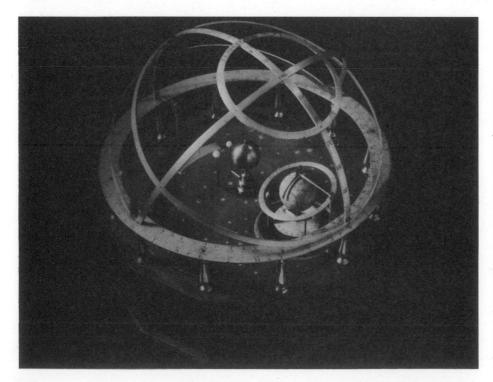

Orreries are mechanical instruments showing the relative motions of the Sun, Earth, Moon and planets. They first appeared in the early eighteenth century and were named after the fourth Earl of Orrery, patron of John Rowley, a London instrument maker. The miniature model illustrated was built by Edward Troughton in about 1800: Mercury and Venus (small white spheres) are in orbit around the central brass sphere of the Sun. The Earth turns around the Sun, its axis inclined at $23\frac{1}{2}°$ to the ecliptic, an ivory ball representing the Moon circles the Earth, the hemisphere facing away from the Sun being covered to explain the Moon's phases.

 *Sun*

The Sun is the ruling planet of Leo, and the keywords which assess its astrological significance are power, vitality and self-expression. It is exalted in Aries.

The Sun is the most important inhabitant of the solar system to both astronomers and astrologers, for it is the centre of all life and strength. The sign the Sun was in at the time you were born will influence your character to a great extent. This is also the one astrological fact that everyone knows, because, of course, it depends on one's birth date. If the Sun was, for example, in Aries at birth, you would nowadays call yourself an Arien. Popular newspaper astrology began in the 1930s; before that the most important sign in the personal horoscope was the rising sign, which had to be calculated mathematically.

The Sun works on your image—the face you present to the world. When you read a description of the Sun sign, it is essential to remember that the characteristics listed will be radically modified by the effects of your rising sign. Basically, you are a combination of both your Sun sign and your rising sign, plus the influences of all the other planets in their respective signs of the Zodiac.

If Cancer is your Sun sign, for example, and you read a list of twenty characteristics attributed to Cancer, you would probably conclude that you actually possessed about eight of them as elements of your character, and perhaps an additional two or three might be "about right". If, however, you were born at sunrise, your rising sign and Sun sign would be the same, and, as a result, it would have additional force and more of the characteristics would fit.

If you were born under the influence of the Sun, which rules Leo, you are likely to be an ambitious, tireless worker, with a strong will to succeed.

 *Moon*

Astrologically, the Moon is the ruling planet of Cancer, with response, instinct and fluctuation as its keywords. It is exalted in Taurus.

This is the second most important body in the solar system. It affects such things as the ebb and flow of the tides and your emotions and instinctive behaviour. But the Moon moves from one Zodiac sign to another so quickly that it is impossible to provide simple tables of its position in the sky at the moment of anyone's birth. It endows you with those traits which are often ascribed to the genes, for it describes and relates to your mother and reinforces inherited personality traits.

Since the Moon changes signs every two and a half days, it is the most personal of the planets, passing through all the zodiacal signs in twenty-eight days, a lunar month. It is, after the Sun and rising signs, the most important factor in the birth chart; astrologers who interpret a chart will constantly refer to its position and the way it is affected through the aspects, the relationships between the planets and earth. If it is "afflicted", that is, being battered by negative relationships with other planets, the individual concerned may suffer an unhappy childhood, with an uncaring mother. Or the reverse may be true: if Sun and Moon make a trine aspect, which is a positive planetary relationship, the home life may have been excellent, thus contributing to the development of the individual's well-integrated psyche.

If you were born under the sign of Cancer, the Moon will have a definite effect on shaping your personality. You will probably have the desire to change your occupation or place of residence frequently, since you were born under one of the most changeable planets. The Moon, for example, can make you an extremely sympathetic individual or else a narrow-minded one.

 *Mercury*

Mercury rules Gemini and Virgo, and its keyword is communication, both mental and physical. It is exalted in Virgo.

Since it is placed between the Sun and the Earth, Mercury always appears to be near the Sun in the sky, and in the astrologers' charts must fall either in the same sign as the Sun, or in the preceding or following one. If your Sun sign is Aries, for example, Mercury will either be in Pisces, or in Taurus, or, of course, in Aries.

Mercury is one of the most sensitive planets and helps you to communicate with other people. It influences your desire for knowledge and often makes you feel either the wanderlust or a disinclination to travel. If you had Mercury in Cancer, you are likely to be very sentimental in your responses.

 *Venus*

Venus is the dominant planet in the lives of all those born under Taurus and Libra. Its keywords are harmony and unison, and it is exalted in Pisces.

This planet either occupies the same sign in a birth chart as the Sun, or falls within two signs to either side of it. Venus has always been thought of as a feminine planet and has been traditionally called "The Lesser Benefic". She is known as the goddess of love and beauty. In addition, she is associated with feelings, the urge for harmonious partnerships and an appreciation of art, poetry and music.

Those individuals most strongly influenced by Venus have happy personal relationships, friendly natures and a love of creature comforts. They must guard against laziness and indecisiveness.

♂ Mars

Mars rules Aries, and its keywords are energy and initiative. It is exalted in Capricorn.

This planet has long been associated with aggression and warfare. Those individuals most strongly affected by the position of Mars can control these destructive forces and channel them into such positive forms as ambition and self-confidence. In love relationships, Mars directly influences a person's sexual response.

Mars is the dominant planet of the Arien-born. As a consequence, it often urges them to take the initiative in a variety of situations. It is likely to contribute to their love of freedom and frankness, and it may endow them with great energy to achieve their objectives in life. If Mars is afflicted, however, selfishness and impulsiveness will surface.

♄ Saturn

Saturn rules Capricorn and its keyword is limitation; it is exalted in Libra.

The position of Saturn at the time of birth usually indicates the area of life in which you are likely to face a struggle. There are twelve houses in the birth chart as well as twelve signs. If Saturn is placed in the first house, which represents health, it may indicate a certain physiological weakness; if it is in the second house, representing money and possessions, it will probably indicate that you have to work hard for success, for few, if any, windfalls will come your way.

Saturn does contribute stability, especially if well aspected. When it comes into contact with the other planets in the birth chart, important long-term changes are made, or long-term planning is accentuated.

♆ Neptune

Neptune rules Pisces, and its keyword is cloudiness. It is exalted in Leo.

One of the three modern planets, Neptune was discovered in 1846 as a result of its gravitational effects on Uranus. Since it takes about fourteen years to pass through one sign, it never gets around the Zodiac in an individual's lifetime.

The positive influence of Neptune on Pisceans can be seen in their idealistic, sensitive and imaginative outlook on life. In addition, these individuals are often artistically creative. If badly aspected, this planet may weaken the personality, and such negative traits as deceitfulness, indecisiveness and diffuseness are likely to dominate. On a whole generation, it can signify renunciation, many forms of catastrophe and nervous agitation.

♃ Jupiter

Jupiter rules Sagittarius, and its keyword is expansion. It is exalted in Cancer. Until Neptune was discovered, Jupiter also ruled Pisces.

In old astrological textbooks Jupiter is sometimes referred to as "The Greater Benefic", for it can exert an extremely helpful influence. If it is afflicted, however, it can make you an unrealistic optimist or a practical joker. It is this planet which gives us our "get up and go" and the tendency to take gambles in life. It is also associated with the general enjoyment of life.

When Jupiter comes into contact with other planets in an individual's birth chart, that person generally experiences a positive, productive period in his life. It is usually a time when opportunities present themselves; advantage should be taken of them.

♅ Uranus

Uranus rules Aquarius, and its keyword is change, either disruptive or sudden. It is exalted in Scorpio.

This is one of the modern planets. It was discovered in 1784, at the time of the Industrial Revolution in Europe when drastic changes were taking place in virtually all spheres of life.

Since Uranus is distant from the Sun and takes seven years to pass through one sign of the Zodiac, its influence is usually on whole generations rather than on individuals. It is powerful in the horoscopes of Aquarians, however, and contributes to their humanitarian, friendly, independent and strong-willed natures.

In general, this planet is frequently associated with dramatic events, the unexpected, and also science, particularly electricity and mechanical inventions.

♇ Pluto

Pluto, discovered in 1930, is said to rule Scorpio, although there is a strong influence of Mars in that sign. Its keyword is elimination; no decision has been reached about the sign in which it is exalted.

Pluto stays in one sign for many years, so people living today will either have it in Gemini, Cancer, Leo, Virgo or Libra. Those with Pluto in Gemini will be very elderly; the planet entered Libra in 1971. Astrologers do not stress Pluto too much when interpreting a birth chart, unless the client has Scorpio as a Sun sign or rising sign. In general, its influence is impersonal, extending over entire generations rather than specifically affecting individual lives. Pluto can help encourage good business sense in individuals as well as help them cope with enforced changes and disruption.

The Astral Touch

Astrology has developed strong traditions during the five or six thousand years of its conscious existence. Zodiacal signs have been associated not only with numerous psychological characteristics, but also, for example, with places, herbs, gems, minerals and colours.

Modern astrologers will quote these associations only for amusement. They will tell a client, for example, that Gemini is traditionally the sign of the city of London, or that the Sagittarian colour is purple. They would not, however, dream of seriously suggesting that a Gemini should take any job that is offered in London, or a Sagittarian never wear any colour but purple.

Many of the ancient associations do, however, often seem to be meaningful. One of the traditions of astrology, for example, associates the zodiacal signs with parts of the human body. Doctors who are interested in astrology find that a patient's birth chart can offer clues to the development of injuries or some diseases, and modern science is beginning to explore this area. For the astrologically-orientated lover, the birth chart can offer many hints for getting to know the body of a loved one; in giving and receiving pleasure.

In the modern permissive society, there is constant discussion about freedom of sexual expression. The inhibited Victorian attitude towards sexual expression has given way to a completely open consideration of the techniques of lovemaking. Although there are hundreds of books and manuals that describe these techniques in great detail, almost all of them ignore the importance of astrology, which can often guide the lover to those areas of the beloved's body which are most susceptible to touch.

Aries, for example, rules the head and any Arien will enjoy caresses to the head, from the soothing touch of fingers at the temples to stroking of the hair. The Arien will also be attracted by his or her partner's head, ears and soft throat. Libra, the opposite sign across the Zodiac, shares this attraction, and Librans are also often sensitive in the lumbar region of the back.

Scorpio is the opposite sign to Taurus, which rules the throat and neck. Both these types will love the caress of fingers down the neck, while Taurus will share Scorpio's strong sexuality. Although the sexual organs are the main

♐ **Sagittarius**
hips and thighs
As with the Virgoan, the Sagittarian is perhaps fortunate in that while he may find the hips susceptible to sensual pleasure, weight may also concentrate there; massage may thus serve two purposes.

♎ **Libra**
lower back
A major erogenous zone the lower back and butto are invariably sensitive. To the Libran this is particularly so, and a certain frivolity may wel enable them to enjoy playful patting or spank

♏ **Scorpio**
sexual organs
Traditionally, Scorpio me and women are highly sexed. More perhaps than anyone else, they are liker to respond to the most dire and uninhibited lovemakin

♍ **Virgo**
stomach
Quite apart from the slimming advantages of tightening the muscles of the stomach, this body are can be an excitingly sensu one, especially for Virgoan

♓ **Pisces**
feet
Feet can be sexually very attractive to some people, and those with Pisces emphasized may find that a tickling, light massage of the soles of the feet is very stimulating. Firm pressure on the instep can also give great pleasure.

♒ **Aquarius**
ankles
Beware of sprains. Aquarius also rules the circulation, and a general body massage not only improves the circulation of blood but also gives sensual pleasure.

♑ **Capricorn**
knees and calves
Perhaps knees do not naturally seem the most erotic part of the body, yet they and the calves are centres of pleasure for Capricornians.

focus of everyone's sexual feeling, the fact that Scorpio rules this area of the body indicates the powerful immediacy of the Scorpio's sexual needs. Scorpios are sexually inventive and relish a direct physical approach.

Cancer rules the breasts, perhaps the second greatest area of tactile pleasure, and Capricornians will share the instinctive attraction. Capricorn rules the knees, perhaps not usually considered an erogenous zone, but nevertheless surprisingly sensitive.

Virgo rules the nervous system as a whole, and any Virgoan will be quick to respond to a gentle caress. They frequently seem more sensitive to touch than those of

other signs. The polar sign of Virgo is Pisces, and Pisceans are also extremely sensitive to touch, while Virgoans share the Piscean's sensitive feet, which can often caress a lover's body as sensitively and tenderly as hands.

Sagittarius rules the hips and thighs, extremely susceptible to a tender caressing touch. Geminis will enjoy this—and will have, generally, slender hips which it is a pleasure to caress. Sagittarians will share the Gemini's most sensitive body area, the shoulders and arms. And, finally, the Aquarius and Leo polar signs share the back as a sensitive body area. Caresses which sweep the whole of the back are sure to arouse them.

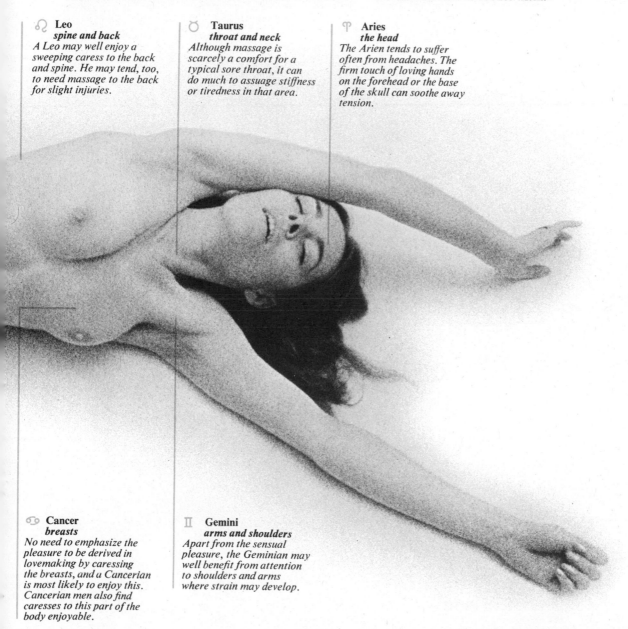

♌ **Leo**
spine and back
A Leo may well enjoy a sweeping caress to the back and spine. He may tend, too, to need massage to the back for slight injuries.

♉ **Taurus**
throat and neck
Although massage is scarcely a comfort for a typical sore throat, it can do much to assuage stiffness or tiredness in that area.

♈ **Aries**
the head
The Arien tends to suffer often from headaches. The firm touch of loving hands on the forehead or the base of the skull can soothe away tension.

♋ **Cancer**
breasts
No need to emphasize the pleasure to be derived in lovemaking by caressing the breasts, and a Cancerian is most likely to enjoy this. Cancerian men also find caresses to this part of the body enjoyable.

♊ **Gemini**
arms and shoulders
Apart from the sensual pleasure, the Geminian may well benefit from attention to shoulders and arms where strain may develop.

23

The Aries Woman

March 21st – April 20th

Ruling Planet: *Mars*
Triplicity: *Fire*
Keyword: *Enthusiastic*
Jewel: *Diamond*
Flowers: *Honeysuckle* ✳ *Thistle*
Trees: *Thorn-bearing Trees* ✳ *Holly*
Cities: *Naples* ✳ *Florence* ✳ *Utrecht*

The Aries Woman in Love...

The Arien woman is an enthusiast; she has a zest for life and is always eager to experience new things. Conversations with her are bound to be witty and informative. Possessing a warm-hearted disposition, the female Arien makes friends easily. And once she realizes that she is in love, she will not waste any time making sure that the object of her affections knows exactly how she feels. Because she lives her life at a hectic pace, it is too easy for her to fall quickly in and out of love.

Patience is certainly not one of her virtues, and so she must try hard to adopt a more level-headed approach in her private affairs. It is important for her to guard against being too aggressive in her relations with the opposite sex. Otherwise the man of her choice may find her directness somewhat unfeminine, especially if he is rather conventional, or sensitive, or slightly inhibited.

Basically, the Arien is straightforward, and does not want to waste time making trivial conversation. But she must remember that if she is not discreet, in the long run, she may spoil some of her chances. Since the Arien woman does not spend enough time considering the pros and cons of any situation, she must be extremely careful that she does not hurt a current lover in her eagerness to form a new and apparently exciting relationship. The Arien's major failing is her selfishness. Unfortunately, she is likely to consider her needs and feelings above those of others; she will often employ whatever means she can to obtain the results or conditions so fervently desired, without giving much thought to obstacles, human or otherwise, that confront her.

The Arien woman is passionate, and while she is sexually generous, she must be sure that in other aspects of a relationship she is equally forthcoming. In most cases, her partner will enjoy a fulfilling sex life with her, but he may find that he will not receive the psychological support or practical help that is necessary to keep their affair running smoothly.

She must, for example, be ready to encourage him in his career and business interests, as well as offer to share domestic chores and concerns.

It may be easier for the Arien woman to commit herself sexually rather than emotionally. Frequently, her sexual needs are high, but a deep emotional involvement with one man may become a source of conflict, because she needs a certain amount of personal freedom. It would therefore not be unusual for her to become restless within a marriage or a long-lasting partnership, particularly if her partner makes great emotional demands upon her. The Arien woman loves life, and wants to get a great deal out of it.

with Aries

An Arien woman who is in love with an Arien man will discover that his approach and attitude to life harmonizes with hers. Within the relationship, she will find the freedom that she needs, and she will guard it jealously. Although these two should be sexually compatible, there is an element of risk inherent in the nature of this sign: two Ariens may find it difficult to form a genuine partnership, because each wants to be dominant. Consequently, they will need to work at establishing mutual understanding, and the woman will have to use her feminine intuition to sense her partner's physical and emotional needs. The outlook for the pair will be brighter if one party has his or her Sun in Aries and the other has an Aries ascendant. It is of little consequence if they share a common Sun sign or rising sign. A permanent relationship between the Aries woman and man will be based on a deep friendship and a desire to do things together. They must make an effort to relax with each other.

with Taurus

A straightforward comparison of the characteristics of Aries and Taurus seems to indicate potential difficulties in their relationship. The position of Venus, however, can often be a mitigating factor. The Arien woman will find her Taurean mate slow to arouse, but he will be extremely sensuous. It should be easy for her to identify with the passionate side of his nature if her Venus falls in Taurus. If his Venus is in Aries, the ties between them will be strengthened; should they marry, no serious problems are likely to arise. The Taurean male is known to be possessive, however, and she may rebel against this because she needs a certain amount of freedom. If Taurus is his rising sign, his possessiveness could be expressed as jealousy. The Arien woman must try not to provoke jealousy or the Taurean temper, which can be ferocious. Remember that Aries is a fire sign. Arien exuberance and Taurean patience should help them build a solid partnership.

with Gemini

A Gemini operates on a different emotional level from that of an Arien. Her passionate attitude towards love will find but dim reflection in the Gemini's intellectual, flirtatious approach. Since he does not take his love life seriously, he will understand and sympathize with her desire to maintain some degree of freedom, even in marriage. If Gemini is his rising sign, he will not irritate her with detailed questions about her every action, and he will also be more passionate towards her. The partnership will be an extremely lively, carefree one, as both live life at a hectic pace. If Aries has Venus in Gemini, friendship and affection will develop, and their rapport will steadily deepen throughout the years. The combination of an Aries Sun sign and a Gemini ascendant has the greatest chance for success. In any event, if they make a concerted effort to develop mutual interests, their affair should be firmly cemented. If they marry, both will work hard to see that the union flourishes.

with Cancer

Inevitably, an Arien woman who gets involved with a Cancerian man will find that in some ways their personalities will clash. Aries is a strong, powerful, masculine sign; Cancer is gentle, sensitive, and essentially feminine. These descriptions do not imply that an Arien woman is masculine, nor a Cancerian man effeminate, but rather stress that the Arien woman is basically independent, and may resist her Cancerian lover's desire to be too protective. She will, however, have to make allowances for this difference. Both Aries and Cancer have outgoing personalities. He is a sensuous and passionate lover, and this couple's sex life should be a happy one. If Cancer is his rising sign, he may be more critical of her; he may be more sentimental towards her if Cancer is his Sun sign. A Cancerian makes a good husband, and is often prepared to assume more domestic responsibility if his partner wishes to pursue her professional career after their marriage.

The Aries Woman in Love...

with Leo

Both Aries and Leo are essentially extroverts. As a result, they tend to argue about who is to be the dominant partner. The Arien woman is extremely forthright, and will resist any attempts to be influenced, particularly by a Leo. It is imperative that she recognizes this possible source of conflict, and learns gently to persuade her partner to share any decision-making or joint responsibilities. Sex problems will be minimal, although he may be more conventional than she. The position of Mars at the time of her birth will have considerable influence on this aspect of the relationship. If his Venus was in Cancer, she may find him surprisingly sentimental. Overall, this is an excellent pairing, particularly if Aries and Leo are the Sun signs. If Venus falls in Gemini for both signs, the Leo man may have a slightly less conventional attitude towards sexual behaviour. This couple is temperamentally well-suited and will be friends as well as lovers; together they will enjoy life to the fullest.

with Virgo

It does not matter whether Virgo is the man's Sun or rising sign, his approach to love, sex and life will be quite different from the Arien woman's. But these differences need not divide the pair. Sexually, he will be less demanding than she, and his attitude towards emotional relationships may be somewhat clinical. If Virgo was rising when he was born, he will tend to be cool, but kind and considerate, towards her. The positions of Venus and Mars at the time of his birth are of great importance because they could decisively affect his sexual responses and his ability to give and receive affection warmly. The relationship will be helped if his Venus was in Leo, but it is least likely to develop if it was in Virgo with the Sun. Although allowances will have to be made in this partnership, the lively, assertive qualities of Aries will be good for Virgo. In turn, he should be able to help her view life more critically, carefully and less tempestuously. They would do well to cultivate a joint interest.

with Libra

While most women would find a Libran lover easy-going and amenable to any suggestions, the Aries may have the greatest difficulty adjusting to his indecisiveness. Prospects for the partnership will look more favourable if she has an Aries Sun sign and he has a Libra ascendant. There are, however, some interesting psychological differences between this pairing. Many times she will put herself first, but he will always think in terms of his partner. This Libran trait is so strong, that many of those born under this zodiacal sign do not feel that they are whole people until they are settled into a permanent relationship. Consequently, the Arien woman needs to be on her guard. It is much too easy for Librans to fall in love with the idea of love, and thus rush into a marriage prematurely. Since the Arien woman is a born enthusiast, she may also commit herself to the relationship, but for different reasons. The Libran man will be attentive, but he can be resentful at times.

with Scorpio

An Arien woman and a Scorpio man have the potential to share one of the most highly charged of sexual and emotional partnerships. She will soon learn he is a more complicated person than she—subtle, secretive and possibly jealous. Sexually, they will be compatible, and if they can find constructive outlets for their tremendous energy, they should have a rewarding relationship. Their lives will never be dull, but each is capable of hurting the other. Should the Arien woman persist in her demand for freedom, her lover could be unpleasant; if she really loves him, she may have to make some sacrifices. Mars has considerable influence on both of them, and the sign in which it falls furnishes insight into their attitudes and emotional levels. She will benefit most if Venus was in Libra at the time of his birth. If the relationship seems to be waning, there should be a complete break. For Aries and Scorpio, it is all or nothing, and it is better for them to part than to torture one another.

with Sagittarius

A particularly healthy and uncomplicated attitude towards sex will be shared by Aries and Sagittarius; the relationship should be an excellent one—fun-filled, honest and lively. Even more than Aries, he needs to have considerable freedom of expression; she will readily understand and accept this. Sagittarians are often either intellectuals or sportsmen; occasionally they need someone to help them balance their interests. Both would benefit from exercise, and Aries should be able to persuade her mate to get outdoors more regularly. Psychologically, this pair should have a good marriage, with few personality clashes. If Sagittarius is his rising sign, a more light-hearted and less passionate side of his personality may emerge as the relationship develops. She may find this surprising and even mildly annoying, but she should be able to manage well if her Venus is in Gemini. If it is in Taurus, however, she may not be able to cope with his flirtatious manner.

with Capricorn

The pioneering spirit of Aries combined with the ambitious nature of Capricorn should ensure success in whatever endeavour these two undertake together. Both will work hard, with Capricorn exerting a positive influence on Aries to be more practical and constructive. Sexually, some problems may arise. While the Arien woman will enjoy the challenge of arousing a Capricorn man, she may find that he is not so deeply involved, as his basic emotional level is considerably lower than hers. He does not believe in flirting and therefore will not give his heart lightly. But if he has Capricorn rising, it is likely that he will be delightfully protective and possibly more sensuous towards her. On psychological and platonic levels, the partnership could be a rewarding one. The positions of his Mars and Venus are important in outlining sexual boundaries. If Venus is in Aquarius, he will accept her independence more readily. As the relationship grows, she will realize that Capricorns are faithful.

with Aquarius

The independence and love of freedom that are so characteristic of Aquarius indicate that any affair with him will probably develop at a slow but positive pace. It is not unusual for the Aquarian-born to marry late in life. Friendship often forms the foundation of love. Surprisingly, he may be set in his ways, and reluctant to change his individual life-style to harmonize with what she has in mind. This could be a challenge that the Arien woman would do well to accept, as long as she remembers that he will probably not be as emotional as she. Unfortunately, this difference may become a source of conflict between them, and one that he could find draining in every sense. If Aquarius is his rising sign, he will relate more warmly towards her than if his Sun sign is Aquarius. There are times when she could feel somewhat distant from him. If Uranus, the ruling planet of Aquarius, is in Aries, there is an interesting possibility of an increased dynamic attraction between them.

with Pisces

An Arien woman involved with a Piscean man should be prepared for a reversal of his usual role. In this pairing, it is not unusual for the female to have the stronger character of the two, and thus be left to make most of the major decisions. Although she is extremely competent, she must be diplomatic and careful to give the impression that he has had the final word. This tactic may not be easy for her to employ, but it should be tried, otherwise Pisces may become lackadaisical and complacent if he realizes that he can afford to leave everything in her hands. Sexually, she will probably be satisfied, although their sexual approaches and attitudes, as well as their emotional qualities, are quite dissimilar. He is tender and sensitive; she is lively and fiery, and must consciously keep these differences in mind. If she does, she can certainly give his life direction, which most Pisceans sorely lack. It will be easier for her if she has Venus in Pisces, or if he has Venus in Aries.

Making the Most of Aries

All Ariens have a pioneering, adventurous spirit, a need to be first, ahead of everyone else. This is an admirable trait, but it is essential that they do not become too aggressive or ruthless in the pursuit of their ends. Ariens have great difficulty slowing down and considering their next move carefully. They are frequently impulsive and begin things which they do not always complete. This scattering of their energies can be a major drawback in their business endeavours as well as in their personal relationships. The capacity to plan in detail, and to think slowly and constructively, are qualities which must be consciously developed if Ariens are to make the most of themselves, and not provoke antagonism in others.

On the credit side, Ariens have the ability to spur others into action, which is a powerful asset. They will make good leaders in community affairs and in public life. Most people will inevitably be infected by their enthusiasm and warm-hearted nature, especially when it is a question of forming personal relationships. And in the latter circumstance, if their lovers are not caught up in their exuberance, then it is the responsibility of the Arien-born to recognize when they and their affections are not wanted. Once they accept the situation, Ariens have the ability to forget failure easily, and are able to look around almost immediately for new and more responsive partners. They fall in love quickly and are ardent lovers.

The Arien-born have a quick wit, and usually can be relied upon to make their friends laugh. Although it might seem unlikely, as they have so many positive qualities in their favour, Ariens are extremely forgetful, particularly about small, daily concerns. This is due in part to the hectic pace at which they live, as well as to a streak of carelessness in their character. It is important for Ariens to work hard to counter this tendency. Perhaps the best advice the Arien-born can be offered is to make a deliberate effort to consider their partners. This complete turnabout in their normal motivation will not be an easy one, for it is characteristic of Ariens to put themselves first, rather than to think initially of fitting others into general plans. If, however, they can gradually think in terms of a genuine partnership, and of truly sharing, their personal relationships as well as the general tenor of their lives will benefit enormously.

In matters of dress, Ariens prefer casual attire, especially an old jacket or colourful sweater, even if they look well in formal clothes. It suits their hurried pace. Women of this sign usually feel their best in clothes that are comfortable but stylish. The favourite Arien colour is red, and a red silk shirt and long flowing skirt would make an ideal outfit for evening wear. During the day, the Arien woman prefers wearing trousers that permit her to move as freely and easily as she needs to. Either A-line or permanently pleated skirts are also chosen by the Arien career girl or housewife who usually drives a car and wants to be able to sit comfortably. And most women of this sign wear little or no makeup.

Clothing is one area in which the Arien man does not care to be a leader. An old tweed jacket generally forms an integral part of his wardrobe, unless his wife or girlfriend drops a hint or personally escorts him to a men's store or to a tailor. He can be surprisingly conventional and unadventurous in his choice of clothes. This is worth thinking about, for a style well tried could be tried too often, and he may not find it too easy to change his image. It is more common for Arien men to become bald than it is for men of other signs, so additional time and money spent on hair care when they are young will not be wasted.

Generally, Ariens of both sexes have an abundance of vitality and energy that needs an outlet. Fairly strenuous physical exercise, or sports such as hockey and football, would be appropriate. Aries is the first sign of the Zodiac, and the head sign of the body. It also rules the top of the physical being, and, therefore, many Arien-born are likely to have headaches. They are also accident-prone, and should, therefore, take great care when handling sharp knives, hot dishes, or any power-driven machine tools. They may cut and burn themselves so frequently that they scarcely notice the blood or pain.

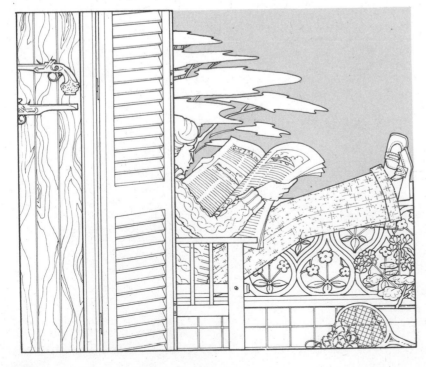

The Aries Man

March 21st – April 20th

Ruling Planet: *Mars*
Quadruplicity: *Cardinal*
Keyword: *Enterprising*
Metal: *Iron*
Countries: *England ✳ France ✳ Germany ✳ Poland*
Animal: *Sheep, especially Rams*
Colour: *Red*

The Aries Man in Love...

The combination of naivety, which can be quite disarming, and of spontaneity makes it comparatively easy for the Arien man in love to express his feelings. However, these same qualities can cause him considerable pain, especially if he is young. Should he be spurned, the Arien-born will suffer more of a shock than most men. It is not a question of his being hypersensitive, but he will be perplexed and his pride will be hurt.

The Arien man likes to excel in everything he attempts, and inevitably, he will be attracted to the best-looking woman in his particular group of friends, even if she is involved with another man. The "battering-ram" aspect of his personality ignores any previous entanglement, in his haste to get what he wants as soon as possible. He needs to learn patience.

Most women find the Arien man passionate and highly sexed. Selfishness will be apparent in one form or another, but his basically uncomplicated motivation can be admirable. Love, for him, must be as straightforward as his attitude towards it. He will not want to be concerned with such trivialities as his partner's

changes of mood, and, thus, he must guard against behaving insensitively towards her. Fortunately, a natural sense of fun and a great zest for love and life will make it easy for him to lift his mate out of any depressing moods. In addition, the Arien man must make a deliberate effort to learn exactly what her sexual needs are, for in his eagerness to gratify himself, his inherent selfishness may prevent him from satisfying her fully.

It sounds as though the Arien lover is a blustering, brash individual, but, in general, this is not an accurate description. He tends to be extremely generous and charming. He delights, for example, in giving her small, unexpected presents, especially if he knows he has recently been selfish or inconsiderate. He is good at apologizing, but he must not rely too much on his charm.

The Arien has a definite need for

personal freedom. He does not function well if there are restrictions in his work or in his personal affairs. If Aries is the rising sign, he will have a tremendous amount of energy to burn up, but he must remember that his frenetic activity can exhaust his partner, and his insatiability can sap her vitality and strain her nerves. In other areas of his life, this vitality manifests itself in the many projects he begins but seems never to finish.

with Aries

Sexually, the Arien man and woman are extremely compatible. In addition, he will discover that his lively Arien partner shares his enthusiasm for life and action. Of course, these similarities are bound to bring pleasure and satisfaction to both individuals. They could reach an impasse, however, if she puts her own interests first. But if he is honest, he will have to admit to having a similar inclination. A good partnership between these two cannot be taken for granted, even though they share the same zodiacal sign; it will be necessary for them to work at building a mutually satisfying relationship. Tensions could run high at times, and there is the likelihood of stormy quarrels. Since she is basically as straightforward as he, and dislikes a strained atmosphere, it should not be difficult for her readily to forgive any upset. It is important for him to study the positions of Mars when both were born. Mars is the ruling planet of Aries, and the sign in which it falls will influence both personalities.

with Taurus

An Arien man will have to be on the defensive if he falls in love with a Taurean woman. Although he will find her charming and probably quite attractive, each has certain characteristics that are bound to cause problems between them. She is reliable, but has a possessive streak that may annoy him if he gets the impression that she considers him as just another one of her treasured possessions. On the other hand, she will not find it easy to accept his love of freedom. The Arien man will enjoy her sensuous nature and the challenge of arousing her passion. There will be greater harmony between them if Venus, her ruling planet, falls in Aries, or if his rising sign is Aries. The Taurean woman may have a calming influence on him, and, if this is the case, they should be able to build a stable, permanent relationship. It will also be necessary for the pair to recognize their major weaknesses—the Arien's selfishness and the Taurean's possessiveness—and put them into proper perspective.

with Gemini

There may be a lack of communication in regard to sex between the Arien man and the Gemini woman, who is basically an emotional lightweight. But the fact that they may not be using the same terms of reference will perhaps encourage the adventurous Aries. He will be surprised to learn that she is not uninterested in sex, although she may not consider it in as serious a vein as he. She tends, however, to be more eager to engage in sexual experimentation. If Gemini is her rising sign, he may find her more passionate than if it is her Sun sign; and the sexual bond will certainly develop as the affair settles into a permanent relationship. Gemini likes her freedom as much as Aries, but he must not forget her strong inclination to flirt. He may appear to accept this, but, in reality, he is liable to be upset and become short-tempered. It will not be difficult for them to gradually build a firm friendship within marriage. The Gemini versatility will help them discover mutual interests.

with Cancer

It would not be unusual for the Arien man who is having an affair with a Cancerian woman to decide suddenly that she would make the best partner for him. Basically, they are hardworking and will share a determination to overcome any obstacle to their happiness as partners and as parents. The maternal element is very strong in the Cancerian-born. She is a tender, sensuous and romantic female, who does not take her sex life lightly. Unfortunately, the Cancerian woman does tend to be moody and to cling to her man. At her worst, she will nag him. Although he may want to try teasing her out of her moods, her Arien partner would be wise to use a gentle but firm approach. The position of Mars in her birth chart should be consulted. If it is in a fire sign, he can help channel her energy in more positive directions and also increase her sexual responsiveness towards him. His efforts will be complicated, however, if the planet of sex falls into another triplicity. She may be defensive if he rushes her.

The Aries Man in Love...

with Leo

If an Arien man is involved in a relationship with a Leo woman, he may find her somewhat domineering at times. Furthermore, he may think that she stands on ceremony too deliberately. But there are aspects of her personality that he will enjoy: her love of and enthusiasm for life, and her warmth and passion. The Leo woman certainly likes her comforts, and will be her most charming and dramatic when she is entertaining her lover in relaxed, elegant surroundings. On a more serious level, it will not take him long to discover that she is a sensitive, highly sexed and faithful mate. Before this pair can think in terms of marriage, they will have to reach a compromise on their approach to life, as he views virtually everything more casually than she. Moreover, they may have some difficulty working out their roles, for both will want to be the dominant partner. Theirs can be a satisfying relationship, with the Leo woman offering security and constancy to her Arien man in an appealing way.

with Virgo

The Arien man must curb any impetuosity in his approach to a Virgoan woman. She is naturally shy, and false modesty is a stranger to her. He must be prepared to understand and accept this part of her character, as well as the possibility of her having a low sexual response. These may be problems that the Virgoan woman is trying to resolve herself, especially if she is young and has yet to come to terms with her total personality. If Virgo is her rising sign, she may find it easier to relate to the Arien man than if it is her Sun sign. Special attention should be given to the position of Venus, which can be an enormous help or a hindrance; if it is in Leo or Libra, she tends to be affectionate; and if Neptune is in either of these signs, Virgo may be more disposed to romance. Should Venus fall in Virgo with her Sun, however, she is likely to be critical and even more sexually reticent than is expected of a Virgoan. She makes a careful, perhaps fussy, wife and parent, with a lively intellect.

with Libra

Libran indecisiveness may prove the most difficult obstacle that the Arien man has to face. He will be under considerable strain, especially in the early stages of the relationship, waiting for her to make up her mind. He must try to develop patience, however. Psychologically, this is an interesting pairing. Aries and Libra are opposite, or polar, signs of the Zodiac, and in many ways complement each other well. She will be understanding and affectionate, but sexually not as demanding as he. Basically, Libra is a romantic, but because of sheer laziness or her preference for doing things at a leisurely pace, she may not want to make much of an effort in bed. In addition, she may find that making love with an Arien is an exhausting experience. If Libra is rising, she may be eager to marry. In fact, it is often important to her on many levels of her personality to settle into a permanent relationship. Potentially, Aries and Libra should be an outstanding combination.

with Scorpio

The Arien man has much in common with the Scorpio woman, particularly in relation to their attitudes towards sex. She is passionate, emotional, and can often be provoked to jealousy. The marked difference between the two is that his approach to life is straightforward and uncomplicated, and hers is intense and often unfathomable. It is advisable for him to find out the sign that Mars was in when they were both born, because Mars, along with Pluto, is the ruling planet of Scorpio as well as Aries. Its influence on their personalities cannot be underestimated. If Mars falls in a fire sign in her chart, his prospects are brighter. Her sensuality will be heightened if it is in a water sign. The Arien man will have to come to terms with possible possessiveness if she has Scorpio rising. Both parties must realize that theirs is potentially a powerful combination, and that a relationship between them will be highly emotional, requiring considerable sexual involvement if they are to feel fulfilled.

with Sagittarius

In terms of sex, friendship and intellect, a partnership between an Arien man and a Sagittarian woman should prove mutually enjoyable as well as sexually satisfying. He will find that she is an interesting conversationalist and has an infectious enthusiasm for love and life. If she has Venus in Libra, he will discover a surprisingly romantic side to her nature, which he considers refreshing, but which she may be reluctant to acknowledge. The Sagittarian woman will probably be franker and more freedom-loving than her Arien lover, so there should be few jealous scenes, unless she has Venus in Scorpio. He will not find his partner too demanding emotionally; she is a fun-loving and amusing companion, who will display a sense of humour at the most unexpected moments. If they decide to marry, the future bodes well as long as they respect each other's need for freedom. A word of warning: since both are strong-minded types, they will need to make a determined effort to think in terms of a real partnership.

with Capricorn

The fun-loving side of the Capricorn woman will please her Arien partner, but he may consider her too remote for him. Should her Venus fall in Scorpio or in Sagittarius, she will be more likely to give and receive love warmly. There is a strong possibility that her sexual needs will not be as great as his; her emotional level certainly is lower. The Capricorn woman will take an active part in promoting his career interests, because she is ambitious. She tends, however, to complain. Should Capricorn be her rising sign, she may show more tenderness to her lover, but also could become more dependent on him. Although the Arien man will appreciate her need for protection, it could make him feel somewhat smothered in a permanent relationship. Allowances would have to be made for this, as well as for their different attitudes towards life. The Arien man is carefree and optimistic; the Capricorn woman is serious, calculating and possibly pessimistic, though not humourless.

with Aquarius

The Aquarian woman will enjoy friendships with other men, which her Arien lover may find hard to accept. Furthermore, he may be surprised by both her coolness and unconventional attitude towards her love life. But if he is patient and faithful in the early stages of the relationship, he will reap the benefits. Her need for freedom and independence will attract the Arien man, who prefers these traits to more dependent, weaker ones. He may find that she can be quite stubborn, especially if her ruling planet, Uranus, is in "fixed" Taurus. Once she has made up her mind on a course of action, or established a particular life-style, she may be extremely reluctant to change it. In fact, she often prefers living alone to moving in with her lover. Although she is a good friend and humanitarian, the Aquarian-born can be a loner as she prefers to remain personally detached. When she marries, the Aquarian woman will be faithful, and will bring a lively and friendly spirit to the union.

with Pisces

Neighbouring signs of the Zodiac are usually very different, and such is the case with the Aries and Pisces combination. In terms of love between people of these two signs, the position of Venus needs to be carefully studied, as it will play a decisive role. If it is in Aries or Pisces with the Sun, for either partner, the relationship will be considerably strengthened. Should an Arien find his Piscean woman somewhat disorganized, he is likely to be annoyed. In general, she is a passionate woman who does not have a strong character; this is most apparent when positive action is necessary. Consequently, the Piscean may rely too much upon her Arien man, so he must guard against allowing such a situation to develop. If Pisces is her rising sign, her attitude towards her partner may be matter-of-fact and slightly critical. It will be worthwhile for them to develop common interests; otherwise he will concern himself solely with athletic activities and she with intellectual pursuits.

The Way to the Aries Heart

If you are attracted to an Arien, it would be to your advantage to make the first move as soon as possible. People of this sign have little patience. Arrange an informal get-together with other friends or suggest a lunch-time drink. The invitation should be accepted readily, but remember that Ariens are inclined to be selfish and will put themselves first, so do not be surprised if they excuse themselves at the last moment by saying they have to work late, or that they must leave on an unexpected business trip. Actually, they have been asked somewhere else that seems more exciting.

It is not difficult to see through the Ariens' little white lies, since they cannot tell them convincingly. You can either tolerate or complain about this kind of selfishness. But when you do finally meet, the Arien will probably arrive offering apologies and a small but thoughtful present. He has a charming manner and knows just how to assuage the injured party's feelings.

Impulsiveness and ardour also characterize Arien love affairs. A sensitive or inhibited person could easily be put off by these qualities, particularly if he or she has been uncertain beforehand. Ariens are passionate, generous partners who like their liaisons to develop quickly. Physical contact will not be long delayed. On the other hand, they cannot tolerate boredom. Consequently, they will not hesitate to end a relationship as soon as possible if it does not live up to their expectations, or if they realize that they have misjudged their choice of partner.

It is very important that Ariens have a sufficient amount of fresh air because their sensitive nasal passages tend to get easily clogged in a stuffy or hot room. Depending on the temperature, adjust the air-conditioning, or keep at least one window open. In fact, most Ariens of either sex will enjoy participating in outdoor activities, so you will not go wrong if you plan a picnic for the Arien woman or suggest a ball game for the Arien man.

You will find that Ariens are witty, refreshing and informal people, so particularly during the early stages of the relationship, keep things relaxed, light-hearted and fun-filled.

Tranquillity and serenity are rarely appreciated by the Arien-born. Wherever they live, they seem to prefer a noisy atmosphere—in their kitchens you will hear a great deal of activity as they handle saucepans, dishes, domestic appliances, cutlery; and there will always be a television, stereo or radio loudly playing in one of the rooms.

If Ariens are asked to do any household jobs, whether it is ironing shirts or fixing the iron itself, have a good supply of bandages and dressings ready. Usually, they are so accident-prone in minor ways that if they cut or burn themselves in the process, they take little notice. In their workshops chaos seems to reign supreme, but actually they know where every tool is located.

Ariens are generous, and will often spend a great deal more money than they should on gifts for their friends. In turn, they are not difficult to please. Possible items the female Arien would enjoy receiving are hair-dryers and beautiful scarves; the males of this sign would appreciate tools for their particular hobbies, or would prize an antique pistol, as many of them collect weapons. Both sexes favour carved ornaments, especially if they are from the Far East or from South America.

Since Mars is the ruling planet of Aries, it is not surprising that a fair number of Ariens seem to enjoy eating curry. But it is also true that it can have an adverse effect on their stomachs afterwards. Of course, the fact that they have enormous appetites also has to be taken into consideration. So if you are inviting an Arien to dinner, you would do well to serve a vegetable soup that contains onions, which is traditionally an Arien vegetable. For the main course, serve a crown of lamb and a good Burgundy wine. Top off the meal with Baked Alaska.

To accentuate the romantic atmosphere, dim the dining-room lights and try to have something red —the favourite Arien colour—on the table, perhaps a tablecloth or napkins. When you are entertaining an Arien woman, place a spray of honeysuckle, if it is summer, or a single red rose next to her plate. For background music, play some records that are fairly spirited.

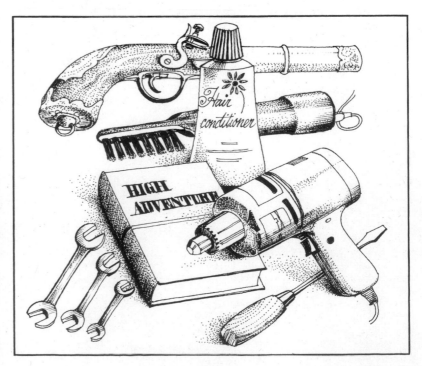

36

The Taurus Woman

April 21st – May 20th

Ruling Planet: Venus
Triplicity: Earth
Keywords: Practical * Stable
Jewel: Sapphire
Flowers: Rose * Poppy * Violet * Foxglove
Trees: Ash * Cypress * Vines * Almond
Cities: Dublin * Lucerne * Leipzig * St Louis

The Taurus Woman in Love...

The Taurean woman will always be absolutely sure of her ground before admitting, even to herself, that she is in love. And she will go through a process of very careful forethought before she commits herself to any man. Caution is her keyword, because a rebuff will hurt her more deeply than it will most other women. Her psychological motivation in a love relationship is likely to centre on her need for security. A transitory or casual affair is not for her.

Usually the Taurean woman has a conventional outlook on life, and this is most apparent in her love affairs. She will not be enthusiastic about engaging in sexual experimentation. And once she has settled into a relationship, she will demand faithfulness from her partner. Sexually, she is often extremely passionate, especially if Venus, her ruling planet, falls either in Aries or Taurus. If she has Taurus rising, her attitude towards her partner will be even more intense. She can be slow to arouse, and it is much too easy for her to become impatient with a partner whose pace of lovemaking differs from hers. Unfortunately, this is often the case. To allow her sensual nature its full expression, the Taurean woman must try to recognize that many men, particularly in the early stages of a relationship, could find her slow response frustrating. She should, therefore, make every attempt to convince her lover of her desire to express love through sex, so that he realizes that if he is a considerate, understanding partner, his efforts will be fully rewarded.

The Taurean woman has a natural, instinctive eye for beauty. Possessions are important to her, and she would be reluctant to part with any of them. She must remember that she has a strong tendency to regard her lovers as possessions, but they may well resent this.

She will soon learn that one cannot possess another person, and that if she persists in her attempts, injury and pain will inevitably follow. Possessiveness can be an all-consuming aspect of her personality, and she will have to come to terms with it in a love relationship.

with Aries

A Taurean woman may find an Arien man somewhat exhausting because he leads such an active life. He is always eager to visit new places, to play or watch various sports, or drive his fast car along country roads. Sexually, too, she could find his pace, and the speed at which he will expect the relationship to develop, overwhelming. But the faults in this pairing are not those of Aries alone; the Taurean-born has her share. While he is certainly the most impatient of all types, wanting a great deal to happen at once, she is equally slow both in her sexual needs and reactions. Because she is passionate, she will satisfy him, but he will have to learn to be patient. These signs are neighbours in the Zodiac, and when Taurus is the Sun sign, her ruling planet Venus can be in Aries. If this is the case, the Taurus and Aries partnership will benefit enormously. If she has Taurus rising, the relationship will be highly emotional. These two can learn a great deal from each other, but theirs may not always be a calm affair.

with Taurus

The Taurean woman will find that she shares many of the Taurean man's personality and character traits, but she must not expect him to be an identical twin. The position of Venus when they were both born will contribute to their individuality. Of course, it is possible that this ruling planet will be in the same sign; if this is so, the chances are increased that they will react to and express affection in a similar manner. Perhaps the Taurean tendency to be possessive is at its height in this partnership, and although this trait could permanently cement the relationship, it may do so in a negative way. Since both partners like routine, they are liable to get in a rut and may begin to take each other for granted. They will have several interests in common, so that the outlook for a lasting relationship or marriage is promising. In the sexual sphere, their demands should not cause any friction, although if Taurus is rising, their emotional levels are likely to be intensified.

with Gemini

The Taurean woman may find herself on a completely different wavelength from a Gemini man, unless he has Venus in Taurus. She must remember that he is usually light-hearted, somewhat flirtatious and unemotional, and does not take his love life seriously. She will have to learn to accept this side of his nature if she wants to be happy with him. Should she have Venus in Aries or Gemini, she will, undoubtedly, find she has fewer problems; and if she gives Gemini a chance to be himself she should benefit further. The Taurean woman will soon learn that he will not allow her to get into a rut; he will help broaden her outlook so that she can form more intelligent opinions, which is not easy for her to do. However, it will not take the Taurean-born long to realize that her Gemini partner will not be possessed. There is an inherent duality in Gemini, and he will enjoy having other relationships. Moreover, he will probably enjoy sexual experimentation, which may present a problem for her.

The Taurus Woman in Love...

with Cancer

The Taurean woman will respond warmly to her Cancerian's instinctive inclination to look after and protect her. His sudden changes of mood, however, disturb her. Generally, she is temperamentally calm, except for rare outbursts of bull-like temper, and this tranquil nature will help her deal effectively with his moodiness. It would not be unusual for him to be attentive one moment and defensive the next. The Taurean woman will be attracted to her partner's sensuality and thoughtfulness; they will feel secure with each other. If she has Venus in Cancer with his Sun, the bonds between them will be strengthened considerably. If he has Cancer rising, they will be concerned with developing their partnership and mutual objectives. Although the Cancerian man is considerate, there are times when she may feel taken for granted. Friendship will be an integral part of their relationship. Joint interests will be easily discovered, such as collecting beautiful objects for their home.

with Leo

Everything on a material level that makes life worth living—luxury, comfort, good food, music and the arts—will delight both the Taurean woman and her Leo man. As long as he has enough money, he will enjoy spending it on her. Psychologically, they are well-suited. At times, however, her stubbornness and his tendency to dominate may produce a stalemate. She must then rely implicitly on her intuition to help her out of such a situation. He will be an enthusiastic and passionate lover, and although he may be sexually demanding, he will also be considerate. Both require comfort and the right atmosphere for lovemaking, and neither will want to be rushed. The Taurean woman may have to learn to tolerate some flirtatiousness on his part if he has Venus in Gemini. Should both have Venus in Cancer, they will have a sensitive, perhaps even sentimental, attitude towards love. The Taurus and Leo combination should work out well. Even though both are strong personalities, they are flexible.

with Virgo

The Virgoan tendency to be critical, clinical, even fussy, may irritate the more sensual and passionate Taurean, but Taurus and Virgo are both earth signs, and that tie should serve as a good base on which to build a partnership. He will consider the relationship from a completely practical viewpoint, so that his endless discussion about the future, the size of the bank balance and the house they may hope to buy could spoil Taurus's vision of their life together. If Virgo has Venus in Libra, there is bound to be more joy and happiness in the pairing. The Virgoan man will be somewhat less matter-of-fact if the romantic planet Neptune was in Virgo with his Sun at the time of his birth. Emotionally and sexually, he may demand less than she, but should he have Virgo rising, it is likely that he will be more romantic and, perhaps, sentimental towards her. A marriage between the two has a good chance of success, as they share a practical outlook on life, and they feel secure with one another.

with Libra

These signs share Venus as their ruling planet, which suggests that they could have a remarkably romantic and happy partnership. It is possible, however, that Taurean possessiveness may clash with Libran resentment and mar the relationship. Furthermore, Librans have a tendency to shelve decisions, while Taureans tend to be lazy; here are two traits which have the potential to create chaos. On a practical level, to avoid such problems, the Taurean woman must be sure that she knows precisely what is expected of her, and what she expects of her Libran mate. She will discover that he prefers a peaceful life, avoiding upsetting scenes and quarrels; he favours routine and regularity. Sexually, they are compatible, and his languidly romantic and considerate nature is very appealing to her. They should enjoy building a friendship and developing mutual interests; the latter frequently revolve around music. If Libra is the rising sign, she may have to tolerate a certain amount of selfishness.

with Scorpio

A partnership between a Taurean woman and a Scorpio man will be a powerful and conquering one. The polarity of the signs helps explain their strong mutual affinity. Despite their many opposing characteristics, they complement and often need each other. Even in the early stages of the relationship, Scorpio's jealous nature and Taurus's possessive streak will be apparent. Neither will like these negative traits in each other, but they will be able to understand and tolerate them. Scorpio is the most passionate and demanding of the zodiacal signs, and, consequently, she will soon know whether this will be a permanent partnership, or whether she should end it immediately. It would be too difficult for her to cope with a slowly dying affair. In general, these two should have plenty of fun together. If Scorpio is his rising sign, there will be significant psychological identification. Careful study must be given to the position of Mars and Venus, as their influence is considerable on this pairing.

with Sagittarius

In an affair with a Sagittarian, a Taurean has to be realistic and accept that there will be basic differences between them. He needs freedom within a marriage or a permanent relationship, and she must never expect to possess him. There is a duality in his nature, and he is therefore not likely to be completely faithful to her. The Sagittarian man is considerate, broadminded and passionate, but he will not regard love in as serious a vein as she. The bonds between these two will be strengthened immeasurably if the Taurean woman has Venus in Gemini or Aries, or if her Venus is in Gemini and his ascendant is Sagittarius. Usually, Sagittarians love the outdoors and enjoy exercise; most Taureans, too, need to be more physically active. Joint participation in a sport will provide a common interest for this pair to develop. However, Sagittarians are not too concerned about creature comforts, while Taureans want them. On the positive side, they both share an interest in and a love of good food.

with Capricorn

Taurus will admire Capricorn's approach to love, which is as cautious as hers. A relationship between the two should prove mutually satisfying on many levels. She may discover, however, that he is not as emotional as she, and possibly is less sexually demanding. If he has Venus in Scorpio, he is likely to be more sensual, but he will consider other areas of his life more important. The Taurean woman will admire his ambition and persistence, although she sometimes feels frustrated by them. Should they marry, it will not take him long to realize that he has chosen an excellent partner. Friends and business associates will enjoy visiting them, especially since she is a gracious hostess. The Taurean woman's possessiveness manifests itself in her desire for beautiful possessions. Consequently, she is inclined to be extravagant, spending a great deal of his hard-earned money. This is a potential source of conflict, so restraint is needed. Capricorn will be kind, although possibly remote at times.

with Aquarius

There is virtually no aspect of a relationship between a Taurean woman and an Aquarian man that will not be affected by their fundamentally different personal traits. Although he was born under one of the friendliest and kindest signs of the Zodiac, he is the most independent and emotionally controlled. The Taurean mate is unconventional; he develops his own life-style early and it is likely to be very different from what she would choose. There are bound to be conflicts between their sets of values, and since both are probably stubborn individuals, deadlock can often result. Together they must make a deliberate effort to be more flexible; she will have to come to terms with his need for freedom and independence. Despite these pitfalls, great admiration, respect and love can develop as the relationship matures. Should they marry, Aquarius will find his Taurean woman a faithful partner. If his ruling planet, Uranus, falls in Taurus, the outlook should be more promising for their future.

with Pisces

The Taurean woman's practical ability, plus her psychological and emotional strength, are precisely what a Piscean man needs. In turn, she will find him a sensuous, romantic lover —intuitively aware of and responsive to her every need. However, he may be uncertain as to future objectives, and he may have a disorganized lifestyle. The Taurean woman can be extremely supportive under such conditions. If her lover is creative, she should openly and enthusiastically encourage his efforts and offer positive suggestions to him. If he has a Pisces ascendant, she may find him slightly critical, and occasionally a clinical attitude could emerge to dampen his ardour. Luckily, the Taurean woman will be able to cope with either complication. In this partnership, Taurus's possessiveness may take on a positive hue, for it could make her mate feel even more secure. Overall, an affair between these two will be rewarding on both a sexual and a practical level. It will certainly be an easy-going partnership.

Making the Most of Taurus

Over the years Taureans have earned the reputation of being the most attractive-looking people of all the zodiacal types. Taurus's ruling planet is Venus, and although Venus also rules Libra, its influence on those born under the sign of the Bull seems more direct. Despite their natural physical attributes, Taureans are not always careful to maintain their looks and figures. They are not particularly active people, but the primary reason for their weight problems is that Taureans love food, and the richer and sweeter it is the better. In general, as they become more prosperous, they tend to frequent more expensive restaurants and choose calorie-laden dishes.

Taureans procrastinate about starting diets. And once they do begin, they can easily be tempted to forget their good intentions if they are invited to a business lunch or to a romantic dinner, or are given a box of chocolates. It is difficult to advise Taureans about their eating habits; they should realize, however, that it will be difficult for them to retain their good looks if they continue to be self-indulgent. Physical exercise should be encouraged.

Taureans are great plodders, who think carefully and will not be rushed or frightened into decisions. They dread anything new, or any disruption in the established order, preferring the familiar. And when they have made up their minds, they can rarely be persuaded to change them. Like the Bull, which is the symbol of their sign, Taureans are tenacious. But a more flexible attitude needs to be developed, otherwise important opportunities for success may be missed.

Although the Taurean-born are not enterprising, and rarely initiate projects, they are excellent at interpreting the inspired ideas of others who are more dynamic, at filling in the details and at offering constructive suggestions that help bring ideas and plans to fruition.

Whatever profession they choose, their primary concern is security. They work best when they follow a routine and are earning a regular salary. This assurance gives them peace of mind, for they abhor debts. Consequently, Taureans prefer not to work in a freelance capacity, relying on random employers and never being certain when the next project will arise.

The Taurean-born do have good business sense, a high degree of integrity, and a willingness to work hard. They can do well on their own in professions and trades such as banking, architecture, hair-dressing and sculpturing. Generally, they excel in work which requires a sense of true proportion, and they seem to have infinite patience and persistence.

Since Taurus rules the throat, it is not surprising that there are usually several Taureans in any choir, singing group or musical society. It is also true that music satisfies a deep psychological or emotional need for many Taureans. In addition, there are a number of actors and actresses who are born either with the Sun or Moon in Taurus, or with a Taurus ascendant.

Occasionally, the Taurean woman's choice of clothes tends to be too frilly. She looks marvellous in soft blues and pinks—the colours of Venus, her ruling sign—and is inclined to buy dresses or blouses that have a bow or ruffle at the neckline. She will look best when she combines her liking for soft, extremely feminine clothes with a restraining and critical eye.

The Taurean man is usually conventional in his choice of clothes, and looks handsome in a three-piece business suit. He wears ties and shirts in Taurean colours to brighten his otherwise conservative appearance. The young Taurean man frequently chooses jackets and jeans in light-denim shades for casual wear.

In general, Taureans prefer a country atmosphere, although many of them are involved in such city careers as banking, law, market research. If the latter is true, they should aspire to buying a country house where they can relax, get away from the stresses of business, and indulge in their favourite hobby, which for many is gardening, or flower-arranging or embroidery.

As might be expected, a stereo will occupy a prominent place in the **Taurean home, and a large record collection will make constant demands** on any available space. A piano is also likely to be found there.

The Taurus Man

April 21st – May 20th

Ruling Planet: Venus
Quadruplicity: Fixed
Keyword: Resistant to change
Metal: Copper
Countries: Ireland ✳ Switzerland
Animal: Cattle
Colours: Pale Blue ✳ Pink

The Taurus Man in Love...

The possibility that he may make a fool of himself, or may even suffer rejection, will prompt the Taurean man to think twice before he declares his love for any woman. In addition, he will relive every recent meeting, word and glance between his loved one and himself. Then, feeling sure of his position, he will approach her conventionally, although warmly and affectionately. Unless she is also ruled by Taurus, he may discover that she does not appreciate a careful approach in the early stages of an affair. So it would be to his advantage to think in terms of her possible reactions as well as his own powerful need for security and assurance in love. In addition, he would do well to express his deep feelings and show his appreciation of her good qualities more readily.

The Taurean usually has no problem attracting a partner, as he has a great deal of natural charm and is frequently good-looking. Moreover, he is a passionate and considerate lover. Despite his sexuality, he may be somewhat surprised, and, at the deepest level of his personality, even shocked if his mate tries to be the dominant partner. He wants to think of his beloved as essentially passive, but may soon realize that his opinions will have to be revised. It would never be easy for him to change his views about anything once he had made up his mind, but it would be even more difficult when it concerned his love life. The Taurean male is not known for his adaptability, but rather for a bull-like tenacity.

Taurus's need for security within an emotional relationship is of the utmost importance, and consequently, he will do everything within his power to keep his loved one interested. He will treat her well and enjoy spending a great deal of money on her, partially in the belief that it strengthens the bonds between them. Once the Taurean male marries, he will make a good provider and a faithful lover. He thrives on the security that domesticity brings, and works best when inspired by a wife's and a family's love.

The glaring Taurean fault is possessiveness, which is linked to his need for security. He will shower his love with presents, and, admittedly, attention in this form is enjoyed by many women. If, however, his partner has and wants to maintain her independence, he must make every attempt to counter his possessive tendency, although it will be very difficult for him to control. If he has Taurus rising, he could become particularly jealous of her career and of her attitude towards love. In extreme cases, he may regard every man she meets as a potential rival.

Detail from The Bright Cloud by Samuel Palmer. Reproduced by courtesy of The Tate Gallery, London

with Aries

In an affair with an Arien woman, the Taurean man is likely to experience some surprises, and may even be somewhat shocked by certain developments. He will soon become aware of her independent nature and her love of freedom. Although he may be slow to arouse, she is a passionate woman, who is capable of awakening and stimulating his sensual side. The Taurean man should consider the sign Mars was in when his Arien lover was born. Mars is her ruling planet, and thus will have a strong influence on her personality as well as her attitude towards sex. The Arien woman is affectionate, refreshing and uncomplicated. Since Taurus and Aries are neighbouring signs of the Zodiac, it is possible they could have Venus, his ruling planet, in the same sign. If this is so, the bonds of affection will be strengthened between them. However, there are likely to be definite differences in temperament. As their relationship matures, periods of adjustment are inevitable.

with Taurus

If the Taurean man is cognizant of his sign's characteristics, he might be tempted to believe that any Taurean woman's responses will be similar to his. He will be sadly mistaken, however. Although the chances that they will react in a like manner will be greater if their ruling planet, Venus, falls in the same sign, there are several other factors in their birth charts which will ensure their individuality. Certainly, they will have many interests and characteristics in common. Music is frequently a mutual love, and expressions of possessiveness are likely to be voiced if either partner shows any interest in a member of the opposite sex. The Taurean woman will be sensual and passionate, but does not want to be hurried; in this respect, she will find her lover sympathetic. Basically, they operate on the same emotional level, but if Taurus is her rising sign, she may feel even more deeply towards him. Both parties must be aware that there is always the slight danger they will get into a rut.

with Gemini

The Gemini woman always has a younger outlook on life than the Taurean man, whatever their respective ages. In general, she does not want to develop any permanent relationships or make any firm commitments—she will refuse to possess or be possessed by a partner. The relationship has the greatest chance for success if he has Venus in Gemini or Aries, but he will have to be prepared for some shocks. Her inherent quality will extend to her love life, and her emotional level will be lower than his. Although she is interested in sex, she will not want to get too involved, and he may find this difficult to accept. In many respects, a partnership with a Gemini, whether that is her Sun or rising sign, is a good experience for a Taurean. She will make him reconsider his outlook on life. They will never have a dull moment together, and should enjoy developing mutual interests. Gemini is always eager to discover new subjects and Taurus will not allow her to view anything on a superficial scale.

with Cancer

The Cancerian woman is affectionate and motherly, but the depth of her character may not be revealed to the Taurean unless she is placed in a position that requires her to defend her opinions or attitudes. Still, if necessary, he will not find it difficult to persuade her to change her mind. He could learn something about flexibility from her, for stubbornness is one of his failings, especially if Uranus is in Taurus. Sexually, her romantic and, at times, sentimental nature will further enhance the partnership. Unfortunately, she is inclined to worry a great deal and also to change her moods often. But the Taurean-born is quite capable of handling both problems. If she has Cancer rising, there may be occasions when she seems to adopt a cool, practical posture. Known for her shrewdness and good business sense, the Cancerian woman will work hard to build her marriage and to protect those whom she loves, and, in turn, she will enjoy feeling protected and secure with her Taurean partner.

The Taurus Man in Love...

with Leo

The slow, safe and steady approach that often characterizes Taurus may prompt his Leo woman to pay more attention to the purely enjoyable side of love. Naturally more spirited and cheerful than he, the Leo woman may find his careful advances somewhat tedious. A relationship between the two, however, has a good chance for success. Taurus will look after his mate well, and can expect to be rewarded for his generosity. Emotionally and psychologically, the Leo woman needs to be encouraged; he will find that because of his support, she is likely to idolize him. The position of Venus at the time of her birth is of great significance. If it falls in Cancer, their affair could progress more smoothly because she will probably be less exuberant. Problems could result if she has Leo rising, as she will look for the unusual or the unconventional in her partners. His basically conservative nature may prevent him from satisfying this desire. Stubbornness is not uncommon to either partner.

with Virgo

Virgo is often a shy woman and may be slow to respond sexually. Fortunately, Taurus has a great deal of patience and usually can be relied upon to be particularly affectionate under such circumstances. He will be well rewarded for his patience, although he may find her low emotional level somewhat frustrating at times. Because of her desire for perfection, Virgo can be extremely critical of her partners. Thus her Taurean lover must try to control his temper, which he has been known to lose in the past, and help her relax. The position of Mars and Venus in her chart will help him assess her underlying attitude towards sexual and emotional relationships. The partnership will benefit enormously if Venus falls in Libra, the second Venus-ruled sign. Her problems, coolness and a matter-of-fact outlook on all spheres of her life, will be compounded if it is in Virgo. She will be more romantic towards him if she has Virgo rising. This pair are likely to share a practical outlook.

with Libra

Although Taurus and Libra share Venus as a ruling planet, and frequently have similar ideals, it is not always easy for a Taurean to relate to a Libran with complete freedom and affability. He might, for example, find that Libra is a pure romantic, whose attitude towards sex is languid. She is a fun-loving partner and will tease her Taurean mate in a way which appears to be light-hearted, but is often relevant to the situation at hand. It will not take long to learn that Librans tend to procrastinate, particularly if they have to make decisions; here is an excellent opportunity for the strong-minded Taurean to offer practical assistance. Their future together will be more promising if she has Venus in Virgo, as she tends to be more pragmatic; or if it is in Scorpio, as she is likely to be more sexually and emotionally responsive. The Libran woman longs for marriage or a stable relationship, and if Libra is her ascendant, a selfish streak may influence her attitude towards him.

with Scorpio

Since Taurus is slow to arouse sexually, he will probably be surprised by Scorpio's demands. A love affair between this pair will not be an uncomplicated one, but it will be strengthened by mutual rapport and great solidity. Their harmony can be attributed mainly to two factors: their polar positions in the Zodiac, and their powerful and strong personalities. The major weaknesses of both signs—Taurus's possessiveness and Scorpio's jealousy—will certainly feature in their relationship, whether her Sun sign or her rising sign is Scorpio. Unfortunately, these negative emotions, if unchecked, could eventually play a destructive role. A partnership between these two either will be tremendously rewarding or totally disappointing. Should the latter case be true, both have the ability to forget the affair within a few weeks. Mars and Venus are important factors, for Mars shares with Pluto the rulership of Scorpio. Even at its zenith, the relationship demands much of the two people concerned.

with Sagittarius

It will not take long for the Taurean man and the Sagittarian woman to discover that they are different in many respects. She is basically independent and freedom-loving, and tries to enjoy life to the fullest. Sagittarius probably has more than one emotional involvement at a time, although she will never allow herself to be totally possessed by a lover. It is perhaps this trait that is the most significant, for Taurus may want to possess her completely. Sexually, she is passionate, but as a fire sign, her emotions do not have the depth which characterizes Taurean love. Her sense of humour may be revealed at the most unexpected times and under the most unorthodox circumstances. The Sagittarian woman loves challenges of every kind, particularly in her love life. Her affectionate nature will be deepened if she has Venus in Scorpio. Should Sagittarius be her rising sign, she will be even more determined not to get married, and is likely to be more fascinated by a man's intellect than by his looks.

with Capricorn

An affair between the Taurean male and the Capricorn female would appear to have several positive factors working in its favour. Both have a definite need for security and permanence within a love partnership; both are endowed with common-sense and both share the same objectives and will enjoy working for each other in a permanent relationship. If Capricorn is her rising sign, he can expect her to be more tender towards him. Should her Venus fall in Aquarius, however, she may be cool, with the accent on friendship rather than on passion. If this is the case, problems may be in store for the affectionate and passionate Taurean. His fun-loving characteristics and capacity to enjoy life are just what the serious Capricorn woman needs. Overall, the outlook for a Taurus and Capricorn partnership is extremely favourable and in every respect, theirs should be a dynamic union. There could be arguments about money—Capricorn tends to be frugal, and Taurus extravagant.

with Aquarius

Both Taurus and Aquarius have reputations for being stubborn, and for being reluctant to change their ways; these negative traits can cause innumerable problems should these two contemplate a permanent relationship. Moreover, there are several other areas which are potentially explosive. For example, consider the Taurean man who has established himself in a conventional career, and has a girlfriend much younger than he, who is living alone and determined to preserve her independence. In some respects he may admire her for this, but he will think that her love of freedom is unfeminine and too modern for him to accept. The Aquarian woman will be satisfied with simple ties of friendship; and unless her Venus is in Pisces or perhaps Aries, she could be surprisingly aloof sexually. The position of Mars is also of particular relevance; its influence can be a positive one unless it falls in Gemini, Capricorn or Aquarius, which frequently indicates cool sexual attitudes.

with Pisces

Taurus will find he can satisfy his Piscean woman sexually and psychologically; she is sensitive and highly emotional, but his natural strength and sane outlook on life will have a reassuring effect on her. He should encourage her artistic interests, for Pisceans are usually more creative than they care to admit, and frequently leave the projects which they undertake unfinished because they lack self-confidence. An affair between these two should prove mutually satisfying: the Taurean will find his partner romantic and passionate, and she has the ability to bring out his best qualities. If Pisces is her rising sign, he should be able to appeal to a critical and practical side of her character which is not typical of her sign. He should expect to be criticized, but will be able to take it in stride. The balance between the couple may be delicate, but she needs direction, which generally he can provide. It is a question of finding a tactful approach, but the patient Taurean should be successful.

The Way to the Taurus Heart

Persuade a mutual friend to drop a hint about your culinary talents to the Taurean that you want to meet, then invite him or her to dinner, and, provided that it is a delicious meal, you may be at the threshold of a beautiful friendship. Those born under the sign of the Bull are usually self-indulgent and love good food. If you are primarily a main-course cook, no doubt the local bakery can provide a rich, fattening chocolate cake that no Taurean will be able to resist. Of course, Taureans will not be satisfied with dessert alone. You should be able to tempt them with a smooth, creamy cauliflower soup, and as the *pièce de résistance*, serve a classical steak dish, such as *tournedos Rossini*. Remember, too, that most Taurean-born are quite particular about wine, so choose with great care. Undoubtedly, good claret or burgundy will meet with approval.

If you are not a cook, then a really fine restaurant will make an equally good impression and is an ideal place for a first date. Or extend an invitation to a symphony or choral concert. Chances are that it will be readily accepted as Taureans have a reputation for being musically inclined.

Basically, people of this sign tend to prefer to live in the country rather than in towns, although, conversely, their careers often keep them in the city. They are happiest, however, working in the garden, and, generally, love growing flowers and vegetables. If you have a garden and your favourite Taurean does not, advice requested will be readily given.

It is not a good idea to make a quick pass at Taureans of either sex. This will simply not stir their passion. In fact, they are surprisingly conventional and could easily be put off. Instead, it will be to your advantage to take your time, use flattery, admire their clothes, and if you visit their home, comment on their general taste and admire their possessions. These are extremely important to them. It should not be difficult for you to do, as Taureans love delicate colours, particularly shades of blue and pink, and will furnish their homes with the accent on comfort. Couches and chairs will be scattered with several decorative cushions of velvet, or of a soft material covered with a floral design. A stereo or musical instrument is likely to be found in the living-room.

Taureans have much natural charm, and are frequently good-looking. Venus, the goddess of beauty, is their ruling planet. So even if your affair is slow to begin, you should be prepared for good company, and for other heads to turn as you pass by together. Since those born under this sign have excellent business minds and a flair for making money, a good approach, possibly more useful for a woman, is to ask for financial advice. The male Taurean will probably know the ins-and-outs of the stock market, so if his lover has some money to invest, or if she wants a better deal on her car or on a life insurance policy, she can usually rely on her Taurean's counsel. In general, Taureans will also be able to help should the stereo break down. They are eminently practical and able to do a thorough repair job on almost any piece of equipment.

Taureans tend to be conservative, but they do not consider their formality artificial. It is simply a means of making life more civilized and elegant. Their leisurely ways and calm manner help those around them to relax. But, perhaps, at times, Taureans relax so well that they are inclined to become lethargic. Their delightful sense of humour and the fact that they can take a joke well, make them favourites among their friends.

Taureans enjoy luxury and the good things of life. Keep this in mind when you are choosing presents for them. In general, a box of chocolates or some accessory for the neck or throat is certain to be appreciated. A mohair or cashmere winter scarf would make a suitable present for a Taurean man. And if you were to choose either a silk printed square in pale blue or pink or a long silk scarf that can be tied in a knot at the throat, female Taureans are bound to be delighted. They also enjoy receiving embroidery, jigsaw puzzles and cosmetics. Even more welcome would be a lovely pale leather vanity-case. Records, too, will always bring a smile to Taurean faces, but find out their preferences first.

The Gemini Woman

May 21st – June 20th

Ruling Planet: Mercury
Triplicity: Air
Keywords: Intellectual * Communicative
Jewel: Agate
Flowers: Lily of the Valley * Lavender
Trees: Nut-bearing Trees
Cities: London * San Francisco * Melbourne

The Gemini Woman in Love...

The Gemini woman's basically low emotional level makes her light-hearted, almost too casual at times, and possibly somewhat afraid of an intense emotional commitment. Frequently, if she finds herself becoming deeply involved in a liaison, her strong natural tendency is to question her feelings and even to suspect them. Basically, she is governed more by her mind than her emotions. As a result, the Gemini woman in love is faced with all sorts of conflicts that she must resolve. She will either want to accept her feelings, or will decide to keep the relationship on a casual basis. If she does not take the latter approach, her inherent duality, which affects every sphere of her life, will soon make its presence felt. It is not unusual for the Gemini woman to become bored with her lover, and, without saying anything, go off in search of another.

It is essential for a Gemini woman to enjoy her partners, and there will always be a strong element of friendship in her affairs. At times, in fact, she may keep, or attempt to keep, a relationship entirely on a platonic level. And within marriage she believes that companionship and intellectual sympathy are necessary for her well-being. Although she is not usually very passionate, she will often enjoy sexual experimentation, for variety and change are important to her general well-being.

The Gemini woman has a flirtatious reputation, and is capable of being in love with more than one man at the same time. Each lover will be respected and admired for different reasons. While this may be difficult for others to accept, it is simply a matter of course for this modern, liberated female. Consequently, the Gemini woman may have to cope with some fairly confusing situations. She is frequently misunderstood and cannot understand why other people are unable to see things the way she does. She is, however, extremely logical and rational and will try to come to terms with herself and with her partners. And if the Gemini woman does commit herself prema-

turely, she can be relied upon to adapt well to the situation, provided there are no serious restraints placed on her freedom and that her partner remains intellectually stimulating and receptive to current thinking.

The Gemini woman makes a vivacious companion, and a relationship with her could never be described as boring. She is quick-witted, fun-loving, eager to learn new things and to spark off lively discussions. But for a love affair to develop fully, she will need to analyse all aspects of the relationship carefully, and place her emotions and feelings in their proper perspective. It is extremely important that the Gemini woman does not view it in a superficial way.

with Aries

Both the Arien man and the Gemini woman like to live life at a fast pace. Since Gemini's approach to life is logical and rational, the enthusiastic, positive nature of the Arien man may prove very appealing to her. If, however, she considers having an affair with him, she must accept the possibility that he may be more passionate and eager for sex than she. It is not a question of her being cool or distant, but rather that she does not consider sex as important, and thus could find him too demanding. The position of his ruling planet, Mars, at the time when she was born, should be carefully studied. If she has Aries in the ascendant, they will be better matched sexually, and theirs could be an excellent coupling, for in other respects they are well suited. It should not be difficult for them to develop joint interests, particularly since they both enjoy being active. If he has Aries rising, he may be more romantic towards her, and they may lead a less frenetic life. They can then appreciate each other's fine qualities.

with Taurus

For the Gemini woman who is restless or suffers from bouts of nervous stress and tension, a relationship with a Taurean man could be an excellent one. He will calm her, be extremely kind, and tend to spoil her. She will appreciate his stable influence, but as their affair develops, she will soon discover his tendency to be possessive. She needs a certain amount of freedom, including friendships with other men, and he may find this difficult to accept, particularly if he has a Taurus ascendant. In addition, all Gemini women like variety, while Taurean men hate change. The Taurus lover can be expected to establish a steady routine, both in his career and at home. She may constantly want to be changing the cushion covers, the breakfast menu, the newspaper they take. In all areas, the Taurean man and the Gemini woman will have to learn to compromise. Frequently Venus, his ruling planet, will be in the same sign. If it happens to be Gemini, their problems will be fewer.

with Gemini

An affair between these two will be based upon a strong friendship and, initially, may be best described as a friendly rivalry. If a Gemini woman and a Gemini man develop a serious interest in astrology, they will have yet another topic to discuss and analyse. For, whenever they meet, they tend to exchange opinions and ideas at a non-stop pace. Occasionally, it is important for them to stop talking and assess how their relationship is developing. The female Gemini may be able to do this more readily than her partner. Otherwise, they will be living their lives purely on an intellectual and mental plane and, as a result, they could miss out on many less important but equally pleasant experiences. It is essential that they learn how to relax. They should allow time for developing joint interests and reminiscing, which will be easier for them to do if either has Venus in Cancer. And listening to music together will provide the proper atmosphere for calming their restless natures.

with Cancer

The response of the Gemini woman to the Cancerian man will depend a great deal on her background and upbringing. In general, she may find him somewhat possessive and protective, but if she did not receive much love and affection as a child, the Gemini woman will respond well to him. Considerable sympathy should exist between the pair if she has Venus in Cancer, or he has Venus in Gemini. There are, however, many basic differences between these two signs. He may expect her to be more devoted to her home and family than she is prepared to be. Gemini women are often reluctant to sacrifice a career for a family. A compromise on this issue may not be too difficult to work out since the Cancerian man enjoys taking an active part in dealing with his children. His sensuous, passionate and occasionally sentimental nature will appeal to her if she has Venus in Cancer. If it is in another sign, Gemini could easily become restless and annoyed by these traits.

The Gemini Woman in Love...

with Leo

There is no doubt that most Geminis like to spend money, and with a Leo for a lover, a Gemini woman will be entertained in grand style. Leo's sweeping statements, possibly dogmatic attitudes and pompous nature will, however, not appeal to Gemini. Of course, many Leo men are aware of their negative traits, and can control them well. If she is clever, the Gemini woman will be able to help her Leo mate recognize and deal with his less admirable characteristics. She will enjoy making love with her Leo partner; although he is passionate, he will be considerate of her feelings and wait for the right time and a comfortable setting. Should the Leo man be creative or extremely knowledgeable about a particular subject, the Gemini woman must guard against offering superficial criticism. If he loves her deeply he may take her disapproving remarks well, otherwise she may be rebuffed. If he has Leo rising, she will find the friendship side of their relationship rewarding as well as demanding.

with Virgo

Gemini and Virgo share Mercury as their ruling planet. Although Mercury has little influence on emotional relationships, it is responsible for giving them certain characteristics in common. They are both busy types who must always be doing something, and in terms of critical natures, each is likely to have met his match. Moreover, the Gemini woman will be able to provide the intellectual companionship the Virgo man desires. It will not take her long to recognize that her partner has a logical and analytical mind, which she will admire in many ways. But, occasionally, she may be annoyed by his practicality. Virgo's attitude towards sex will be cool. The Gemini woman could be frustrated by his low emotional level, as she enjoys sex. But perhaps he is shy, so she would be wise to check her flirtatious, light-hearted tendencies. If he has Virgo rising, he will respond to her in a surprisingly sensitive and emotional way. Should he have Venus in Leo, he will be inclined to enjoy life more.

with Libra

Gemini and Libra are both of the air triplicity and, consequently, are likely to get along very well. They both are light-hearted, and the Gemini woman will particularly admire this aspect of her Libran lover's personality. Furthermore, on an intellectual level they should be mutually stimulated. Despite her need for friendship, she may find him somewhat languid sexually. In addition, she will soon discover that he is the type who frequently keeps a woman waiting a long time before asking for a first date. The Gemini woman will definitely not like his indecisiveness, but she can help him by putting forward her own point of view and questioning him, thus encouraging him to make up his own mind. If Libra has Venus, his ruling planet, in Virgo, he may be slightly critical towards her; she will respond well to this change in his character. Based on a strong friendship, theirs can be an excellent partnership. Should he have a Libra ascendant, it promises to be an even more lively pairing.

with Scorpio

The Gemini woman who gets involved in a relationship with a Scorpio man may find herself coping with someone who is on a totally different emotional wavelength. Although she will probably enjoy making love with him, she will discover that sexually he is extremely demanding and very easily becomes jealous. Should Gemini and Scorpio want a permanent relationship, they will both have to be prepared to make many compromises. He will not be impressed or charmed by her lively, flirtatious manner, and, since he will also take his love and sex far more seriously than she, she could at times find him too intense. If he has Scorpio rising, he has a tendency to be possessive. If they can accept each other's failings and different motivations, they can benefit immensely from a partnership. His depth can counter her superficiality, and should they develop mutual interests, perhaps involving research, their friendship should deepen. Each must learn, however, to trust the other.

with Sagittarius

Gemini and Sagittarius are polar signs of the Zodiac, and although they differ considerably, a natural rapport should readily develop between them. The Gemini woman will immediately admire the Sagittarian's breadth of vision and outlook, and despite his inherent duality, he is less superficial than she. It is often the case that she knows a little about many things, while he knows a great deal about a few, well-chosen subjects. She will also like his rather casual attitude towards sex. The Sagittarian man is passionate, but will not be dependent on his lover, and can tolerate her liveliness. Both have a great love of freedom and a need for individual expression. She may find him more highly sexed if he has Venus in Scorpio; although he will never admit to romanticism, there is likely to be an element of it if Venus was in Libra when he was born. Because they can quickly develop joint interests, a permanent relationship often is based on an excellent friendship.

with Capricorn

In virtually all respects, the differences between these two are vast. While the Gemini woman may find a Capricorn man a bit cool and aloof, she will love his offbeat sense of humour. She will also enjoy discussing things with him and prodding him on in an argument. He is an extremely faithful lover, but has a low emotional response. While she is orientated towards the intellectual, he favours the constructive and practical. These opposite characteristics have the potential to harmonize well. He could be rather formal, and is likely to take his sex life seriously, as he tends to regard it as integral to his whole life, something not to be dismissed lightly. On the contrary, Gemini needs and thrives upon a lot of fun and informality in love. The Capricorn lover could prove to be a steadying influence for her, but she must ask herself honestly whether she wants a steady man. If Capricorn is rising in his birth chart, he may become too dependent upon her.

with Aquarius

Gemini and Aquarius share the same element—air—and if Gemini is often classed as an emotional lightweight, Aquarius is even more so. It will be the easiest thing in the world for a Gemini woman to develop a friendship with an Aquarian man, but that could well be as far as the relationship will go. Both need freedom of expression, and she will find her Aquarian partner extremely independent. Both of them are interested in sex, however, and certainly enjoy experimentation. The Gemini woman is considered to have a modern outlook; so does the Aquarian man. Perhaps these similarities will allow them to establish a happy "no strings attached" liaison. She need not worry that he will care about her affairs with other men, but if they marry, he will be both fair and faithful. These two will have endless discussions and arguments about a variety of things, but, surprisingly; the Aquarian man can become fixed in his opinions. His Gemini partner should be able to help him become more flexible.

with Pisces

Since Pisces is the most emotional sign of the Zodiac, the Gemini woman may have some difficulty coping with him. His behaviour is often irrational, but if she loves him, she will try to understand his motivations. Only if the Gemini woman is able to put them in their proper perspective, can she begin fully to appreciate his good qualities. Piscean man is frequently artistic and creative, and it is in this area that she can be of practical help to him. But the Gemini woman may be amused by her partner's sensuous and sometimes sentimental attitude towards love. She must be careful not to hurt him, for he is a particularly sensitive individual. The Piscean mate will not be so emotional if Venus was in Aquarius or in Capricorn when he was born. The relationship will be a less complicated one if it was in Aries. And should Pisces be the ascendant, she will find that, at times, he can be quite critical of her. She will respond well, however, to this change in character.

Making the Most of Gemini

The world would be an extremely dull place without Geminis. There would be far less discussion, argument and general conversation. In the past, astrologers have likened the true Geminis to small, chattering monkeys, which is not as uncomplimentary as it may sound, for they do tend to talk at a non-stop pace. Generally, everyone enjoys listening to them, since their talk is amusing and stimulating.

Geminis always have an opinion about something, whether it is about a particular subject they are studying, a news item they have just read in a newspaper or magazine, or a piece of information they have recently heard. Luckily, Geminis are quick-witted and able to absorb new ideas readily. They are quintessential interviewers, since they have inquiring minds and a smattering of knowledge about a great many things. But the clever individuals of this sign will, with great skill, give the impression that their knowledge is sound, or, with discipline, research various topics in depth. Communication is their keyword, and it is therefore not surprising that so many Geminis work in the media. Many journalists who write for mass-circulation newspapers are Geminis, as are radio and television commentators. It is in this atmosphere that they thrive and make the best use of their assets.

Restlessness is perhaps their greatest failing. They seem to have an abundance of mental energy and can easily get bored. Unless Geminis make an effort to complete every task, they tend to leave a trail of unfinished projects in their wake, never accomplishing anything in particular. It is important that they have a definite direction or goal in mind for any of their efforts to prove fruitful. Unfortunately, in many cases, it will not be easy for them to define such an objective.

There is a natural duality in all Geminis that should be encouraged. Frequently, in early childhood, Geminis are taught to concentrate on a single issue or on a specific job or even on a particular friendship. In some respects, the sooner they rebel against this teaching, the better. Geminis are simply not single-minded people. They are quite capable, for example, of dealing with a telephone call while they are writing a letter. They will be happy reading more than one book at a time, on completely different subjects. They often have two sources of income, perhaps doing some freelance writing that has no relation to their actual career or profession. Geminis are happiest when they indulge their instinct for duality. It is also true that their restlessness will be minimized once they come to terms with their personality and realize that they can derive a great deal of satisfaction from being able to drop one job, one book, one conversation, and go quickly on to another.

Geminis have the reputation of being the most up-to-date of all the zodiacal signs. They keep abreast of the younger generation's opinions on a variety of subjects, and, in particular, their views on controversial topics. In fashions, both Gemini men and women are eager to wear the newest styles and experiment with their image. This aspect is one which other people may consider superficial, but which Geminis are serious about.

Geminis are often slim and nearly always quick-moving. They are easily identified by their short, quick steps. Both sexes look well in most fashionable clothes; male Geminis seem to favour well-cut suits in interesting fabrics and contrasting-coloured shirts. They are similar to quick-change artists in their approach to clothes, as they generally discard a look as soon as they think it is no longer the current style.

Geminis like change and variety, so it is not difficult to understand why the females of this sign prefer to wear separates—to mix and match skirts, sweaters and trousers—and are adept at making the most of a relatively small wardrobe. They also enjoy wearing the latest cosmetics, particularly those for their hands, which are frequently well shaped and which they prize. As might be expected, they buy a number of hand creams and nail polishes. Since Gemini rules the hands and arms, they are likely to choose dresses that have interesting sleeves. Their arms are frequently adorned with jewellery—fun bracelets and rings, in a variety of colours.

The Gemini Man

May 21st – June 20th

Ⅱ

Ruling Planet: Mercury
Quadruplicity: Mutable
Keyword: Adaptable
Metal: Mercury
Countries: United States of America ✳ Wales
Animals: Small Colourful Birds and Butterflies
Colour: Bright Yellow

The Gemini Man in Love...

Since the Gemini man is so used to having light-hearted affairs, the realization that he is deeply in love will hit him with more impact than it does any other zodiacal type. Although he will know exactly what line of approach to take, his inner feelings will be in a complete turmoil. Rarely does he trust his emotions, and when they flood over him, he will undoubtedly be faced with conflicts. He can give countless reasons why he loves a woman, but he cannot understand why he is feeling this way about her. When his emotions rule his reason, which hardly ever happens, he is perplexed. At the same time, the Gemini man will enjoy being puzzled.

His approach to any woman he likes will not be too direct. He will discover her hobbies and interests as soon as he can, but he will not make it immediately obvious that he wants to make love to her. Books will be exchanged, and there will probably be many long telephone conversations. He will make sure that his date enjoys herself when she is out with him. The Gemini man, however, is not slow or apprehensive. He takes his opportunities as they present themselves. In fact, some of his partners will find it difficult to accept that duality affects this sphere of his life as it does every other. He has a flirtatious reputation and will probably have more than one relationship at a time. As a consequence, the Gemini-born is sometimes considered fickle, although he would not agree. He will admire different qualities in each loved one.

Among his many assets is his lively, fun-loving nature, so a woman who gets involved with a Gemini will certainly not be bored. Since he has an overwhelming urge to communicate, and a strong desire for variety and intellectual satisfaction, conversations with him are bound to be stimulating.

The most notable Gemini fault is restlessness, which, unfortunately, can affect his sex life. He and his lover may not be able to relax in a relationship, or even do only one thing during a day or evening out. It would not be unusual for the Gemini to meet his girlfriend, take her for an early evening drink, then to see a film or to the theatre, have a late supper and perhaps more drinks or coffee. Then off to bed. It is at this sort of pace that most Geminis live their lives, cramming a great deal into every day. A partner will need to have considerable stamina to keep up with him. He has an abundance of nervous energy, which he seems to live on. In general, a relationship with a Gemini will be exciting and will make most women feel younger.

with Aries

The Gemini will probably find his Arien girlfriend as lively and energetic as he, and as eager to keep busy. He will quickly discover that she is passionate and highly sexed, but will enjoy other aspects of their relationship with equal exuberance. He will admire her enthusiasm, and because they both live life at a fairly fast rate, they should enjoy each other's company. Should they decide to deepen their relationship, all indications are that it will work out well. He will not find her jealous if he has light-hearted relationships with other women, but she can be selfish. Both may have Venus in the same sign, which will strengthen their affection and help to develop their love. Sometimes Gemini is too cool and rational, while Aries is too hot and passionate. If she has Aries rising, he will soon discover that she will be even more tender towards him, instead of simply expressing a sexual interest. The partnership has a good chance for success if he has Venus in Taurus. Rivalry is likely in this combination.

with Taurus

If a Gemini man and a Taurean woman love each other, they will have to learn to compromise, for they are totally different in their approach to, and reactions in, love. The Taurus woman is steady and dependable, but she will not permit herself to be rushed into anything, particularly a serious commitment. She is passionate and sensuous, but her lover will discover that she is not easily aroused. Taurus will not appreciate her Gemini partner's somewhat light-hearted approach to love and to women. If she has Taurus rising, she may be provoked to jealousy should she see him having some fun with other women. If he realizes that she will be upset, and that no amount of discussion or reasoning on his part will make her accept it, then he would be wise to adopt a different course of action. If he has Venus in Taurus or Cancer, and she has Venus in Gemini, the relationship should be helped considerably. Of course, their respective rising signs may alter their situation completely.

with Gemini

The Gemini twins, so familiar as the pictorial representation of this sign, will certainly make their influence felt when a Gemini woman and a Gemini man have an affair, regardless of other planetary factors. Versatility will be the most obvious characteristic they have in common. While they will probably both find sexual fulfilment in the relationship, there will be a strong element of youthful friendship in it, too. These partners will delight their immediate circle of friends, for they never stop talking, discussing and arguing. They should perhaps make a conscious effort not to allow talk to occupy too much of their time. Their partnership would benefit tremendously if they relax and indulge in mutual nostalgia, or plan a vacation together; otherwise they could miss out on many rewarding experiences. There should be no serious sexual problems for this couple. If one partner has Gemini rising, they will identify with each other's objectives and psychological motivations.

The Gemini Man in Love...

with Cancer

It is important for a Gemini man to realize that a Cancerian woman is often emotional and sensitive, and can thus be easily hurt. Sexually, she is usually passionate, but far too dependent on her mate. Her whole emotional makeup prompts her to cherish a lover; and it is often true that she views every man she meets as a potential husband, for Cancer is eager to have her own home and family. Therefore, it would not be surprising if she finds Gemini's flippant attitude towards love and sex unattractive; and he could unwittingly hurt her. If he does, either she will let him know verbally, or he will soon feel her displeasure, for she is a creature of changing moods, who can sulk at the appropriate time. Gemini and Cancer are neighbours along the zodiacal belt. If Venus falls in Cancer for him or in Gemini for her, the future bodes well for the pair. Should she have Cancer rising, possible difficulties can be averted, as she is in a position to encourage him to develop his latent talents.

with Leo

It will not take the Gemini man long to realize that the Leo woman likes to enjoy life and love to the fullest. Between them they are likely to spend a great deal of time and money pursuing and enjoying mutual interests, but they will work together as hard as they play. Sometimes, however, he could be irritated by her sweeping generalizations, her lack of attention to detail, and even slightly embarrassed by her occasional displays of pomposity. Sexually, she makes an enthusiastic partner, and although the Leo woman tends to enjoy passionate affairs rather than minor attachments, she will probably not be upset by his openly flirtatious manner. The Leo woman is usually self-confident, particularly about her own attractions, so that she will not feel threatened. Moreover, Leos often have Venus in Gemini, which indicates that they also enjoy the company of male friends. As the relationship matures, she will become more tolerant, and he less superficial.

with Virgo

Caution should be the watchword for any man developing or considering a love affair with a Virgoan. It should be easier, however, for the Gemini male than for some other zodiacal signs because he shares his ruling planet, Mercury, with her. On an intellectual level, they will not have any problems getting on the same wavelength. Virgo will appreciate that kind of approach, as she is likely to be apprehensive about sexual matters, particularly if she is young. Luckily, Gemini also enjoys the friendship stage of a romance, and thus will be considerate and ready to accept her pace. Obviously, it will be a challenge to him. He would benefit by studying the position of Mars at the time of her birth since it has an influence on her sexual needs. Her somewhat cold outlook on love may be softened if Neptune was in Virgo, or if Virgo is rising in her chart. If Venus was in Virgo with the Sun, she will be critical of her Gemini partner, but her logical, analytical mind could make theirs an adventurous union.

with Libra

The Gemini man has precisely the right talent for dealing with the typical Libran fault—indecisiveness. In a light-hearted and friendly way, he can offer every conceivable reason why his Libran woman should deepen her involvement with him, and certainly will not be disheartened by her seemingly endless number of excuses. The Libran woman often puts the accent on romance rather than on sex, but in an extreme situation may even tolerate sex to secure a partner. Basically, Gemini and Libra are excellent for one another, and will share intellectual interests. Of course there may be clashes in their daily life, because he never stops arguing and discussing. Libra wants peace at any price, and he must recognize that it is easy for him to upset her delicate balance. She is ready to give a great deal of herself in a permanent relationship, but if he fails to respond fully, she may become resentful. The Libran woman will be more logical in her Gemini lover's eyes if she has Venus in Virgo, or if Libra is rising.

with Scorpio

The deeply smouldering sexuality of the typical Scorpio woman may surprise the more casual Gemini man. He could find her sexual attitude somewhat claustrophobic in the long run, although he may be delighted to know that she regards him as her ideal lover. He will not appreciate her resentfulness if he eventually develops another attachment. Should she have Scorpio rising, she will want to possess him, and is capable of great outbursts of jealousy, which will annoy him. Temperamentally, the Scorpio woman is the type who wants to delve deeply into every problem and subject, while the Gemini man is concerned only with the more superficial aspects. If they can develop a joint interest that requires research, they will have a practical bond. The position of Mars will have an important influence on her personality, as it shares the rulership of Scorpio with Pluto. Should this couple consider marriage, many compromises would need to be worked out beforehand.

with Sagittarius

This is an excellent partnership, with the polarity of the signs working in its favour. The Gemini man will soon realize that, in some areas, his Sagittarian woman will be his intellectual superior. But she can encourage him to view common interests and concerns in greater depth. Initially, they will have many lively and stimulating conversations, and he may even stay up late studying a subject in which he knows she is interested. It is not unusual for him to take a long time to explain any situation, while she can often sum it up in one succinct sentence. Sexually, the Sagittarian woman needs a certain amount of freedom within a permanent relationship, so she will not mind his lively, possibly dual attitude towards sex. He will find her a warm, enthusiastic partner, but, like him, she has a tendency to be restless. It is advisable that they both try to recognize and deal with such symptoms as soon as possible. If she has Sagittarius rising, she will then be able to identify more readily with his outlook.

with Capricorn

Although this combination of a Gemini man and a Capricorn woman may not be an easy one, there is a lot in its favour. Gemini, for example, will like his Capricorn mate's off-beat sense of humour, which is so different from his cynical or satirical kind, and her natural ability to help him practically and constructively to develop his objectives. These are sometimes quite vague. She will be ambitious for him, but he could find that she tries to push him too hard. Generally, she does not have a high emotional level, although her rising sign will have a direct bearing on this aspect of her character, and if she is somewhat cool, she will relate to him in a different way. Although they can have a great deal of fun, the partnership will have to develop gradually. His light-heartedness might annoy her, and she may consider him too flippant. Obviously, care is needed, but theirs can be a relationship that thrives. She will be a faithful lover, and should she have Capricorn rising, she will show more emotion.

with Aquarius

The Gemini man will admire many qualities in his Aquarian mate, particularly her individuality and her independence. They can build a marvellous relationship, which both will enjoy and accept on contemporary terms. She may not want to commit herself, or move out of a place she has furnished. Both have open minds about sex, and probably enjoy experimentation. If they find that they are sexually compatible, they will get great pleasure from each other's company. The Aquarian woman could be detached and distant if she has Venus with the Sun in Aquarius, or in Capricorn; he will find her much warmer, although her outlook on emotional relationships may not be well defined, if it is in Pisces. Uranus, her ruling planet, will play a more important part in her psychological makeup, so he would be wise to refer to its position. These two are good for each other. She may want to take the lead in a permanent relationship, however, should she have Aquarius rising.

with Pisces

It will probably be a mutual interest, often related to the arts, that will bring Gemini and Pisces together. They must encourage each other in their individual pursuits, and in this relationship the Gemini man should make the most of his own rational and intellectual qualities. He will soon discover that his Piscean mate is often completely ruled by her emotions, and although she is extremely talented, she may not be fulfilled, mainly because her organizational ability is not very good. In this area, he can be of immense help to her. Sexually, she is a rewarding partner, although at times he may find her too demanding. However, should he have Pisces rising, he will like a certain "edge" or a critical attitude in love, and she is bound to express this. She should be able to look more objectively at her love life if her Venus is in Aquarius, and less seriously if it is in Aries. She is sensitive and emotional, but will benefit enormously from his reassurance. Relaxation is important for this couple.

The Way to the Gemini Heart

If you keep in mind the fact that those who are born under the sign of the Heavenly Twins have an overwhelming urge to communicate, you should not have any difficulty attracting the attention of a Gemini. In general, they all enjoy talking on the telephone, receiving letters, answering questions, and sorting out problems for other people. And if those problems are related to books, magazines, newspapers or television, they will be even more delighted. It is essential, however, that your approach is friendly and casual rather than heavy or seductive. More than likely, the Gemini will quickly telephone or will reply by letter, thus giving you the opportunity to develop the relationship further.

Perhaps the easiest and most comfortable way to approach a Gemini is to invite him or her to your place for drinks or coffee, along with a few mutual friends. In such a congenial atmosphere, the Gemini guest can be depended on to initiate and to keep conversation flowing, thanks to a quick wit, an ability to absorb a variety of facts, and an inquiring mind.

In general, Gemini men and women are not interested in sexy seduction scenes in the early stages of a relationship; they might even be somewhat embarrassed. Do not forget that those born under this sign are ruled by Mercury, and therefore have rather low emotional levels but highly developed, sensitive mentalities. Consequently, they will be more responsive to friendship and intellectual stimulation.

Geminis have an inherent duality, which may not be easy for the more possessive or conventional types to accept. It finds expression in all levels of their personality, in their love life as well as in careers and hobbies. It is not unusual for Geminis to have two liaisons at the same time, two sources of income, and for the more prosperous ones, two homes. But this diversity is essential to their happiness and welfare.

Since the majority of Geminis are adaptable, they will rarely question or disagree with any social arrangements that have been made by their lovers or friends. For example, it does not matter very much to them whether they sit in the least or the most expensive seats at the theatre. Stuffiness, however, is something they cannot bear, and they are easily bored by conversation which revolves around business matters or dwells on idle social gossip. In such a situation, they will provoke arguments, making outrageous suggestions and offering outlandish opinions, solely as a means of stimulating an interesting exchange of ideas. This tactic is often successful, but Geminis can be bested if one of the group happens to be well versed on a subject that they have brought up for discussion.

Remember that in all facets of their lives Geminis enjoy living at a fast pace, and cannot tolerate boredom. The mere thought of it fills them with anxiety. Should you become involved with a Gemini, do not plan on a quiet evening for two at home. Suggest a number of activities, and although you may be exhausted and longing for a little peace at the end, your lover will be most appreciative of your efforts. As the relationship matures, get your Gemini mate to relax. He or she lives on nervous energy, and, as a result, is a prime candidate for a breakdown.

Geminis like variety and change in their music and food, too. They enjoy listening to folk, classical and country and western records. The perfect meal for your Gemini guest should include *gazpacho*, which is a cold vegetable soup of Spanish origin, and as a main course, perhaps some sweet-and-sour pork, or the Italian speciality *chicken Jolanda*. Choose a bottle of Moselle or a light claret to accompany the meal. For dessert, serve *zabaglione*.

Should you need to choose a gift for a Gemini, remember that women born under this sign take great pride in their hands and, as a result, pay a great deal of attention to them. They love lotions, manicure sets, bracelets and rings. The last two items need not be expensive, as they seem to favour junk jewellery and colourful plastic bangles. In general, Geminis would appreciate receiving a good dictionary, a portable typewriter, a game of Scrabble, driving gloves or magazine subscriptions. To help them occupy their spare time, consider giving them model kits of such things as vintage cars or aeroplanes.

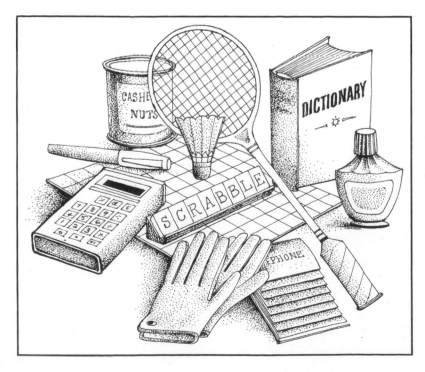

The Cancer Woman

June 21st – July 20th

Ruling Planet: *The Moon*
Triplicity: *Water*
Keywords: *Emotional * Intuitive*
Jewel: *Pearl*
Flowers: *Acanthus * White Flowers*
Trees: *Those Rich in Sap*
Cities: *Amsterdam * New York * Venice*

The Cancer Woman in Love...

Of all the zodiacal signs, Cancer is the most family-orientated. The Cancerian woman can readily see every man as a potential husband and the father of her children. While enjoying the early stages of a love affair, and possibly a rather speedy marriage, she will really come into her own when she is pregnant. All her thoughts and actions will be based on a strong urge to cherish and protect her family.

In this emancipated age, however, the Cancerian-born may react to love in precisely the opposite way, firmly stating that she is not prepared to be tied down to a family and to neglect her business interests, career, or other objectives in life. If the Cancerian woman does adopt this attitude, she will make use of her powerful psychological defence system—the Cancerian "shell" will act as a buffer against such pressures—thus making it easier for her to resist the home-making urge. And her innate shrewdness will serve her well in whatever business endeavour she undertakes.

At some point, however, the tide will turn abruptly, and the defensive shell will crack. Then the Cancerian woman will break down whatever barriers—sometimes self-imposed—exist between her and the object of her affections.

It will not take the man of her choice long to feel the full force of her change of attitude. Although she is normally a sensual and highly responsive partner, she will seem suddenly to come alive when she is sure that she is in love. But she does need to proceed with care, for she must accept the possibility that her lover may not be quite so seriously involved as she, and consequently, she could get hurt. The Cancerian woman will find it difficult to give her loved one up if he wishes to end the affair. She tends to be clinging and sometimes too sentimental, inclined to look back to the days when everything was

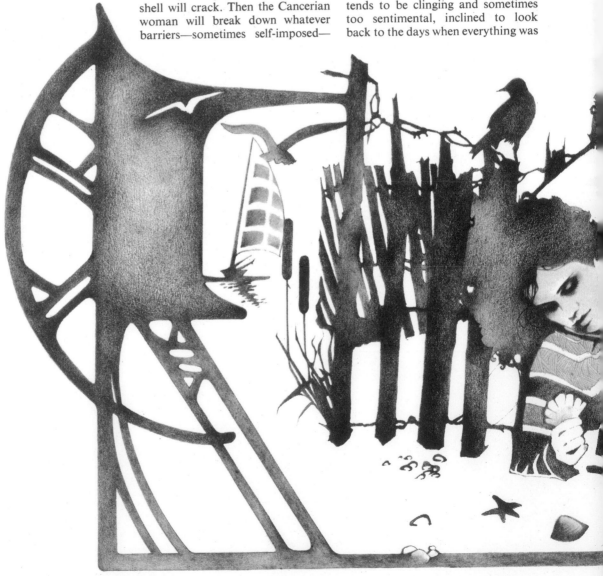

with Aries

going well between them. He, on the other hand, could find this tedious and may be forced to break away by resorting to gentle but firm measures.

In love, the Cancerian woman must try to control her natural but disconcerting tendency to change her mood from moment to moment. She easily becomes confused by inner conflicts and by other people's reactions to her. At her best, she is a marvellous romantic partner, but many superb relationships have been seriously marred by the Cancerian's abrupt mood swings. She can readily change from a tender, kind, considerate woman to an ill-tempered crabbed one, who is prone to making hurtful remarks to friends and loved ones.

The Cancerian woman must be willing to recognize and accept that the Arien man's outlook on life, and indeed his whole motivation, are different from hers. As the relationship matures, however, they will both discover how complementary many of their character traits are. He is brave, in a somewhat blustering but pioneering way. She is brave, too, and has great tenacity of purpose. Together they will strive for progress in life, and will both desperately want to be successful. She must be particularly careful that she does not bother him, for he is independent and freedom-loving, and may not enjoy being fussed over. She must also remember that his worst fault is selfishness. If she is subtle and cautious, she should be able to find ways to help him control this weakness. A relationship between the two will be influenced by the positions of both Mars, his ruling planet, and Venus. He will be sexually demanding, but how he expresses pure affection will relate strongly to the position of Venus in his chart.

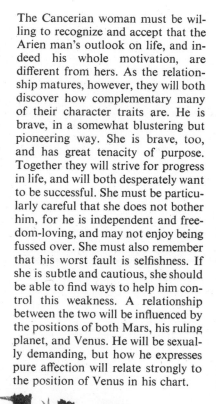

with Taurus

The Taurean man can give the Cancerian woman precisely what she needs in terms of security and sensual pleasure, and she, in turn, can help him view life in a more interesting, imaginative way. One point worth remembering is that the Taurean-born is slow and steady, and does not like change or even a simple disruption in his daily routine. Cancerians, on the other hand, like change, and the Taurean man may get somewhat upset if, for example, his loved one changes the arrangement of the furniture, or tries to spur him into activity that will further his career. But she is shrewd, and therefore, it should not be difficult for her to pick the most appropriate time to make useful suggestions. The Cancerian-born are more prone to worry than those of other zodiacal signs, but her Taurean lover should be able to calm her frayed nerves and allay any fears. If he has Taurus rising, he may relate to her more emotionally, but she must expect him to be jealous or possessive on occasion.

with Gemini

The rising signs of the Cancerian woman and the Gemini man may indicate stabilizing factors which could positively influence an otherwise restless partnership. Because both are inconsistent types and love variety, there may be misunderstandings between them. Basically, these are not unpleasant or negative qualities, but Cancer's changeability is reflected in her moods and feelings, while Gemini's is related to his mental and intellectual states of mind. If the Cancerian woman can recognize this difference and learn to cope with it, she may be able to instil some of her patience into her Gemini partner. In addition, she must acknowledge that he is not highly emotional, and be willing to accept that he may occasionally find it difficult to accept or even trust his emotions. If he has Venus in Cancer, and she in Gemini, theirs can be an excellent pairing. Should he have Gemini rising, she will have to learn to admire his breadth of vision as well as come to terms with his need for freedom.

The Cancer Woman in Love...

with Cancer

For the Cancerian woman who is longing to settle into a permanent relationship, a meeting with another Cancerian might certainly provide the opportunity. Having decided on mutual objectives, they will both work hard to attain them. They could, however, find themselves getting irritable too easily, and worrying over trivialities. Should this be the case, they must try to relax more, particularly if they have any children, who will undoubtedly suffer more than their parents realize. Sexually, the Cancer couple should be well matched, but the position of Mars at the time each was born needs to be carefully studied. If they have Venus in the same sign, prospects for a happy future together look promising. If he has Cancer rising, his attitude towards her could be somewhat remote, and possibly less emotional. She will know that he can be relied upon to be a faithful partner, giving her a sense of security. Cancerians will enjoy sharing hobbies which each has developed before they meet.

with Leo

A combination of Cancer, which is ruled by the Moon, and Leo, which is ruled by the Sun, is the perfect blending of the masculine and feminine types, and of power and vitality with response and instinct. These qualities can create a wonderful partnership, although some compromises will be necessary. The relationship may be complicated by the Cancerian's need to be an individual in her own right and to pursue a career. She will have strongly to impress her Leo partner with her attitudes. In the long run, he will respect her for it, and encourage her. But should she be willing to settle down to domesticity, he may tend to become over-dominating. He makes an excellent if demanding father and a warm and enthusiastic lover, so, overall, she should be relatively content. In this pairing, it will be primarily her responsibility to see that she is treated on equal terms. The Cancerian woman has a choice: she can assert herself, or allow her loved one to rule her.

with Virgo

The Cancerian woman may find the Virgoan man a rather reticent lover, for he can be fussy and clinical in his attitude towards sex, and he is not as emotional as she. In addition, he is likely to be somewhat critical of her, but she can certainly cope with this, since she is not lacking in quick verbal wit with which to defend herself. These problems need not prevent a Cancerian and Virgoan from building a good relationship. She will admire his practicality and his simple, although analytical, approach towards life. The Virgoan will not be particularly affectionate and warm towards his loved one, but should he have Venus in Libra or a Virgo ascendant, he could well be a more responsive partner. Neptune, the planet of romance, could exert a positive influence if he was born with it in Virgo, near the Sun. Before they can consider a permanent commitment, each one must try to take life as it comes, for of all the signs in the Zodiac theirs are the two most prone to worry.

with Libra

Although the Cancerian woman will find the calm, lyrical qualities of her Libran man appealing, his indecisiveness could be a constant source of worry. In the early stages of their relationship, she will have to wait around while he makes up his mind whether to ask her out for dinner; later, it will manifest itself when they have a practical problem that requires a prompt and positive solution or action. She will find her Libran lover pleasant and not too demanding, but he may be more passionate than she suspects if Venus, his ruling planet, is in Scorpio. While the Cancerian woman will be eager to have her own home and family, he is usually even more interested in developing a permanent relationship, and often has a tendency to rush into marriage. It will be necessary for her to bring her admirable defence system into play, because his romanticism could easily sweep her off her feet. The Cancerian woman should give herself more time to think before committing herself.

with Scorpio

This is an extremely emotional and highly sexed pairing; it is one in which both the Cancerian woman and the Scorpio man will have difficulties remaining rational. Undoubtedly, there will be some fantastic times which neither will want to forget, but these could be offset by outbreaks of Scorpio's jealousy or Cancer's moodiness and harsh manner. Should they be able to recognize and control these character weaknesses that could damage a potentially excellent union, they can have a wonderful life together. On a more practical and routine level, the Cancerian woman will find her Scorpio lover an intensely hard worker, and their partnership is certain to grow in a material sense. Likewise, she can contribute to this growth by using her natural shrewdness to pursue some business undertaking. Joint interests are advisable, for it is important that their strong emotions have outlets other than sex. Should he have Scorpio rising, he will be kinder, but perhaps more possessive.

with Sagittarius

Allowances will probably have to be made on both sides when a Cancerian woman becomes involved with a Sagittarian man. Basically, her interests centre on the home and family, while he needs a certain amount of freedom within a permanent relationship or marriage. So if she wants their affair to progress, she will have to learn to cope with his independent streak; otherwise she is likely to start nagging him and the bonds between them will inevitably weaken. He cannot tolerate possessiveness or jealousy. Although the Sagittarian man is demanding in love, he is not a romantic. In fact, his honesty often causes him to be blunt or tactless to a loved one. The Sagittarian man needs a partner who is intellectually stimulating. He will make a devoted and appreciative husband and a wonderful father. He will be eager to teach and encourage his children, particularly in sports or in intellectual activities. This pairing could have its complications should he have Sagittarius rising.

with Capricorn

The fact that Cancer and Capricorn are opposite signs across the Zodiac seems to indicate that they will complement each other well. Although it should not take the Cancerian woman long to realize that she and her Capricorn lover differ in many respects, she will respect his nobility, straightforwardness and faithfulness. In sexual matters, she could find him rather cool and aloof, and certainly his emotional level will be much lower than hers. But gradually she will discover his admirable qualities. Both are inclined to moan and complain about their individual lot at times, but as long as they both maintain their sense of humour, theirs can be an excellent combination. The Cancerian woman, above others, can help him attain his goals; Capricorns are known to be ambitious, and frequently are successful in reaching the top positions in whatever careers they choose. So should she notice that he is holding back and not seizing his opportunities, the Cancerian woman must ease him out of the doldrums.

with Aquarius

It would not be unusual for the Cancerian woman to meet her Aquarian lover while each is pursuing some interest or hobby, perhaps archaeology or history. If it does not happen this way, however, it is important that they develop some joint interest in the early stages of the relationship, so that they will have an opportunity to get to know each other. They are completely different types. She will find the Aquarian man interesting, possibly modern in outlook, and certainly unemotional. Because their motivations are dissimilar, they meet with certain difficulties. It is unlikely that he will want to settle into a permanent relationship with one woman and may only be interested in the Cancerian woman from the point of view of friendship and/or sex, but not marriage. So she must take this into consideration before she gets too involved. This can be a partnership in which each can do a great deal for the other, with their widely different characteristics complementing rather than clashing.

with Pisces

When a Cancerian woman gets involved with a Piscean man, it will not take her long to realize that he does not have a great deal of psychological strength. Because he was born under an impressionable, emotional sign, she would be wise to study the positions of Mars, which influences sexual energy, and his rising sign to see if these add power to his chart. Sexually, they will be quite compatible, but in a long-term relationship she may well find that it will be necessary for her to attend to such matters as making sure that the bills are paid on time. There is a strong possibility that the partnership may not develop and, as a result, slowly grow stale. The Cancerian woman may have to be brave at this point and make a final break, or adopt a constructive attitude to cope with the lack of direction. The position of Neptune, his ruling planet, is more important to Pisces than it is to most other people. There may be a strengthening factor to the partnership should he have Pisces rising.

Making the Most of Cancer

Cancerians are natural-born worriers. As soon as one problem is resolved, they find another that needs their attention. In addition, they have to contend with being teased about their strong tendency to worry because their facial expressions so readily reveal their inner turmoil. As tension increases, a tell-tale vertical line appears between their eyes. Get a Cancerian to relax, and the usually somewhat pale complexion will have a beautiful glow.

It is delightful to have Cancerian friends, for they will be truly concerned and sympathetic about your well-being. If, for example, you are not feeling well, the Cancer-born will be the first to arrive with something light and delicate to tempt your appetite. Friendships formed with those born under the sign of the Crab will undoubtedly last a lifetime, regardless of the distance between you or lapse of time between meetings.

Cancerians have powerful instincts and generally live by their intuition; most of the time they will be right if they rely solely upon their feelings. In their careers and in their domestic life, they demonstrate extreme shrewdness. Many Cancerian-born have built business empires from scratch, and they are unlikely to let anyone take advantage of them. Moreover, their innate tenacity prevents them from giving up any ideas or projects easily.

In love, Cancerians are probably the most romantic and imaginative people in the Zodiac. Often, however, they are reluctant to display their feelings to others because they are naturally shy and fear rejection or ridicule. Once they overcome such obstacles and profess their love, Cancerians show themselves to be affectionate and protective. Unfortunately, they are inclined to cling desperately to partners. They must make themselves more aware of this tendency, otherwise they can unwittingly make their lovers feel smothered. Cancerians are sensitive and very easily offended, but sometimes it is they who show a rather hard streak, and hurt others more than they realize. It is not easy for them to grasp this fact, mainly because any pain they inflict will be an expression of their elaborate self-defence system, which both sexes share.

Cancerians should strive for a certain softness in their appearance. The females of this sign look well in soft crêpe or fine wool dresses in shades of pale grey, blue or green. The males, particularly on formal occasions, will enhance their image by wearing fine wool suits and pale-coloured shirts and ties.

Cancerians often are not concerned with wearing the latest styles of clothing. Indeed, they may even be guilty of keeping new items in a clothes closet for months before actually wearing them. So it is perhaps best for Cancerians to choose outfits that do not date easily. Unfortunately, Cancerians are likely to spoil their outward appearance by slight carelessness: a shoulder-strap will show, a button will be missing, or casual shoes will be worn with an expensive business suit. They should try to make a habit of checking their overall appearance before going out on a date or to the office.

The usually delicate Cancerian skin will not respond well to the strong rays of the sun. Consequently, holidays by the sea, which Cancerians look forward to, may be dearly paid for in the form of a severe sunburn. They would be wise to do their sunbathing in careful stages, always using an effective tropical suntan lotion, and making certain that they do not fall asleep in the sun, even for a few minutes. Those born under the sign of the Crab look their best in full moonlight.

Wherever the Cancer-born live, they will make it feel and look quite home-like. They do have a tendency to be untidy so when visitors are expected, they often have to make a last-minute dash around the living-room to make sure that toys and magazines which have been left in odd piles are picked up. By the time guests sit down to dinner, all signs of clutter will have disappeared from the room. Cancerians of both sexes are excellent cooks, and would not consider serving any course that they had not made themselves. Cancerian women will set their tables impeccably, with a fine display of silver. Bowls and vases of flowers, in delicate arrangements, will be found throughout their homes.

The Cancer Man

June 21st – July 20th

Ruling Planet: The Moon
Quadruplicity: Cardinal
Keyword: Outgoing
Metal: Silver
Countries: Scotland ✳ *Holland* ✳ *New Zealand* ✳ *Paraguay*
Animals: Those with a Shell Covering
Colours: Pale, Smoky Grey and Green

The Cancer Man in Love...

Although the Cancerian man in love may try to hide his feelings underneath a seemingly indifferent façade, there is bound to be inner turmoil. When he is first attracted to a woman, he will use a cautious approach, as he fears being ridiculed or rebuffed. And even if the Cancerian man is convinced that she is interested in him, he will continue to act with care. Once committed, he will be an extremely kind, considerate and protective lover. In fact, he is inclined to be too attentive, so that his loved one could easily feel overwhelmed by his care and affection. He may find that his partner needs more freedom than he will feel able to allow her; she will probably get quite annoyed if she sees her independence being gradually curtailed, or that her Cancerian lover is beginning to father her.

Sexually, his sensual, passionate nature should satisfy his partner fully. But a word of warning: when in love, the Cancerian sensitivity is at its peak, and, as a result, his typical moodiness can become almost intolerable. What is a blissfully romantic occasion one moment can suddenly turn into sheer misery the next. He can become harsh and far more unkind than he realizes. The situation can further deteriorate if his loved one retaliates. Overall, an affair with a Cancerian can be marvellous, with some notable high spots, but it can also plummet unexpectedly to the depths. Like the Cancerian woman, the male of this sign is motivated towards marriage and having a family and a home of his own. Should he be single, he probably views every woman he is attracted to as a potential wife. But he will not rush into a permanent commitment, for he is too cautious and would hate to make a mistake. If this happens, his powerful memory and tendency to look to the past rather than the future can play havoc with him, and consequently, make him miserable. It is never easy for the Cancerian man to forget in a hurry, and sometimes this inability is coupled with a strong sentimental streak that can be rather tedious for his intimates should adverse conditions prevail.

It is more than likely that the Can-

cerian man will prefer a conventional marriage to a mere liaison; he tends to feel insecure without a religious or legal contract between his wife and himself, particularly if there are children involved. The Cancerian man can be relied upon to work extremely hard for their mutual spiritual and material progress, and is capable of making great sacrifices for his loved ones. He has many qualities that will make him an excellent father. Should any difficult problems arise, his children know that he will be kind, understanding and ready to give practical help and advice. Furthermore, the Cancerian man is highly imaginative, and will delight in making up bedtime stories for his sons and daughters.

with Aries

The Arien woman is so straightforward and uncomplicated that the Cancerian man initially may feel somewhat apprehensive about starting an affair with her. He is her opposite—a complicated, evasive man, who does not always find it easy to be direct. In this pairing, however, he should try to be, as the Arien woman could get bored just waiting for him to ask her out. Once the liaison develops, he will find her a passionate and sensuous lover, but there is a good chance that she may not take the relationship as seriously as he. If this is the case, he could get hurt. The Arien-born likes her freedom, while he has a tendency to depend on a loved one too much. Should he react sharply towards her, he could be on the receiving end of an Arien temper tantrum. If she has Venus in Pisces, she will be more sensitive, and the ties between them should be strengthened. Her worst fault is selfishness, but if the Cancerian man has Aries rising, he could help her deal with it.

with Taurus

The Taurean woman's sensuous and passionate nature should prove quite appealing to the Cancerian man. She has a definite need for security on all levels, and particularly in emotional relationships, which she takes seriously. She enjoys being pampered by her Cancerian lover, and although he is not the most freedom-loving type, he must remember that she is capable of being very possessive. Since he usually has a strong urge to protect, he may not mind this trait too much. Moreover, he will appreciate her good sense and practical outlook. The Cancerian man will need to be patient in the sexual sphere; although she is a passionate lover, the Taurean female may be slow to arouse. They should discover that they have similar attitudes towards life, love and future objectives. Some tension could arise if she has a Taurus ascendant, for she might show a jealous streak, at times, when he knows there is no basis for it. Should Venus be in Cancer, prospects are excellent for their future.

with Gemini

Since the Cancerian man and the Gemini woman have completely different character traits, it would be to his advantage to proceed with caution before definitely committing himself to a permanent relationship with her. She is basically unemotional and light-hearted, avoiding any serious involvement with one man, particularly when she is making substantial progress in her career. It is not uncommon for the Gemini woman to change her outlook and opinions, while he is more likely to change his moods and feelings. Her friendly nature will appeal to him, but he may find it difficult to accept her need for sexual freedom. Cancer and Gemini are neighbours along the Zodiac, so it is quite likely that they will have Venus in the same sign. Should this be the case, they will have a better chance to develop a more harmonious and affectionate partnership. Each will be fascinated by the other's motivation: Cancer responds emotionally and intuitively, Gemini rationally and logically.

with Cancer

If Cancerians of opposite sexes begin an affair, it will not take them long to realize that they share many of the same objectives in life, regardless of whether Cancer is the Sun or rising sign. But the fact that these two people were born under the sign of the Crab does not mean that they will be identical. Environment and heredity will ensure the development of distinctly different individuals. They should be in accord, however, in their attitudes towards sex and emotional relationships. As the partnership develops, the Cancerian man may well find that his loved one is prepared to take him seriously. Problems could arise if she has to sacrifice a promising career. In general, the Cancerian woman is inclined to give in to her extremely powerful maternal instincts, and opt for marriage and a family. In turn, the Cancerian male will have as strong an urge to cherish and protect her and their children as she has to mother them. There is a risk that they may cling to each other, even if the love has died.

The Cancer Man in Love...

with Leo

In this particular partnership, there is likely to be an element of role reversal. In the male, the motherly intuitive influence of Cancer is operating, in the female, the active fatherly influence of Leo. These tendencies should not have a negative effect on this coupling, but, as a result, it is conceivable that their individual approach to life may be markedly different. It would not be unusual for the Cancerian man to find his Leo partner too domineering and forthright. If this is so, he must point this out to her, for these are the worst Leonine faults. On the other hand, she could be quite annoyed by her Cancerian lover's more complicated and evasive nature. In the sexual sphere, each can learn a great deal from the other. Should they share the position of Venus, their relationship will be helped enormously. If the Leo woman can learn to blend her extremely constructive characteristics, the pair could be very happy. They would do well to develop mutual interests.

with Virgo

The Cancerian man's approach to a Virgoan woman should be as evasive and indirect as possible. More than likely, she will be genuinely reticent and shy. It would be to his advantage to study the position of Mars at the time of her birth, as it could accentuate her sexuality. But if Venus, the planet of love and affection, was in Virgo with the Sun, she may well be inclined to criticize him about niggling, petty things. Because of this tendency, there will undoubtedly be occasions when he is sufficiently provoked to make sharp remarks to her. The modest Virgoan, however, will be most appreciative of and responsive to his natural sensitivity and strong protective urge. Since the women born under the sign of the Virgin generally have low emotional levels, the couple will have to make some allowances. Should she have a Virgo ascendant, her lover may be surprised at the extent of her affection for him. Since both are prone to worry, their union would benefit from joint interests.

with Libra

At heart the Cancerian man and the Libran woman are romantics, but their motivation and outlook on life are quite dissimilar. Unfortunately, an affair between the two may never have the chance to develop into a serious relationship if he is too cautious in his approach to her, and if she takes too much time deciding whether to get involved with him. Should they get together, they will probably regret that they took so long to do so. The Libran woman will like his romantic, sensuous attitude towards love and sex, but, unless her Venus is in Scorpio, she is likely to be less emotional than he. It is essential that the Cancerian man recognizes that his lover needs to lead a peaceful existence; she will do everything possible to avoid quarrels and controversial issues. Should he start carping or nagging, her equilibrium will be upset for days. Consequently, the tranquillity of their home will be disturbed. This is a pairing that will require their attention, particularly if she has Libra rising.

with Scorpio

A very exciting, highly charged emotional relationship awaits a Cancerian man who starts an affair with a Scorpio woman. Undoubtedly, blissful moments will be offset by some unpleasant scenes. He may find that his Scorpio lover has a tendency to become jealous, even when there is no basis for it. Should their affair be deteriorating, it is quite possible that she will be the one to take the initiative to break away, while he may want to continue. He would be wise to let her go, otherwise the strain on their nerves and emotions may become intolerable. Since they share the same element, water, their type of emotion is almost identical. Theirs can be a memorable relationship as long as they remain clearheaded and keep their sense of perspective. Prospects are favourable for a long-term partnership, particularly if she has a Scorpio ascendant. He should study the position of Mars, which is her co-ruling planet along with Pluto, at the time of her birth. It will influence her emotional state.

with Sagittarius

If the Cancerian man and the Sagittarian woman want their partnership to be permanent, they will have to give it a great deal of careful and serious thought. In general, she is not the type of woman to devote herself exclusively to a home and family. Should the Sagittarian woman have a university or college degree, or have made substantial progress in her career, she will be thoroughly conditioned to a life of intellectual challenge. In addition, she needs to have freedom of expression. So if a Capricorn man believes that his lover should be content to be a wife and mother, he will have to readjust his thinking if he has married a Sagittarian. Once married, she is likely to find raising a family a challenge, but it certainly will not stimulate her enough. Sexually, the Cancerian man will find her a fulfilling partner, but she may not regard sex as seriously as he. If Venus was in Scorpio at the time of her birth, she may express her feelings towards him with more intensity.

with Capricorn

In a relationship between a Cancerian man and a Capricorn woman, there is bound to be a degree of rapport, as they are polar signs across the Zodiac. He may find her slightly remote, almost cool, if Venus was in Capricorn or in Aquarius when she was born. But he is in a strong position to cope with her low emotional level. Since she is more cautious than he, the Cancerian lover would do well to proceed with more than his usual care, particularly in sexual matters. Generally, she is an ambitious woman who can be a tremendous asset if, for example, her partner is in business. He will soon notice that she is able to make original suggestions, and should he bring his boss home for dinner, he knows that he can rely upon her to be a gracious hostess. The Cancerian man will be in an extremely good position if she has Capricorn rising, for they will be able to identify with and respond to one another. If there is any difficulty in this pairing, it may be on the sexual level.

with Aquarius

In virtually all respects, these two signs could not be more dissimilar. So if a Cancerian man finds himself attracted to an Aquarian woman, it would be to his advantage to find a common interest for them to develop. Both are fascinated by the past; perhaps an historical or archaeological topic would be a good starting point. Or, since the two are known for their kindness and humanitarianism, mutual involvement in a charitable cause may prove to be a suitable vehicle. Nevertheless, it will not take the Cancerian man long to discover that his loved one prefers to be completely independent, having already established her own life-style, and often living alone. Potentially serious problems could arise between them because she may well not want to be loved and protected in the way that he feels she should be. In fact, she is likely to find him too overbearing. Sexually, her approach may be too unconventional for him, and, in addition, she may not want to be tied to one deep emotional relationship.

with Pisces

If a Cancerian man gets involved with a Piscean woman, he will soon discover that she does not have a very strong personality. Unfortunately, life is frequently difficult for the Piscean-born, so he would be wise to show her the full extent of his kind and protective nature. In organizational terms, the Cancerian man can also do a lot for his loved one, so that her creative and artistic potential can be realized. If he can encourage her and give her a feeling of stability, she, in turn, will see that their sex life is a fulfilling one. Since the Piscean-born are known to be the most emotional, he should not be surprised to see a tearful look in her eyes most of the time. Consequently, he must be careful not to lose his temper or make a cutting remark, for she is very sensitive and may simply not be able to take it. He will find her slightly more matter-of-fact and critical towards him if she has Pisces rising. Neptune, her ruling planet, is more important to her than to any other zodiacal type.

The Way to the Cancer Heart

If a liberated career woman begins an affair with a Cancerian man, she must act cautiously. Otherwise the liaison may quickly develop into a long-lasting partnership, because those born under the sign of the Crab generally are more strongly motivated to marry and have a family than any other zodiacal member. The majority of female Cancerians do not feel completely fulfilled until they have children; males often expect their spouses to give up their professional life and devote themselves exclusively to domestic matters. In turn, they will use their tenacity and loyalty to build their marriage, to see that their family is well provided for and to do everything in their power to make it a permanent union.

Should you decide, however, to try and win the heart of the Cancerian-born, remember that they are usually excellent cooks and will be impressed by an individual's culinary skills. But do not forget that they are rather shy and could easily be intimidated by the suggestion of an intimate dinner for two at your place. For a first date, you would be wise to arrange a small dinner-party with mutual friends. They would also appreciate being invited to your family home for Sunday dinner. In general, you will find that Cancerians get along well with parents and younger brothers and sisters in the immediate family circle. In fact, there will be times when you may feel neglected.

It is important that you are careful, however, because the Cancerian-born are true romantics and are extremely protective of those they love. If necessary, they are capable of great sacrifices. They are usually very generous individuals, who expect little in return. So if your feelings for one another are reciprocal, the future bodes well. But if yours change, it will be your responsibility to break away in a gentle but firm manner. Cancerians are usually unable to end a love affair, even when they know it has lost its sparkle.

The major Cancerian faults are a crabbed, short temper and moodiness. On occasion they will even snap at or make cutting remarks to friends. Minor events, which would not bother the less sensitive, can upset Cancerians and spoil many good times. It is difficult for them to find a balance between their extremes of feeling and action. They do not respond well to being teased about their feelings. Should you do so, their mood can blacken to such an extent that everything is permeated with their gloom. The best thing to do is to ignore these bad times, if possible, because their swings of emotion change very rapidly.

Cancerians of both sexes would thoroughly appreciate receiving any gift that was made of silver, which is the metal of this sign. It is not unusual for wealthy Cancerians to collect silver cutlery, tableware, curios or antiques. By nature, the Cancerian-born are the collectors of the Zodiac; if they do not collect, they hoard. If you want to make an impression on a person born under the sign of the Crab, find out in advance what is collected, and then add a suitable item to it. Perhaps it will be matchboxes, postage stamps, or fossils.

A less original present, but one which would be most acceptable to either sex is an umbrella. Cancerians tend to be pessimistic and usually take one with them, even if the sky is clear. Females enjoy receiving toilet water that has a delicate scent, or gadgets that could help them save time in the kitchen. Males seem to favour any item that would improve or add to their camping or fishing equipment. Basically, the Cancerian's interests are either of a relaxing nature, or of a harsh and aggressive one; some love quietly boating, fishing or playing chess, while others enjoy shooting and sports car racing.

When you finally decide that the time is right to invite your Cancerian lover for a romantic dinner, have some lyrical, classical or pop music playing in the background. Set the table with highly polished silver cutlery and a pale grey tablecloth or napkins. These touches are bound to delight the Cancerian eye. The ideal menu should contain some smooth, bland recipes. As an appetizer, serve vichyssoise or salmon pâté; for the main course, choose *sole à la bonne femme*, or chicken à la king. A light white wine, perhaps a Rhine, will make a suitable accompaniment to the meal. Undoubtedly, you can expect to receive a return invitation.

The Leo Woman
July 21st – August 21st

Ruling Planet: The Sun
Triplicity: Fire
Keyword: Enthusiastic
Jewel: Ruby
Flowers: Sunflower ✳ Marigold
Trees: The Palm ✳ Bay ✳ Walnut
Cities: Rome ✳ Prague ✳ Damascus

The Leo Woman in Love...

When the Leo woman realizes that she is in love and that her feelings are reciprocated, she will really blossom, wearing her most flattering clothes, or perhaps even buying a completely new wardrobe. Her glowing expression of happiness will assure friends and relatives that everything is going well for her.

She will idolize her loved one, putting him on a pedestal in the belief that he is the epitome of perfection. This could prove quite disconcerting to him. The Leo woman will be extremely generous in expressing her love, emotionally, materially and sexually. She will try to make every meeting a memorable occasion, and will do everything possible to ensure that her man is happy, pampering him and deriving a great deal of pleasure from seeing him obviously comfortable and satisfied.

The Leo woman has a great deal to give to a lover, and inevitably, will make him the centre of her whole existence. Whatever she does will be a reflection of her love for him and an expression of her joy and exuberance in their relationship.

Since the Leo woman has such a strong personality, she needs to keep her inclination to be domineering in check. She has the inherent leonine tendency to rule and, as a consequence, she may try to assume a dominant role in an emotional relationship, particularly if her lover has a weaker personality or is less extroverted than she. The Leo woman will want the affair to develop steadily on all levels, and should her partner be reticent, she will certainly do something to encourage more positive responses.

Unfortunately, in her eagerness to have a spectacular and passionate affair, she may not show care, forethought and tact, but rather act in too eager and too impulsive a manner. In general, the Leo woman

is the type to indulge in love relationships on a grand scale, having perhaps fewer affairs than many other zodiacal types and treating each one with special care. Her love is very constant.

When things go wrong for the Leo woman in love, she will probably suffer in silence, with her pride hurt as well as her tender emotions. She can be surprisingly sensitive and depressed for such a positive personality. It will not take her long, however, to bounce back, perhaps bravely feigning happiness rather than allowing anyone, especially her ex-lover, to see how miserable she is.

with Aries

Whether she is madly in love with an Arien man or merely attracted to him, a Leo woman will have to come to terms with traits in his basic character that she will either disapprove of or be unwilling to accept. He is passionate, and generally likes to develop his affairs quickly. Unless his partner is young and enthusiastic, she will object to being seduced in an uncomfortably small car or on damp grass. In addition, she will soon realize that he can be somewhat selfish, but she will approve of his approach to love, and his endearing if sometimes simplistic attitude towards life. Since Mars is his ruling planet, she would do well to discover the sign it was in at the time of his birth, as it will add an important dimension to his personality. If he has Venus in Pisces, the Leo woman will probably find him more tender and affectionate than usual, which will make him an even more appealing partner. Should he have Aries rising, the selfish element may be even more pronounced.

with Taurus

Leo will adore being taken to the finest restaurants and hotels that her handsome Taurean lover has discovered. She, in turn, will make sure that she looks fantastic, wearing her most stunning outfit for the occasion. He is passionate and sensual, but may be too serious in his attitude towards love and sex. Moreover, she is likely to be disconcerted by his tendency to be possessive. Even if she wants to be possessed, nothing will stifle her independent streak, and she must make him aware of it. While not particularly unconventional herself, she could find her Taurean partner rather too conservative. Since he can be stubborn, the Leo woman may have some difficulty in getting him out of any rut into which he may have fallen. In fact, it is quite likely that she may be too sympathetic to his almost compulsive routine. She will probably be in the most favourable position if he has Venus in Aries. Should he have Taurus rising, he will be an extremely passionate and intense partner.

with Gemini

The Leo woman is likely to find her Gemini partner's constant questioning and requestioning about minor details of a situation somewhat tedious, particularly if she has fully and succinctly summed it up already. These two, however, should never have a dull moment together, whether in a brief affair or a permanent relationship. Sexually, she will like the challenge of her Gemini lover's inventiveness, but may find that he is less emotional than she, preferring a slightly intellectual approach to the most passionate interludes. She will inevitably have to cope with his inherent duality, which permeates every sphere of his life. As long as the Leo woman remains young at heart and stimulating, she need not worry about her loved one's flirtatious nature. In fact, she will have duality in her love life if she has Venus in Gemini, and, therefore, will be even more sympathetic towards her Gemini lover. Should he have a Gemini ascendant, he will have a broader, less fussy outlook on life.

with Cancer

It would appear that the Leo woman and the Cancerian man have irreconcilable character traits. Should they fall in love, however, an affair would have a good chance to develop if each could recognize and learn to accept the other's different qualities. The Leo woman will find her partner highly emotional, although his means of expression is unlike hers. In addition, she must expect considerable changes of mood to have an effect on their relationship. More than likely, it is this characteristic that she will have to come to terms with, and it may not be too easy for her to do so. He is passionate and extremely kind, but she may occasionally get the feeling that he is somewhat frightened of her. In fact, it is only his natural defence system coming between them. There is a distinct possibility that both may share Venus in the same sign, which would be excellent for the relationship. Should he have Cancer rising, there may be a more ambitious and practical side to his nature.

The Leo Woman in Love...

with Leo

A relationship between these two will either be marvellous or disastrous. Consequently, the partners must give careful consideration to their respective rising signs and the position of the other planets in their birth charts in order to assess more fully the situation and its possibilities. In general, a great deal of exuberance, happiness, passion and fun should be in store for this couple. Should a liaison progress along these lines, it will be memorable, but perhaps brief; if it is permanent, then it will undoubtedly be an excellent partnership. There may, however, be psychological difficulties; if either partner begins to feel these emerging, they should be discussed in detail. Basically, a joint rulership in the home is the preferable arrangement, but the Leo woman would do well to think of her role as the power behind the throne. She will in no way be subservient, but rather will be developing the best of her leonine qualities and using them in the wisest way.

with Virgo

If the Leo woman is her usual self, she may overwhelm the Virgoan man, especially if she lavishes attention on him immediately, He may be naturally shy and modest, so if she wants the relationship to develop, she will have to be much subtler than usual. Once she has met him, the Leo woman would do well to invite him to a small party at her place rather than to an intimate or a formal dinner. She should exhibit a willingness to let him set the pace of the conversation; although quiet, he enjoys stimulating conversation. The Virgoan man will have no difficulty establishing a friendship, but in the sexual sphere things will develop more slowly, His sensuality could be heightened, depending on the position of Mars. If the Leo woman is considerate and gentle, and takes her time, her efforts should be rewarded. Should he have Venus in Leo, or she have Venus in Virgo, their relationship promises to be rewarding. He will respond more emotionally if he has Virgo rising.

with Libra

In an affair with a Libran man, the Leo woman should feel relaxed and fulfilled on many levels. She may, however, find her lover too languid at times, and, therefore, will need to coax him into action. She may well be the dominant partner, taking responsibility for organizing their daily lives, as he tends to leave more of the decision-making to her, and becomes less inclined to act on his own initiative. The Leo woman should be able to encourage her loved one's strength of character without making it so apparent that she is the dominant partner. In turn, she will enjoy being the object of his romantic nature. Sexually, the Leo woman may be more responsive than her partner, but on the whole, will prefer his approach to that of a lover who might treat her roughly or ungraciously. Should he have Venus in Leo in his birth chart, the partnership will be strengthened; if he has Libra rising, chances are his attitude towards her will be more passionate, but occasionally selfish.

with Scorpio

The differences in temperament between a Leo woman and a Scorpio man should ensure that their affair will be exciting, eventful, strong and dramatic. She must remember, however, that Scorpios are highly sexed, emotional, jealous and secretive individuals, but like Leos, they enjoy doing things in grand style. If both these strong types can keep pace with each other, their relationship will have many rewarding and lively moments. It is essential that the Leo woman recognize and accept that her Scorpio lover's motivations are quite unlike hers. He is intense, complicated, and sometimes difficult to understand, and, in general, will approach problems and life in a way that is alien to her. Consequently, should these two fall in love, they would do well to spend as much time with each other as possible, perhaps developing a mutual interest, before committing themselves permanently. Then each will be in a better position to see how the other acts and how well they can get along.

with Sagittarius

In general, a relationship between the Leo woman and the Sagittarian man will be positive and easy going. But the Leo woman may soon find that her Sagittarian lover is too informal for her. She will like his breadth of vision and straightforward, honest approach towards life; he, in turn, will admire her intellectual powers. The Leo woman must make a conscious effort to curb her pompous tendencies, which are certain to annoy him. Although she will enjoy his fiery passion, she must accept that her partner will not take his love life seriously. In addition, he needs to have a great deal of freedom, and, therefore, the Leo woman is likely to have rivals. Because her loved one is so adaptable and has so many good qualities, the Leo woman should be fulfilled whether theirs matures into a permanent partnership or lasts for a brief time. The Sagittarian lover may be less emotionally responsive if he has Sagittarius rising. Should he have Venus in Libra, a future together looks most promising.

with Capricorn

The combination of a Leo woman and a Capricorn man involves the two most ambitious signs in the Zodiac. She will certainly admire his progressive outlook and will encourage and support him in whatever he undertakes. It will not take her long to realize that they have many different character traits. He is practical, logical and rational; frequently his emotional level is comparatively low. Her drives are motivated by enthusiasm and optimism; his by careful, calculated planning and pessimism. If the Leo woman can accept this, and if the Capricorn man can come to terms with her more exuberant and positive attitude towards life, they could develop an excellent relationship based on mutual admiration. Sexually, she may be far more demanding than he, but Mars will be influential in this respect. The liaison will progress more easily and quickly should he have Venus in Sagittarius; she will find him more gentle and loving if he has a Capricorn ascendant.

with Aquarius

If a Leo woman wants an involvement with an Aquarian man, she will not find it easy to progress from the stage of a kind and interesting friendship to a deep, emotional affair. She will quickly discover that her Aquarian partner is far less conventional than she, and more modern in outlook. But should these two fall in love, there is an excellent chance that they will be able to come to terms with their contrasting characteristics. It is perhaps more difficult to generalize about Aquarians than about any other sign, for they are the individualists of the Zodiac. Leos, however, will sympathize and be able to cope with this aspect of their personality. There could be some power struggles, as the Aquarian man has a strong sense of pride, and can also be stubborn. Although she is more emotional than her lover, the Leo woman will still be attracted to him, especially if he has Venus in Aquarius or Aquarius rising. The position of Uranus should be carefully noted.

with Pisces

Although the Leo woman operates on a totally different psychological level from the Piscean man, their emotional, romantic and usually creative traits harmonize well. In the early stages of the relationship, her generous nature will be apparent; she will want to encourage him, not only in the sexual sphere but also in his various interests and career. He needs her steadying influence. Even though he often has creative potential, the Piscean man is not always able to direct it as positively as she. So the partnership can be fulfilling on a practical level, as she will help him use his talents to their best advantage. Sexually, she will find him a rewarding partner, but the Leo woman needs to proceed with care because of her strong psychological tendency to dominate. Consequently, he could begin to rely on her too much, although this would be less true should he have Pisces rising. The position of Mars in his birth chart will give additional strength, if it is in a fire or earth sign.

77

Making the Most of Leo

If there is one virtue that the other eleven signs of the Zodiac can learn from Leos, it is how to make the most of themselves. And this is something they do quite naturally. They are always very conscious of their appearance, and whatever task they are engaged in, even if it is cleaning the kitchen or a shed, they make sure that they are suitably dressed. If they have to wear such mundane garments as overalls or aprons, which they will don for as short a period as possible, these will be of good quality and probably colourful and flattering.

But it is on formal occasions that Leos of both sexes come into their full glory, wearing their long, sweeping dresses, jewels, or most elegant suits. Their love of opulence occasionally contributes to a lapse of taste. It is therefore important that the Leo-born stop and take a serious look at themselves, asking if they might not be too ostentatiously dressed. Have they put on one ring too many? Should they be wearing a fur coat to the launderette? Do they need such an expensive car? Usually, however, Leos will want all their possessions to look right.

Although generosity abounds in Leos, there may be times when they would do well to curb their natural expansive instinct. It is true that what they spend on others is done with the best of intentions, and, indeed, does give the Leo-born great satisfaction, but it can be misconstrued as showing off, particularly by less well-off friends. So Leos who have progressed faster than many of their friends need to take care in this area.

Admittedly, there are times when leonine magnanimity turns into condescension; if, for example, they suddenly become successful and are only able to think in material terms. In general, however, their common sense will prevail.

Virtually all Leos need a creative outlet. Some may find it through fine art or any craft; others through more indirect means such as photography or film-making. Anything that has a tangible end product will be psychologically rewarding to both sexes. Leos are not hobby-orientated because they always try to reach a professional level in whatever they undertake. It would be rare indeed to hear Leos confess that they are amateurs. They may be in the sense that they are not paid for what they have created, or because they do not sell it. But Leos set high standards and willingly work long hours to become as professional as possible. If a Leo woman wants to make a special evening dress, she will be ambitious enough to get an *haute couture* pattern and work on it until she has made a perfect copy of the original. Similarly, the amateur photographer will save up money to buy the best camera on the market, and then take the trouble to learn how to make high-quality prints in his own darkroom.

In general, those born under the sign of the Lion have a great deal of self-confidence, quick minds, and the ability to make wise decisions without wasting too much valuable time. They have excellent breadth of vision and can immediately grasp the essentials behind new ideas, although they have a tendency to ignore the detailed points.

Physically, most Leos tend to think they are far stronger than they are. Particularly as they grow older, Leos must be on guard not to undermine their health for they work exceptionally hard and are often emotionally involved in their careers. They would find it extremely difficult to slow down. Unfortunately, most people do not realize or appreciate their efforts, for Leos organize their activities so well that they never appear rushed or overworked.

Those born under the sign of the Lion are most likely to suffer from ailments connected to the heart, spine and back. Leos need a lot of exercise to keep their bodies in good shape; dancing of any type would be especially good for them. Although Leos must be careful not to strain their backs, they should try gently to strengthen them through exercise.

Leos enjoy town and country life; wherever they live, they will make a warm, elegant, cheerful home, which will be an extension of themselves and a joy for anyone else to enter. They should beware of pride and condescension, however, when welcoming friends. These are the worst leonine faults and are most likely to surface when they entertain.

The Leo Man

July 21st –August 21st

Ruling Planet: The Sun
Quadruplicity: Fixed
Keyword: Resistant to change
Metal: Gold
*Countries: France * Italy * Romania * Sicily*
Animals: All the Felines
Colours: Pink to Deep Orange

The Leo Man in Love...

When the Leo man is first attracted to a woman, he will very carefully plan his date with her, having taken her preferences and dislikes into consideration. He will be particularly pleased if she enjoys the theatre, but if she is not interested in plays, opera or ballet, he will try to find some other form of live entertainment, or, as a last resort, a highly acclaimed film that would meet with her approval. Later in the evening, he will take her to a restaurant whose excellent menu will undoubtedly be above his income bracket. Indulging himself and his partner with the best is not done simply to show off, but rather because he is genuinely in-terested in doing things as well as possible in a grand and dramatic way. The object of his affections will certainly remember any dates she has with him, for he will make certain that they are all memorable occasions.

Although there is a regal side to Leo, he can be a willing slave to the one he adores when he is in love. He will think so highly of her that he is likely to put his loved one on a symbolic pedestal. She, however, must be a person whom he can fully respect. In addition, the Leo man may well forget his typically gran-diose manner. He will, nevertheless, dress even more brilliantly than usual, and perhaps consider dieting if he has gained too much weight.

The Leo man does not become starry-eyed in love. Instead, his feelings will spur him into more creative and positive action in his private affairs as well as in his professional life. This aspect of his character will be emphasized if he happens to fall in love with someone who is already committed to another man. He will state his case forcefully, and with dignity, although he will accept a refusal once it is given.

Sexually, he is a passionate and demanding partner, but it is difficult to imagine a Leo man, under normal circumstances, being rough or selfish or inconsiderate. He is usually able

to make his loved one the centre of attraction, lavishing attention and praise on her. In addition, he is a constant lover and will do everything in his power to make his present involvement more fulfilling than either has experienced previously. He will not act hastily in love, making quite sure that the time is right before committing himself. If he is rebuked, his pride will probably be hurt. The Leo man is more sensitive than most people realize, but he does not readily show it. His moments of depression in love will be when, or if, his powerful feelings are not reciprocated. More than likely, he will then want to be left alone for a while to adjust.

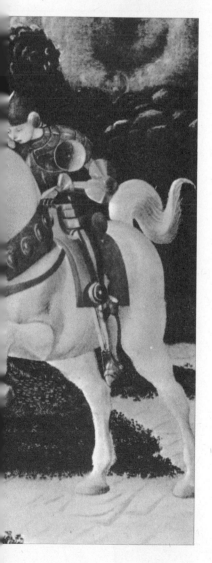

with Aries

The Leo man must be prepared for a few surprises when he gets involved with an Arien woman. She will probably be less formal than he and may well want to be the dominant partner in their sexual relationship, for she is extremely passionate. Since the Leo man is basically conventional, he may admire his partner's independent ways, but may also think that they make her slightly unfeminine at times. He will soon discover that she likes living life to the fullest. Both Leo and Aries are fire signs, so they should approach their affair with a lively enthusiasm. There could be rivalry between them, as each has a strong personality. It will not take the Leo man long to realize that his partner can be rather selfish; he may have to use all his tact and dignity to prevent her from frequently placing her own feelings above his. The Arien woman will be more affectionate and slightly restrained if she has Venus in Pisces; should she have an Aries ascendant, she may want to rush into marriage.

with Taurus

Admiration of the beautiful, the artistic and the expensive could bring a Leo man and a Taurean woman together. He will admire her beauty, and she his artistic flair. Together they will enjoy spending a great deal of money. The Leo man will find his Taurean partner passionate and emotional, and will be delighted to discover that she also likes luxury and comfort. The worst Taurean fault is possessiveness, but because the Leo lover is loyal and faithful, he will be better equipped to come to terms with this particular trait than will many other zodiacal types. In general, they will enjoy their relationship, but there is a chance that it could become too intense. Should the affair deteriorate and become a habit, it will probably be Leo's responsibility to end it because Taurus dislikes change. If they marry, the partnership will be a stable one, but they would be wise to cultivate joint interests. Should she have Taurus rising, Leo will find her even more passionate.

with Gemini

The Leo man may be slightly bewildered by the Gemini woman's light-hearted attitude towards love, and his pride will probably be hurt when he discovers that she often has more than one affair at a time. But he will have to accept her natural duality. It is quite unlikely that they will ever be bored with one another, for Gemini's lively mind will stimulate endless discussions, and Leo's optimism and enthusiasm for life will bring interesting and rewarding experiences. She may well not share her Leo lover's flair for grand passion, but she will love all the memorable evenings he will organize for her. Joint interests will not be difficult for these two to develop, and their partnership will see many fun-filled moments. Gemini is the most youthful of all the zodiacal signs, so she should be able to keep her loved one feeling that way too. It will be to their advantage if they share Venus in the same sign, or if she has Gemini as her rising sign.

with Cancer

In an affair with a Cancerian woman, the Leo lover will have to make allowances for her changing moods and high emotional level; she is extremely sensitive and easily hurt. But it is also true that he is similarly vulnerable, although she may not realize it. The Leo man would be in a better position if he could develop a protective shell like his Cancerian partner; otherwise he becomes deeply upset, even though he does not readily show his distress. In this combination there is a marvellous traditional blending of the most powerful masculine and feminine expressions in the Zodiac. The Sun is Leo's ruling planet; the Moon is Cancer's. If both partners have a mature outlook on life, they can harmonize their different characteristics, and help each other understand their respective weaknesses. Should she have Cancer rising, care is needed, for they will have serious temperamental differences. The position of Venus will be revealing for both.

The Leo Man in Love...

with Leo

A Leo man who is attracted to a woman born under the same sign should not expect to share exactly the same qualities and tendencies. In fact, it will be fun for them to work out which personality traits they have in common, and how their rising signs, and the various planets in their birth charts modify them. They will inevitably be in sympathy in many areas, and should have no difficulty in identification. There is an individual streak in each Leo and, consequently, some rivalry between them is possible. If they are true to their sign, however, graciousness will dominate, and there should be a happy joint rulership. Sexually, they should be equally demanding, but the position of Mars at the time of their respective births will provide interesting information about this sphere of their lives. In addition, the influence of Venus cannot be underestimated, for it can make both or either partner gentler and more affectionate. Extravagance is quite likely to be a joint fault.

with Virgo

When a Leo man starts an affair with a Virgoan woman, he would do well to forget his usual enthusiastic and ardent advances. Undoubtedly, he will make more progress if he is considerate, gentle and friendly towards her. She will appreciate and respond well to this approach. If he is planning to take her to dinner, he might try some pleasant *trattoria* or Greek restaurant rather than his usual stomping ground, which is likely to be too grand and imposing for a young Virgoan. And should he suggest a vegetarian restaurant, his Virgoan partner will probably be delighted, as she is likely to favour natural foods. The Leo lover will soon discover that she does not have a high emotional level, and therefore, he should not be surprised to find her rather reticent in their sexual encounters. The Virgoan woman will criticize her Leo man if she feels he has marked weaknesses or if she thinks he is too pompous or boastful. The position of Venus will influence the way she shows affection.

with Libra

Although Leo will be the more dominant partner, this affair should prove easy and undemanding for both. A great deal will depend on the Libran woman's rising sign. He will not, however, find her eager to make her own decisions, or to contest his. He will not mind taking the lead in this respect, and his excellent organizational ability and determination should have ample opportunity to develop more fully with a Libran partner. But if he is clever, the Leo man will try to help his loved one think for herself, otherwise she will inevitably become too dependent on him. The couple will certainly be happy together and will enjoy life, giving parties that will always be unforgettable occasions. Both are inclined to be extravagant; they place great emphasis on luxury and quality. Leo will soon realize that he is involved with a pure romantic; she is affectionate and loving, but may be less passionate than he had been led to expect. Some allowances may have to be made in this area.

with Scorpio

A partnership between these two will either be absolutely marvellous or a complete disaster. Should the couple begin to quarrel, it will probably be best for them to part. They will soon know whether the affair is worth developing, because both are such strong types that neither would find it easy to take a passive role in any situation. If they make a success of the relationship, it will be dynamic, and both will derive benefits from it. Care will be needed, particularly in the early stages when they are coming to terms with each other's high but very different emotional levels. The Leo man will find the Scorpio woman highly sexed and jealous at times; he should, however, be able to cope with these traits. In turn, his Scorpio partner may think he has a tendency to be domineering, but will enjoy his magnanimity. He should consider the position of Mars at the time of her birth, as it is her co-ruling planet along with Pluto. He will benefit most if it was in a fire sign.

with Sagittarius

The Leo man will be attracted by the Sagittarian woman's enthusiasm for life, her pleasant optimism and open manner. He will be even more pleased as she is bound to take an immediate and intelligent interest in whatever he has to say and whatever he does. It would not be uncommon, however, for him to find her too informal, or for her to consider him somewhat pompous. While she will enjoy the luxurious evenings to which he is accustomed, he must also remember she will like walking in the country, watching sporting events and eating in a local bistro. Sexually responsive and fun to be with, the Sagittarian woman likes her freedom too. She may seem rather unconventional, for she probably will not take her relationships as seriously as he. In general, this is an excellent, lively pairing, with each showing great consideration of the other. She should be more affectionate towards her Leo partner if she has Venus in Libra, or if Sagittarius is her rising sign.

with Capricorn

While Leo will find Capricorn's offbeat sense of humour most amusing, he will also recognize that she is less emotional than he, and sometimes slightly distant. There is an element of the loner in every Capricorn. Leo will admire her aspirations and ambitions, however, and will appreciate her efforts to help him advance in his professional life. He should not have many problems helping her adopt a more positive and cheerful outlook. And unless she is so weighed down by heavy burdens and responsibilities that she is unreachable, he will get through to her. In turn, his Capricorn lover will probably persuade him to indulge in some modest social climbing. Sexually, she may not be too responsive, so they will have to work out a compromise. She will react more positively towards him if Capricorn is rising. In addition, he should find out the positions of Mars, her ruling planet, and Venus, which influences love matters, at the time of her birth.

with Aquarius

There should be a lively rapport between the Leo man and the Aquarian woman; they will find it easy to sympathize with one another and to express a readiness to learn about the other's contrasting character traits. The Leo man will perhaps have some difficulty in coming to terms with his unconventional partner's traits, and may also find her somewhat unpredictable. In addition, she can be as stubborn as he, so their mutual attempts to harmonize their temperamental differences could make the partnership even more dynamic. Activities which have an air of glamour will appeal to both. Sexually, he will quickly discover that she has a fairly low emotional level; consequently she may prefer ties of friendship. But the Leo man should have the necessary qualities to melt her chilly heart. Should the relationship deepen, it could become permanent, as both types are faithful. They will be happy together if he has Leo rising, or if she has Aquarius rising.

with Pisces

The Leo man will find his Piscean woman sensitive, emotional, disorganized and romantic. The intensity of her feelings can easily upset her equilibrium. Fortunately, the Leo man is the right type to give her some much-needed self-confidence. She, in turn, will teach him humility. It will not take them long to discover that they have a great deal in common, for both signs are among the most creative in the Zodiac. Although a partnership between them could have a few difficulties in the early stages, it should also bring many rewarding experiences. The Leo man's emotion is passionate and the Piscean woman's is illogical and deep. As a result, she is often near to tears, and never far from despair when things are not going well for her. Leo, with his natural exuberance and encouragement, can help her blossom. Sexually, they will be quite compatible, responding well to each other. She will have a slightly harsher outlook if she has Pisces as her rising sign.

The Way to the Leo Heart

There is one golden rule to follow when seeking the way to the Leo heart: whatever you do, do it well. Leos, more than any other zodiacal type, love quality and a touch of the magnificent. They have extremely high standards. If you are planning a quiet dinner at home with Leo, make sure that the evening has been perfectly organized, with no careless timing, or minor omissions; strive for an air of luxurious ease, comfort and graciousness. Do not allow anything to happen until the appointed time, and be careful not to pour any coffee into the leonine saucer; Leo will not be amused. Those born under the sign of the Lion take notice of everything, and will thoroughly and warmly appreciate the effort that has been made. Goodwill and happiness can permeate the atmosphere, under the right conditions.

The leonine sense of drama is also well known, so the bigger and more dramatic the seduction scene, the better. The lighting should be modified, if it seems unromantic. In any case, Leos detest glaring lights. Remember that they like to be comfortable, so keep your place warm. They sometimes have slight circulation trouble, and never flourish in a remotely chilly room. Scatter a number of cushions on your sofa. Place the accent on relaxation.

It is not surprising that Leos love the theatre, with their flair for the dramatic. An invitation to a play will be readily accepted, and the Leo-born will arrive looking resplendent, probably in a dinner jacket or opera cape or elegant dress. You should also make a special effort to look your best. Although Leos are not particularly fashion-conscious, they are eager for the attention and compliments of others. You would be wise, however, not to cater too much to their need for flattery.

It is not necessary, however, to spend a fortune on Leos, although most people think the contrary. In fact, they would be embarrassed and upset if they discovered that you had put yourself into financial difficulty merely to entertain them. It is quality that matters. So if you cannot afford dinner at a smart restaurant, for example, suggest meeting in the bar for drinks. They will respond enthusiastically. Leos are generous, so soon it will be your turn to enjoy evenings at his or her expense. Expect to be entertained royally.

Sexually, Leos may like to play hard-to-get for a while. But this attitude will not last for long, for Leos love sensual pleasure, and are enthusiastic and passionate about their sex life. Futhermore, their emotional level is very high. The Leo-born are constant and loyal partners, but their loved ones must be people whom they can fully respect.

Although those born under the sign of the Lion are not particularly sentimental about love, they are far more sensitive than most people realize. Consequently, they can be very easily hurt, but may not show this. In fact when they are particularly miserable, they often put on a brave face and keep up a steady stream of social activity. This is the best way for them to respond to unhappiness and emotional distress. In addition, their magnanimous natures and ability to forgive help them adjust more readily to unpleasant conditions.

It is not always easy to choose appropriate presents for Leos, but if you think in terms of quality, whatever you finally select is bound to please. If you decide to give a Leo woman a box of handkerchiefs, she would infinitely prefer a linen one to a box of six made of cotton. Since Leos love the sun, a large tube or bottle of suntan lotion will always be acceptable, not to mention airline tickets to some exotic climate. The tiniest piece of gold will delight Leos, for it is their metal. They will not only treasure gold for its value, but also for its glow.

When you invite the Leo-born to dinner, plan the menu around good classical dishes. They love meat, so choose either *boeuf stroganoff* or *canard à l'orange* for the main course. Most Leos know their wines fairly well, and if you can afford it, serve champagne. Otherwise, a rich warm claret will appeal to their opulent tastes. For dessert, make something that shows flair, but will not require you to spend too much time in the kitchen during the evening. Pears in wine would certainly meet these qualifications, as well as impress your Leo guest.

The Virgo Woman

August 22nd–September 22nd

Ruling Planet: *Mercury*
Triplicity: *Earth*
Keywords: *Practical * Stable*
Jewel: *Sardonyx*
Flowers: *Small Brightly Coloured Flowers*
Trees: *Nut-bearing Trees*
Cities: *Paris * Boston * Jerusalem*

The Virgo Woman in Love...

When the Virgoan woman realizes that she is genuinely in love, she will probably be somewhat apprehensive, and perhaps frightened of her own feelings and reactions. She will use her analytical and critical faculties to look at herself and the situation, remembering even the most minor details of the affair. As a result, she may get so bogged down by the minutiae that she will forget to review the broader aspects of the relationship and, therefore, could miss out on a lot of the most enjoyable, fun-filled aspects of being in love.

If the Virgoan woman is young, and is involved in her first affair, she must make a deliberate effort to relax and enjoy the relationship. Since she is a perfectionist, she may find herself being overly critical of her lover's habits and mannerisms. This tendency to nag must be resisted if she wants the rapport between them to deepen. She must concentrate on his good points and remember either to show him her appreciation or to offer some words of praise.

Men are often attracted to the Virgoan woman's genuine modesty and charm. In her youth, she tends to be too talkative, thus hiding her natural shyness. As she matures, Virgo should use these natural assets more wisely.

The Virgoan woman in love must accept that she has a rather low emotional level, and she will then understand why she finds certain types of men too demanding. It may become increasingly important for her to reassess her feelings. She needs an understanding partner who can guide her through difficulties.

The Virgoan woman tends to put work before pleasure, caring little about its rewards but deriving great satisfaction from helping others. Although it may be admirable of her to offer to babysit for her sister or to take her elderly aunt out to lunch every week, she should not use such obligations as a convenient excuse to miss an opportunity to go out with an attractive man. For some Virgoan women, family commitments can become a psychological protection against emotional involvements.

with Aries

The moment the Virgoan woman hints that she is attracted to an Arien man, she will find herself swept off her feet. He is highly sexed, and will probably not want to waste time waiting for her to make up her mind. So she should enter the relationship with her eyes open and expect to be often overwhelmed by him. She will like her lover's enthusiasm for life, and will enjoy being outdoors with him, taking excursions into the country, attending sporting events and going on picnics. His straight-forward approach to everything will inevitably appeal to her. He tends to gloss over the surface, ignoring what to her might be important details. Although these two are completely different types, they can learn a great deal from each other. The Virgoan woman should find out what sign Mars was in when he was born. It, along with Pluto, his ruling planet, will have a powerful effect on their partnership. The position of Mars in her birth chart is also important, as it affects her sexuality.

with Taurus

In many ways a Taurean man seems to be an ideal partner for a Virgoan woman. She will admire his practical outlook and common sense, and will feel very secure with him. In turn, she will be good for him, for he tends to become set in his ways, and she, being infinitely more flexible than he, will not allow this to happen. Sexually, he is very passionate when aroused, but will be patient and considerate with his loved one. Both these types are of the earth triplicity, which explains why they have a number of character traits in common. It should not take the Virgoan woman long to discover that her lover's worst fault is possessiveness. More than likely, he will want to make their relationship a permanent one long before she has made up her mind. Generally, most Virgoans will not commit themselves prematurely, but they may be tempted to do so for a charming and handsome Taurean. Should he have a Taurus ascendant, jealousy could be a serious problem for her to face.

with Gemini

Although there can be considerable sympathy between Virgoans and Geminis, mainly because they share the same ruling planet, Mercury, they can also irritate each other. A Virgoan woman who is attracted to a talkative, sometimes restless Gemini will have a great deal of fun and pleasure with him; there will certainly be no dull moments because, no matter what else they are doing, they constantly engage in discussions and arguments. Since the Virgoan woman is known for her practicality, she should find it easier to set aside some time to consider and understand the relationship. While she will approve of his attitude towards sex, she may be distressed if she feels he does not take her seriously. Geminis are known to be flirtatious, so there is a strong possibility that he will have other involvements. Should he have Gemini rising, he may be more passionate than she. The position of Venus will influence his ability to express affection; she will benefit if it is in Cancer.

The Virgo Woman in Love...

with Cancer

The Cancerian man in love is kind, considerate and particularly sensitive. In the early stages of an affair, the Virgoan woman will also become aware of his romantic and sensuous nature. Basically, he is a good partner for her, although she may be irritated by his emotional character and his abrupt mood changes. Undoubtedly, she will think that her Cancerian partner is too easily swayed by his feelings, and, therefore, she is likely to concern herself with finding the reason for it. She will find none, however, and will have to accept these fluctuations as being an integral part of the Cancerian personality. One negative trait that both Virgoans and Cancerians have in common is a tendency to worry. For the relationship to develop, they must acknowledge this potentially harmful aspect, and work together to minimize its effect. The Virgoan woman will find her loved one less emotional if Cancer is rising. Should he have Venus in Gemini, the partnership should succeed.

with Leo

The Virgoan woman who is having an affair with a Leo man may be embarrassed at times by his flamboyant manner. She is a careful, somewhat economical type, while he is happiest when he has the opportunity to spend a great deal of money. Indeed, if their relationship becomes permanent, this particular difference could become a source of considerable conflict. She should remember, however, that although he does like the best of everything he is not as bad at balancing the budget as she may fear. The Leo lover is emotionally generous and passionate, and probably can help his Virgoan partner to learn about and enjoy the good things of life. In addition, she will benefit tremendously if she can learn to rely on his ability to organize. The Virgoan woman will be well rewarded once she can curb her restlessness, for then her individuality can be appreciated. Should she have Venus in Leo, she will find it easier to accept his life-style. But if he has a Leo ascendant, he is likely to be bossy.

with Virgo

A Virgoan woman who finds herself attracted to a Virgoan man will enjoy a lively, intellectual rapport with him; they will discuss their favourite hobbies or pastimes, such as gardening and outdoor sports, and, if asked, will offer critical appraisal of each other's work. The Virgoan woman, however, must be careful that she is not too harsh, or else she may spoil what might have become a more romantic relationship. The Virgoan man could well be shy and easily put off, although he is in an excellent position to offer resistance. In general, an affair between them will develop slowly. There is a tendency for both to live on their nerves, and to worry about everything. The sign Venus was in when each was born is extremely important; if it was in Leo or Libra, they will be warmer and more responsive towards one another, and if it was in Virgo with the Sun, the accent will be on friendship. The Virgoan woman will appreciate her lover's less clinical approach if he has Virgo rising.

with Libra

The Virgoan woman is likely to be extremely irritated by her Libran man's indecisiveness. In fact, she may find it intolerable to wait for him to make up his mind about everything—from deciding where to go for their next holiday to choosing a restaurant for dinner. Her reason for disliking this trait, however, is not the typical one uttered by others who are affected by Libran procrastination. It is simply a trait that her sharp, quick mind will find difficult to accept. But it is often the case that Librans have Venus, their ruling planet, in Virgo. When this occurs, the Virgoan woman will have considerable affinity with her Libran partner, recognizing and enjoying his positive qualities, while tolerating his more negative characteristics. These two would benefit immeasurably by the development of a joint interest. If he has Libra rising, the Virgoan woman can expect her lover to be more passionate. In general, Librans like to be settled in permanent relationships, and this should be an interesting pairing.

with Scorpio

When a Virgoan woman gets involved with a Scorpio man she will quickly discover that he is very emotional, and sexually demanding. Consequently, she may be somewhat overwhelmed. If she has had other relationships with men, she will probably be able to cope with his demands, but if the Virgoan woman is quite young and relatively inexperienced, she will need to proceed with care. Should curiosity get the better of her, she may become deeply involved too soon, and, as a result, his passionate nature may become repugnant to her. She would do well to study the position of Mars when he was born, as this planet is particularly important to him. In addition, Virgo should note the position of Mars in her chart so that she has a general idea of how she will respond to him. If it is in an earth or air sign, she will be less sympathetic than if it is in a fire or water sign. The relationship may be more harmonious if he has Scorpio rising. She must beware of his jealousy.

with Sagittarius

The initial attraction for the Virgoan woman in this pairing may be the Sagittarian's excellent mind. He, in turn, will admire her natural quickness and genuinely bright, lively qualities. In a sexual relationship, she will find him a passionate partner, but she will soon realize that he does not take his love life too seriously. She must guard against becoming emotionally involved prematurely; otherwise she could get hurt. Sagittarians are known to be restless as are Virgoans, so a mutual concern is needed to prevent this trait from damaging the relationship. They should not have any problem developing common interests, particularly since they both enjoy the outdoors. Activities such as camping, playing tennis, walking and riding would probably suit them well. Theirs can be a stimulating partnership with its many challenges. The Virgoan woman may think that her Sagittarian lover is too bold in manner, too broad in outlook, and too casual in regard to details.

with Capricorn

This relationship should be mutually rewarding. The Capricorn man can encourage the Virgoan woman to develop her positive qualities. In turn, she will help him realize his ambitions, for she is one of the hardest-working types of the Zodiac. He will find her practical and intellectual strengths invaluable in developing both their personal relationship and their material existence. Although the Capricorn lover is not particularly emotional, he is faithful. Once their partnership has been cemented, it is likely to last. There should not be many sexual problems, for he is patient and willing to let the affair develop at a pace which suits her. If he has Venus in Capricorn or Aquarius, he may appear to be unapproachable or remote at times. Should it have been in Scorpio or Sagittarius at the time of his birth, the Capricorn lover's passionate side will be more apparent. If he has Capricorn rising, he will relate to his loved one in a kind and tender way.

with Aquarius

The friendly intellectualism and kindness that are characteristic of an Aquarian man will appeal to a Virgoan woman. In turn, he will be stimulated by her inquiring, critical mind. At times, however, she could find him too forward-looking and unconventional. In addition, she is likely to discover that he does not want to be committed to her alone, for basically he has a freedom-loving nature. They should have no difficulty cultivating common interests, as both enjoy theatre, films and scientific subjects, and then their relationship will have a solid basis. There will never be a dull moment for either of them: conversation will flow rapidly and easily. Psychologically, they are good for each other, but tensions could arise between Virgo and Aquarius. Although the Aquarian man is not very emotional, she could discover that he has a romantic streak; should she have Venus in Libra, it will strongly appeal to her. He is likely to be warmer towards her if he has Venus in Pisces.

with Pisces

Opposite signs of the Zodiac are found in this combination. The Virgoan woman must expect to find her Piscean lover disorganized and more emotional than she. The natural rapport between them, however, will help alleviate any problems that may arise from such differences. She, with her more practical attitude towards life, will encourage him to make the most of his potentialities, which are sometimes neglected because of his slightly muddled sense of priorities. In turn, her Piscean lover will teach her to relax sexually and show her the warmer, more emotional side of love. He will be extremely kind and considerate of her, and consequently the relationship should work out well. Both have a tendency to worry, so care is needed. Since Neptune, his ruling planet, has a definite effect on the Piscean man, his partner would be wise to find out what sign it was in when he was born. Should he have Pisces rising, she will be able to identify with his reactions towards her.

Making the Most of Virgo

Virgo is the sign of the Virgin, and, as a result, both sexes often have a slightly puritanical attitude towards sex. It is also possible that it may be clinical because they are so analytical and set such high standards for themselves and their partners. Of course, the position of Mars and Venus and the rising sign in each Virgoan's birth chart will modify these statements. Psychological conflicts can occur, however, when the clinical, clean, tidy elements clash with the deeper, earthier and more instinctive areas of the Virgoan personality. Most individuals born under this sign are ruled by their intellect rather than their emotions. They tend to be practical rather than sentimental.

Virgoans are frequently attractive-looking people. The women under this sign have a genuine charm which many men find beguiling. When they are interested in attracting the opposite sex, they are likely to choose high-waisted dresses with a tiny floral print designed to enhance their modesty. Usually, however, they prefer to wear simple, conservative suits, well-tailored dresses or classic-style skirts and sweaters. They strive for a basically neat, clean appearance. Male Virgoans tend to be conventional in dress. They look good in dark green or brown formal suits, but sometimes add a dash of colour with a small floral-patterned or spotted tie. Tiny spots and small patterns seem to be Virgoan favourites. For their fresh-air activities, they choose comfortable clothes.

Those born under the sign of the Virgin often have a deep interest in health and hygiene. They love natural foods, and many are vegetarians. Female Virgoans usually enjoy good health, but they should have regular medical check-ups, despite the inclination of some to feel that they will do better without conventional medical treatment.

Virgoans are extremely happy outdoors; they love to walk in the country, or grow flowers or vegetables in their gardens. Many are accomplished gardeners, and should they live in an urban environment, Virgoans will lavish tender and loving affection upon house plants.

The Virgoan-born tend to be high-strung, and like those born under the other Mercury-ruled sign, Gemini, they live on their nerves. Exercise, preferably in the fresh air rather than in a stuffy gym, is essential. Bicycle riding is also recommended for Virgoans of both sexes. Tension and worry can play havoc with their sensitive nervous systems. As soon as Virgoans become worried, their stomachs get upset and their digestive systems complain. Perhaps this is one reason why so many Virgoans are interested in dieting, and make a point of staying away from foods they know will not agree with them.

Some of the lighter forms of sport are good for the Virgoan-born, such as tennis, badminton and golf. They seem to enjoy individual athletic participation as opposed to team effort. But apart from this kind of exercise, Virgoans find it difficult to sit still and relax. They seem to always be in motion, scurrying to the kitchen, tapping their fingers, swinging their feet, and these nervous mannerisms can be often irritating to friends and lovers.

The Virgoan-born are kind and quite eager to lend a helping hand, although they can occasionally carry this too far. If they are entertaining, they should make a conscious effort to get everything done before the guests arrive, so that they do not have to spend most of the evening in the kitchen while their company is left to its own resources.

Virgoans who are artistically inclined should consider doing some craft work to express their creative talents. Perhaps they might enjoy weaving, pottery, or fabric printing. Many females of this sign make good dress-makers, but in spite of their ability to pay attention to detail, they are sometimes in too much of a hurry to get the detail right.

In general, those born under the sign of the Virgin are workers; they require jobs that will keep their lively, restless minds constantly challenged. Virgoans are frequently good at research, and any project that requires them to spend hours patiently sifting through scientific papers or biological specimens will attract them. Their persistence and nervous energy may partly explain why many of them choose areas of study that others would consider too demanding.

The Virgo Man

August 22nd – September 22nd

Ruling Planet: *Mercury*
Quadruplicity: *Mutable*
Keyword: *Adaptable*
Metal: *Quicksilver*
Countries: *Greece* ✳ *Turkey* ✳ *Brazil* ✳ *Switzerland*
Animals: *Small Domestic Pets*
Colours: *Dark Grey* ✳ *Brown* ✳ *Navy Blue*

The Virgo Man in Love...

When the Virgoan man realizes that he is in love, there is a distinct possibility that his logical, analytical mind may force him to suppress his true emotions. He may also have a tendency to belittle himself, wondering what his loved one could possibly see in him. He may even become depressed if he succeeds in convincing himself that he is unworthy of her. The Virgoan man is not the type to rush into a relationship, although in all other respects the general pace of his life is hectic. Either he will try to build up his self-confidence and devote time to developing a love affair, or else he will allow his natural reticence to dominate his feelings, thus losing an opportunity to share hours of happiness and fun.

By nature the Virgoan man is not particularly emotional, and his tentativeness makes its mark on his sensuality. He can be extremely clinical and curious at times, analysing himself, his partner and her reactions towards him. Since his standards are so high, it is not unusual for him to marry late in life.

In love, however, he will work as hard at contributing to the relationship as he does at anything else. Permanence and stability are essential to him. He dislikes change. Should he marry, he will enjoy family life and will always be willing to lend a helping hand. Sometimes he is such an eager worker that his partner will have to call a halt to his constant activity—cleaning the car, emptying the garbage, offering to run errands, doing work he has brought home from the office. As a rule the Virgoan husband is conscientious regardless of what he undertakes, and thus makes an excellent provider.

It is important for the man as well as the woman born under the sign of the Virgin to learn to relax in a relationship. The Virgoan male should try not to be too logical, not to put up psychological barriers between himself and his loved one. In fact, the more real these seem to him, the more he must try to overcome them. Furthermore, he must guard

against trying to impose his ideas or principles on anyone.

The man born under this sign has many excellent qualities that his partner will soon learn to appreciate. Consideration and helpfulness are two which she will most easily recognize in the early stages of their friendship. If only he can persuade himself to unwind, to stop worrying so much, to change his usually critical eye to an admiring and appreciative one, the pair should find happiness together. The self-critical Virgoan can learn how to become a warmer, more affectionate individual from every relationship, whether it be one based on friendship or on love.

with Aries

Although the Virgoan man may be somewhat surprised, perhaps even slightly shocked, by the Arien woman's sexuality, which is strong and forthright, he will like her independence, her ability not to waste a minute of precious life and her strength of character. He will soon find out that she is demanding in many ways, and may want to be the dominant partner in their love life. This could be a possible source of friction. Basically, the Arien woman is extremely passionate and is not tolerant of a slow, cool approach, so a Virgoan lover will have to change his style should he wish to win her affections. Undoubtedly, he will profit from the relationship, even if they eventually decide to break up. Allowances will have to be made for the differences in their emotional levels, and it is possible that she may take advantage of him. Both will work hard to ensure stability in a partnership, but he may find himself saddled with domestic concerns while she pursues a career.

with Taurus

A Taurean woman may be able to help a Virgoan man discover previously unknown facets of his character. And, should he be feeling nervous or high-strung, she can usually exert a calming influence. Sexually, there should not be any problems. Although the Taurean woman is very passionate, she will not have any difficulty adjusting to his slower pace. The Virgoan male may find that his partner is not as intellectual or as quick to grasp ideas as he, but her reliable ways and her need for emotional and material security will be most attractive to him. Her loved one will benefit most if Venus, her ruling planet, is in Gemini. The Taurean-born is naturally possessive, but will be marginally less so with this placing. In fact, she could even be somewhat flirtatious. Should she have Taurus rising, her reactions towards him will be more intense, and slight pangs of jealousy are likely to be felt at times. If they marry, both will work hard for their material progress and happiness.

with Gemini

Since Mercury is the ruling planet of both Virgo and Gemini, its influence will be strongly felt in this partnership. Each will take great interest in the other's ideas, intellectual attitudes, hobbies and careers. Indeed, it is quite likely that they will have first met at a lecture or at a literary gathering. This sort of beginning, rather than a purely physical encounter, generally characterizes a relationship between a Virgoan man and a Gemini woman. Both individuals are somewhat unemotional, and, therefore, friendship will play an extremely important role in their pairing. The Virgoan man may find that his Gemini partner does not take her love life too seriously; if this is so, he must expect to cope with rivals. She enjoys sex, and will never be a boring partner. This is a good combination, but it is not a relaxing one. Both Virgo and Gemini live on their nerves, and care is needed so that their restlessness does not create tension. This could occur frequently if she has Gemini rising.

with Cancer

Virgo and Cancer may each worry too much about the other, but overall it is a partnership that should bring happiness and fulfilment. Although one will appreciate the other's concern, frequently tension between them builds up over minor incidents. For example, the Virgoan man may have a slight cold; his Cancerian lover, however, will convince herself that it is going to develop into pneumonia. As a result, her digestion will be upset, and the household will be completely disrupted. Sexually, he will find her a rewarding partner, for she is sensuous, tender and understanding. He must remember, however, that she is a woman of moods, and these often change abruptly. Furthermore, she is intuitive and emotional, so there will be definite psychological differences between them. If he can learn to deal with these, the relationship will be strengthened. Should she have Cancer rising, the Cancerian woman will respond to him in a more down-to-earth way.

The Virgo Man in Love...

with Leo

If a Virgoan man is attracted to a Leo woman, he must remember that she likes to do things in grand style and appreciates luxury and good quality. Should he be in the middle of an economy drive, it would be better to ask her out for drinks at a smart, fashionable place than to invite her for dinner at an inexpensive restaurant. She often has a critical attitude that he will find appealing. Discussion and argument will then follow with the greatest enthusiasm. In general, the Virgoan man will be much narrower in outlook than his Leo partner, and may not be able to cope with her breadth of vision. The Leo woman may want to organize the relationship, and perhaps her Virgoan partner should admit defeat here, for she excels at organization. Sexually, he will find her a very passionate and rewarding lover. Eventually, he may decide that she is too demanding in all respects for him. The Leo woman will be able to respond more easily to him if she has Venus in Virgo.

with Virgo

A Virgoan man who is attracted to a Virgoan woman may find that her engagement book will be so full of prior commitments that he will have to wait some time before they can arrange an evening out. This does not mean that she will be busily dating a different man each night, but rather that she will be going to lectures, paying social calls, serving on various committees, doing the laundry and cleaning her house. The Virgo man will soon learn that she will enjoy all this activity, and that, sometimes, it is psychologically important to her. But if he can break through the barrier, theirs could be a rewarding relationship. The positions of Venus in both their charts should be noted. They will find it easier to relax and enjoy themselves sexually if the planet was in Leo or Libra, but if it was in Virgo there may be a greater emphasis on friendship than on romance. Should she have a Virgo ascendant, they will both benefit, as it will be easier for them to identify with one another.

with Libra

The Libran woman is a pure romantic, and if her Virgoan partner cannot cope with this aspect of her personality, it could become a tedious element in their affair. Although there will be other striking differences between these two, each will also recognize similarities. At first, the Virgoan man may be surprised and disturbed when his loved one begins to criticize him, but if he thinks about it, he will realize that he frequently does the very same thing to her. Although the Libran woman does not have a high emotional level, she usually longs for a permanent relationship. Consequently, she may rush into one. Libra gives the impression, nevertheless, that she has all the time in the world to relax. Although the Virgoan man finds her indecisiveness irritating, her easy-going, uncomplicated manner may help him unwind and, perhaps, stop him from worrying so much. These two need to share a joint interest to cement their friendship such as tennis or golf.

with Scorpio

Before the slightly cool Virgoan man begins an affair with a passionate Scorpio woman, he should know that she is usually highly sexed and extremely demanding of her partners. Her emotional level is perhaps the highest of all the zodiacal types, and therefore, it is quite possible that he could find her overwhelming. These two would be wise to develop an absorbing joint interest, so that they can divert some of their powerful, but quite different energies. In addition, it will give them an opportunity to get to know each other better. Otherwise their respective needs are bound to come between them. More than likely, the Scorpio woman will be interested in sexual satisfaction, the Virgoan man in intellectual stimulation. If they can learn to be patient with each other, and come to terms with the powerful individual forces that motivate them, the relationship could become both positive and permanent. The Virgoan lover must not arouse her jealousy, as she is inclined to be suspicious.

with Sagittarius

On an intellectual level, a Virgoan man and a Sagittarian woman should complement each other well. He will admire her considerable breadth of vision, but when he asks her detailed questions about a particular topic, she is likely to gloss over them, much to his annoyance. The Sagittarian lover is highly sexed, and could be demanding. In addition, her Virgoan partner will soon realize that she is on a completely different wavelength from him in regard to love and sex. Her attitude towards her love life is not as serious as his, for she is more interested in having fun. Should they consider a permanent commitment, however, he must accept that she will need to have a lot of freedom within it. The Virgoan man should curb his tendency to nag. If she has Sagittarius rising, they may have fewer problems to resolve, but she will probably be flirtatious. They should not find it difficult to develop joint interests, especially if they involve literature or outdoor sports. Both are restless individuals.

with Capricorn

Should a Virgoan man find himself in love with a Capricorn woman, it is quite likely that they will eventually marry. Both will want the relationship to develop gradually; they are ruled by their heads, not their hearts. In general, this combination enjoys an excellent rapport. She will encourage her partner to progress in his career, and whenever he is worried or upset, he can rely on her sound, practical approach and advice to help him through any difficulties. This is exactly what the Virgoan man needs. Sexually and emotionally they should be extremely compatible, as both may consider this aspect of their lives of only moderate importance. It will not take him long to discover that his Capricorn lover is both faithful and dependable. She is often a person of few words, but whatever she does say, it is laden with good sense. If Venus was in Scorpio or Pisces at the time of her birth, she will be more affectionate; should she have a Capricorn ascendant, he will find her more tender.

with Aquarius

A partnership between a Virgoan man and an Aquarian woman will need to be carefully nurtured. It is best for the Virgoan to approach his Aquarian on an intellectual level at first. He should not have any difficulty because the Aquarian-born are the most friendly of all the zodiacal types. He may find, however, that she is more eager to keep their relationship on a casual, unemotional level than he. Consequently, the Virgoan man may experience many frustrating moments, despite his generally cool sexual attitude. Should they become lovers, the Virgoan man will undoubtedly be surprised by her unconventional and radical attitude towards sex. More than likely, she will not want to commit herself to him alone, and because she is enormously independent, the Aquarian woman will probably be reluctant to give up her way of life for the type of security he could offer her. Since the Virgoan man is more flexible than his loved one, chances are he will be converted to her way of thinking.

with Pisces

Opposite signs across the Zodiac always seem to develop marvellous rapport between them. Although the Virgoan man and the Piscean woman have many different character traits, they will recognize and respect these individual qualities and should have no difficulty developing a mutually satisfying relationship. She is endowed with the emotional and intuitive powers which he lacks, and he will provide the sound, practical background to their lives which she needs. The Piscean woman is very sensuous, and should therefore be an excellent partner for him sexually. In the early stages of their affair, he is inclined to be remote or cool, but it is quite unlikely that he will be able to resist her warmth and charm for very long. A partnership will develop steadily over a long period before it becomes permanent. There will be times, however, when her intuitive, sometimes illogical, characteristics will clash with his critical mind and common sense, but they should be able to compromise.

The Way to the Virgo Heart

When attracted to a Virgoan of either sex, it is important to forget any approach you have previously used and start anew. In affairs of the heart, Virgoans lead the field in their need for care and consideration. Consequently, most people find the seduction of those born under the sign of the Virgin difficult, challenging, and intriguing. Ultimately it will be rewarding.

Shyness in the Virgoan-born can either be a charming asset or a psychological liability. The latter can arise if they are the objects of a seductive approach, or of an emotional involvement for which they are not ready. The passionate lover dominated by a fire sign, or the typical deep-breathing Scorpio must be careful when turning their amorous attention towards Virgoans. Those born under the sixth sign of the Zodiac value intellectual powers more than physical attributes.

Friendship and intellectual rapport are essential ingredients for the cultivation of a Virgoan love relationship. Trust is also an important consideration. The sexual side will develop slowly. In all other respects, Virgoans live life at a hectic pace and need several outlets for their abundant physical and nervous energy. Lovers must try to help them relax and enjoy life.

Those born under the sign of Virgo willingly make sacrifices for members of their families, missing out on a lot of fun so that others can enjoy themselves. Although this is an admirable trait, it can also be exasperating. The Virgoan-born must try to recognize that all the kindness, hard work and energy which they exert on the behalf of others provide convenient ways for themselves to avoid becoming emotionally involved. In extreme cases, Virgoans may even convince themselves that sex is not for them, and then push it out of their minds, channelling their sexual energy in other directions. Such people often find fulfilment in their careers.

Virgoans are the perfectionists of the Zodiac. They have high standards, and consequently are critical of those who do not meet them. In general, the Virgoan-born only want to be helpful and constructive, but sometimes they can nag incessantly about friends' minor character traits which they find unattractive. So even if your affair is progressing well with a Virgoan, and the possible inhibitions have been overcome, you may occasionally be the object of criticism.

Virgoans are more prone to worry than any other zodiacal sign. Their partners can be valuable assets if they can successfully make the Virgoan-born see their particular problems in perspective.

How do you reach the Virgoan heart? One of the best approaches is to suggest a day in the country, with a simple but delicious picnic lunch. After parking the car and choosing a shady spot by a babbling brook, resist the temptation to make a sexual advance. Instead, suggest a long energetic walk, which Virgo will thoroughly appreciate. Then, panting slightly, spread a checkered tablecloth on the grass and unpack your picnic hamper.

When you are planning an outdoor luncheon for the Virgoan-born, do not rely on cooked meats. Create your own salad and also bring along plenty of fresh fruit. The majority of Virgoans are attracted to health foods, and some are complete vegetarians.

As might be expected, Virgoans love receiving practical presents. If they have a garden, rose trees, bulbs, or plants of any kind will be most welcome. Should they live in an urban area, surprise them with an indoor herb garden or with a potted plant. Either gift is bound to look healthy whenever you visit, as those born under the sign of the Virgin delight in growing things. Or consider buying an item associated with one of the many hobbies Virgoans choose for their leisure time.

But to the crux of the matter: how to attract and cement a relationship with the Virgoan-born. The best advice is to proceed with care. Do not attempt to sweep the Virgoans of either sex off their feet. The heaviest French perfume will have the wrong effect on his refined sensitivity; the shirt unbuttoned to the waist will simply irritate her neat instinct for dress. The Virgoan woman and man believe that a well-groomed appearance is important.

The Libra Woman
September 23rd – October 22nd

Ruling Planet: Venus
Triplicity: Air
Keywords: Intellectual ✳ Communicative
Jewel: Sapphire
Flowers: Hydrangeas ✳ Blue Flowers
Trees: Ash ✳ Cypress ✳ Vines ✳ Almond
Cities: Vienna ✳ Antwerp ✳ Lisbon ✳ Copenhagen

The Libra Woman in Love...

The Libran woman is the true romantic of the Zodiac. To her, love means harmony and a peaceful, congenial life; it is the state in which she functions best. But her romantic nature also indicates that she is extremely vulnerable. Should her lover upset her in any way—by failing to do something he has promised, or by saying something she finds offensive —he will have to be very tactful and reassuring in order to restore her sensitive balance. She, like the scales that represent her sign, is easily disturbed by any display of negative behaviour. This sensitivity is also reflected in her relationships with family and friends. She is usually kind, loving and generous, but can be resentful when her emotional equilibrium is upset.

Romance is the keyword for the Libran woman. On the surface her love life seems to pose no problems, but the situation is not as simple as it might appear. It is not unusual for complications to arise if she has to decide between a light-hearted romantic involvement and a full sexual commitment, or when she has to make up her mind about a marriage proposal. On the one hand, the Libran woman does not feel she is a complete person until she is involved in a permanent relationship, and, as a result, she may commit herself prematurely to marriage. She is frequently accused of being in love with the idea of love. However, once she finds her true mate, she will do everything in her power to make theirs a happy union. Harmony is of the utmost importance to her. On the other hand, her indecisiveness may dominate, and then she will keep a considerate lover waiting for months or even years before saying "Yes". Libra needs to give serious thought to these two extreme patterns of behaviour. She must be careful, because either can upset the delicate balance of her personality: a hasty marriage may end in disaster, yet an evasion of an important issue may prove equally injurious.

Sometimes the Libran woman prefers love and romance to sex; hers is an air sign, not an earthy or a passionate one. It is essential that anyone who is involved with a Libran study the sign that Venus, her ruling planet, occupied at the time of her birth. If it was in Leo, she will be sexually more enthusiastic and passionate; if in Virgo, she will probably have a clinical, almost sex-is-dirty attitude. If, however, Venus was in Libra with the Sun, the Libran woman will display even more romantic and indecisive tendencies. And if it was in Scorpio, her emotions will be most deeply felt.

with Aries

In a Libra and Aries relationship, polar, or opposite, signs of the Zodiac are involved. This usually implies mutual rapport but some clashes are inevitable. A Libran woman will quickly learn that her Arien man will not wait too long for her to make a decision about a sexual involvement with him. He is a freedom-loving individual. She will also realize that he can be selfish—a trait she finds deplorable. There is considerable natural sympathy between the two signs, however, and if they can harmonize their differences, theirs can be a good partnership. He can help her adopt a more positive attitude towards life; she can be instrumental in persuading him to be less aggressive and selfish. Libra must remember that her Arien man will probably be sexually demanding, and if their relationship is to be permanent, she must come to terms with the situation. If he has Aries rising, there should be great sympathy between them. Mars will influence his character development.

with Taurus

Both signs are ruled by Venus. As a result, the couple will discover that there is much in common—a desire for luxury and good food, and an eye for everything that is beautiful and comfortable. The Libran woman may find her Taurean too much a creature of habit, but she will feel safe and secure with him. He is possessive, and although she may cherish this facet of his personality, she enjoys being with other men and can be flirtatious. It would be wise for them to reach a compromise on this issue because a friendship between the two should prove rewarding. Libra and Taurus complement each other materially and socially, and will inevitably create a beautiful home. In addition, it will not be difficult for them to share joint interests, which are often centred on music. He will be passionate, yet considerate of her feelings, and, luckily, he is patient. She will find him more emotionally responsive if Taurus is rising. If his Venus was in Gemini, he will have a more light-hearted approach towards love.

with Gemini

Since both Libra and Gemini are of the air triplicity, there is a basic harmony between them. They are likely to have a light-hearted, yet intellectual affair, not a passionate one. The Libran woman may not consider the inherent Geminian duality towards other women much of a threat, for she also can attract and charm men, especially at social gatherings. Sometimes decision-making can be a problem for this pair, and can cause more difficulty to others than to the lovers themselves. The Gemini male will try to discuss every detail of a problem and expect a positive response from Libra, but she will reply, "No, you decide." Frequently, friends and family will find themselves waiting to hear whether or not the couple will come to dinner, or whether these two will make up a foursome for the theatre. In general, this is an easy partnership, since Libran harmony blends well with the Geminian characteristics. The outlook is equally promising if Gemini is rising. Affection will dominate their union.

with Cancer

A Libran woman embarking on an affair with a Cancerian should remember that his tongue can be very sharp on occasion, and she should not allow it to upset her. Instead, she must try to accept that this is one of his less pleasant characteristics, and recognize that this inclination to lash out verbally is part of a complex, but typically Cancerian, defence mechanism—the tongue takes the place of the crab's claws. But, crab-like, the Cancerian is soft beneath his protective shell, and she should be clever enough to use this to her advantage. There will be problems in the early days of the relationship, but it is worth making every effort to solve them. She will find her man emotional, sensual and at heart a romantic. He is often eager to start a family and will make an excellent husband and father. The Libran woman is fortunate if he has Venus in Taurus or Leo. He will tend to be more practical towards her if Cancer is rising in his birth chart. Both are psychologically motivated to give of themselves.

The Libra Woman in Love...

with Leo

A Libran woman will appreciate her Leo lover's generosity and attention. Together they will enjoy life and make the most of the time they spend with each other. He is romantic and passionate, and knows how to make every sensual interlude special. He, more than she, likes to make love in comfort. Although the Libran woman may find him somewhat demanding at times, she will be well looked after. In general, this can be a rewarding partnership. He will be the dominant partner, making decisions for her. She will love this, but should not allow herself to become too dependent on him. She should express her opinions on issues of mutual concern as well as deal with her own problems. If she does not do this, he could rule her life so completely that it might seriously weaken her personality. Venus in the same sign for both of them would indicate excellent prospects for the relationship. If Leo is rising, he will have a more individual and intellectual attitude towards her.

with Virgo

A careful balance is required for this relationship to flourish. The Virgoan man may be reticent about making the first move; on the other hand, if the Libran woman takes the initiative and is too direct in her approach, she could put him off. He may be nervous, so the Libran woman will have to think carefully and use considerable tact if they are to become lovers as well as friends. Striking up a friendship with him should be easy for the Libran, but she will not be able to win his heart unless she can help him relax. Her efforts are more likely to be rewarded if he has Venus in Libra, or if she has Venus in Virgo. These two are neighbouring signs in the Zodiac, and each can learn a lot from the other. He is practical, hardworking and careful. And if she can blend her positive, peace-loving characteristics with his, they could have a healthy, lasting relationship. Temperamental differences between them are inevitable, but he will relate to her more emotionally if he has a Virgo ascendant.

with Libra

Romance in its purest form will soon emerge when a Libran woman finds herself attracted to a male of the same sign. Each may, however, have some minor reservations about their relationship. They may wonder if they are really in love with each other, or perhaps merely in love with the idea of love. The Libran woman seems to be more disposed to this state of mind than the man. And decision-making may present problems for them. It should be shared equally. And if she feels she cannot readily make up her mind on issues, then she must be persuaded to do so. The position of Venus is important in this coupling, as well as that of Mars, which affects their sexual responses. In addition, a number of today's adult Libran population are total romantics because Neptune, the planet of escapism and romance, was in Libra at the time of their birth. They can easily be deluded and disillusioned because of that planet's influence. If he has Libra rising, the outlook for the future is promising.

with Scorpio

If a Libran woman is considering an affair with a Scorpio, she must check the signs both Venus and Mars were in when he was born. If he has Venus in Libra, near her Sun, or if it was in Virgo, the prospects are favourable. But she will find him passionate and emotionally demanding if his Venus was in Scorpio, and physically exhausting if it was in Sagittarius. The Libran woman will soon discover that even without the influence of Venus, Scorpio is the most emotional and highly sexed of the signs. She should, therefore, take her time before committing herself to a permanent relationship. Scorpio, however, may not want to be kept in a state of uncertainty for long. If Mars was in an earth sign when he was born, it will help steady him somewhat; and he may be more accommodating if it was in an air sign. Although the Libran woman could be swept off her feet, the relationship might not be an easy one for either party. He can be jealous and possessive, but he will be more reliable if he has Scorpio rising.

with Sagittarius

In the early stages of an affair between these two, Libra may be slightly put off by Sagittarius's exuberant attitude towards sex. He can be very romantic on occasion especially if he has Venus in Libra, but it would be unwise for his mate to expect this to be one of his dominating characteristics. Moreover, the Libran woman may find that her lover can be too informal and demanding. For example, he may not be particular about where he makes love, while she prefers comfort. He will be an intellectually stimulating partner, but he can be somewhat pedantic at times. Sagittarians generally tend to be seriously interested either in science, history and the humanities, or in the outdoor life and sports, so that adapting to either extreme could prove challenging for her. But if they can reconcile their differences, they should have a fun-filled life, provided that she remembers he is freedom-loving. She may find him less emotionally demanding if he has Sagittarius as his rising sign.

with Capricorn

The Libran woman will discover that her Capricorn mate is an industrious and ambitious worker; and frequently, he becomes a success in terms of prestige and material assets. Should they begin an affair, it will not take them long to realize that their concepts of love differ considerably. She is likely to be an idealist, and is prepared to rush into marriage because she is infatuated with the idea of love. He, on the other hand, has a practical outlook and is frequently lacking in sentimentality. Perhaps the loner in every Capricorn, which is particularly noticeable in the male as he gains prominence in his career, will prove difficult for her to accept. But if Libra is not completely fulfilled, she will not complain, because harmony is all important to her. She will respect her Capricorn man and appreciate his faithfulness. She also has the ability to make him laugh at himself, which most Capricorns are unable to do. Theirs can be a solid partnership, but it will demand a great deal from each one.

with Aquarius

A Libra and Aquarius partnership will be founded on a beautiful friendship, and could remain so for a long time. The Libran woman will not mind this state, for she probably finds the early stages of any affair somewhat of a fantasy. The Aquarian may want to develop the relationship sexually without a strong emotional involvement, because he does not want to be tied down to one partner. Thus, the Libran woman must not be surprised if, even after they have become lovers, he fails to think in terms of a permanent commitment. Should differences of outlook be resolved, there is a sound basis for a deep relationship between these two. They will not have any difficulty developing mutual interests, and the arts will probably be high on their list. She must not forget that he is likely to be unconventional but stubborn, kind but distant, especially if he has Venus in Capricorn or in Aquarius. He will relate more warmly and positively towards her if he has Aquarius rising.

with Pisces

The combination of a Libra woman and a Pisces man could prove to be a weak one, so it is essential that other astrological factors be considered, particularly the rising signs. It is quite likely that a relationship between them may lack shape and direction. And if this is so, a certain amount of dissatisfaction is inevitable. Although they may be sexually compatible, neither will derive much psychological strength from the other. Consequently, if they have been having an affair and want to end it, both parties will hesitate to do so for fear of hurting the other. It will be extremely difficult for either to make a final decision, and a general feeling of being emotionally imprisoned may permeate their lives. If they realize that this can happen, and are able to utilize their energies in a constructive way, they could be very happy together, since both are easygoing signs. If Pisces is rising, their relationship could be additionally strengthened because he will have a critical attitude towards her.

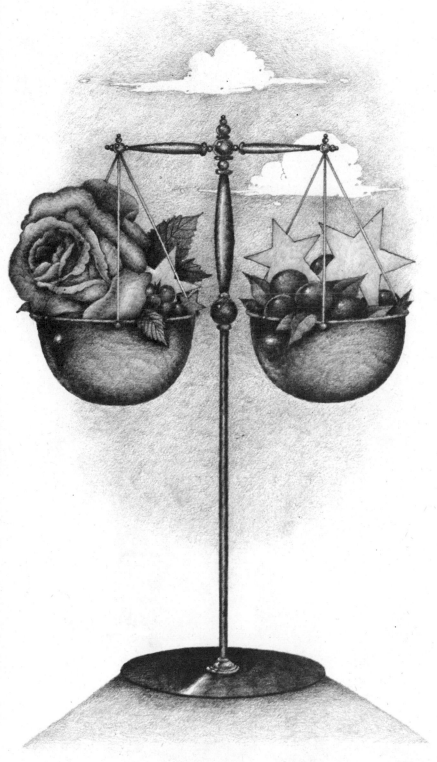

Making the Most of Libra

Venus, the ruling planet of Libra, also rules love and beauty. Librans, and their zodiacal partners, the Taureans, should take notice of her and all that she represents.

Librans have a great need for love. Frequently, they do not feel complete until they are settled in a permanent relationship. Then their romantic natures dominate and sometimes blind them to reality.

When Libran men or women fall in love, they automatically give a great deal of themselves. On a practical level, for example, they will arrange special parties with their loved ones as honoured guests, and will do everything in their power to please them. But, at the same time, they will place their lovers under a certain amount of scrutiny. Are they coming up to the standards Librans consider important? Usually the answer is affirmative. But if you find yourself in the enviable position of being admired and adored by any members of this sign, it is wise to remember that, for Librans to be happy, an affair must be allowed to develop at their chosen pace. As a consequence, they can keep their romantic partners on a string indefinitely while they weigh the advantages and disadvantages of a deep commitment. Librans must be made aware of the damage that this tendency could do to their chances for a long-term emotional relationship. It is unkind, almost cruel for Librans to expect their lovers to remain in a state of continual apprehension. Understandably, they will want to know how they stand with Libra at the moment.

The Libran woman has a keen sense of beauty, and if she wants to attract a particular man, she will expend considerable effort and time on her appearance. She will choose her clothes well and spend as much money as is necessary to keep her hair well groomed. Her style and image may tend to be too frilly, but she does know when to wear a more tailored outfit to contrast with her generally more feminine-looking wardrobe. It would be rare to find Libran women wearing clothes or hairstyles that gave too much emphasis to one side of the face or body,

because this would upset their intuitive desire for balance and harmony.

Similarly, the Libran man is fashion-conscious and dresses well. During his leisure time, he prefers to wear soft colours—shades of blue and of pink, which are associated with Venus. He is likely to have a large collection of jeans and of ruffled shirts that he wears unbuttoned to the waist. In general, Librans should never try to disguise the fact that they are the true romantics of the Zodiac; and when they are in love, they must not hesitate to take advantage of this fact.

Unfortunately, there is a tendency towards self-indulgence in this sign; Librans enjoy eating sweet, calorie-laden food, so it is not surprising to learn that they have a tendency to be overweight. Physical exercise would do them good. Women who are not used to really exerting their muscles could perhaps think of such energetic endeavours as a form of "beauty treatment". Courses which combine exercise machines with massage and sauna are often best for them, and they find that a workout on a bicycle machine can be both relaxing and stimulating to the muscles and figure.

Male Librans would do well to go to their local gyms on a weekly basis. Occasionally, there is an aggressive element present in Librans because the assertive Aries is their opposite sign across the Zodiac. This explains why many of them are interested in karate and judo. Both sexes should give careful thought to pursuing either as a possible hobby.

Libra rules the kidneys; sometimes it is the fate of Librans to have more than their share of headaches. Since these can be difficult to cure permanently, they should have the kidneys checked, as a slight renal defect can be the source of such trouble.

The Libran's desire for harmony and romance will be truly reflected in the home. Each room will be handsomely furnished. Drapes will be made of velvet, of brocade, or of some sheer material. In the living-room, you can expect to relax on a large, comfortable couch that is dotted with soft cushions. It is likely that a musical instrument, perhaps a grand piano, will occupy a prominent position in this room also. Whatever the Libran's taste in music, you can be certain that it will not sound discordant.

The Libra Man
September 23rd – October 22nd

Ruling Planet: *Venus*
Quadruplicity: *Cardinal*
Keywords: *Enterprising * Outgoing*
Metal: *Copper*
Countries: *Austria * China * Japan * Burma * Tibet*
Animals: *Lizards * Snakes*
Colour: *Pale Green*

The Libra Man in Love...

In actuality, the Libran man is as much of a romantic as the woman of that sign. When he falls in love, however, it is likely that he will rationalize his romantic tendencies by telling himself that it is his partner, more than he, who will like the glamour of an evening at a particular place. In doing this, he seems to be trying to justify his romanticism, which he may feel is too sentimental, or perhaps unmasculine.

In love, the Libran has an apparently infallible instinct for doing the right thing at the right time. Like his feminine counterpart, however, he also suffers from indecisiveness. But he will probably have dealt positively with this major failing before getting involved in an emotional relationship. Still, if some attractive woman makes it abundantly clear to him that she is interested, he may keep her dangling for a while, as he makes up his mind whether to commit himself.

Libra will be generous psychologically and materially. He will constantly think in terms of his date—what she would like to do, where she would like to go; and he will consider her moods and reactions carefully. He will not hesitate to spend money on his loved one, arriving at her apartment with bouquets of flowers, bottles of perfume, boxes of

chocolates. Whatever plans he has arranged for the evening, she can be sure that they will be carried through in grand style and in the most romantic setting. But should things go wrong, his generosity will quickly change to resentment. Unfortunately, Libra is frequently guilty of blaming his partner. Before doing so, however, he should ask himself in all honesty whether he has not been the one at fault. While romance, magnanimity and affection are all necessary to build a relationship, they are not sufficient. In addition, he needs to take into account unforeseen factors that could disrupt it. Although the Libran man is acutely sensitive to harmony and discord, he is not perfect. After all, it takes two to make a quarrel.

Most women would agree that Librans make good lovers. Since they are basically easy-going, they will not be too demanding, nor will they exhaust their mistresses emotionally or physically. They readily adopt the pace of the woman with whom they are involved, or at least they skilfully give the impression that they are doing so.

with Aries

Libra will admire the Arien's direct, positive, no-nonsense approach to life. In this combination, the polar, or opposite, signs of the Zodiac are working in a lively and confident way. But in the early stages of the relationship, the Libran man could be slightly dumbfounded by her frank uncomplicated attitude towards sex. And thus he may consider her rather unfeminine until he knows her better and understands her motivation. Libra and Aries could have an excellent partnership, but chances are that it would be one in which she assumes the dominating role. He would not be averse to accepting such a situation, provided that she is tactful and uses her feminine intuition. Mars is her ruling planet, and so its position at the time of her birth should be studied, as it will have a marked influence on her personality. A relationship between these two could be successful if he has Aries rising, but he must beware of her selfishness, which may emerge if she has Aries as either a Sun sign or an ascendant.

with Taurus

The influence of Venus is extremely important in a relationship between a Libran man and a Taurean woman, for both these signs have that planet as their ruler. Therefore, it is not surprising that there are similarities between the two. It is inevitable that the amorous Libran will eventually lose his heart to a beautiful Taurean. He will find her delightfully sensuous and passionate, but in no hurry to rush through the romantic moments of life. The Libran man will learn, too, that the Taurean woman often has a possessive nature. She will be practical, but needs emotional and financial security. She will probably become more self-confident when she feels totally secure in the relationship. Without too much effort, the pair should be able to develop common interests, particularly those related to music. However, he could find an affair with her rather intense at times. Obviously, if she has Taurus rising, the emotional level of the liaison will be heightened. The Libran man will be able to tease her out of any rut.

with Gemini

Although Libra could not possibly be bored while having an affair with a Gemini, he must not be surprised if she fails to take him as seriously as he might like. If he is in a romantic mood, she will enjoy him in a rather detached way. She continually questions her reactions, and does not always trust her emotions. Although she is vivacious and fun to be with, he may find that trying to reach her on an emotional level is exasperating. Luckily, he is in an excellent position to succeed, as their signs are both of the air group. He should focus on her more intellectual approach to life, and initiate conversations. If he makes a determined effort to discuss any problems that may emerge, he will probably win her in the end. Sexually, she will be a lively partner, and may have other lovers, but he can cope with rivals. A very good partnership when it matures, but with the accent on friendship rather than on great passion. The forecast is very positive if she has Gemini rising, and her Venus is in Taurus.

with Cancer

The Libran man, especially if he has a Libran ascendant, will probably be eager to develop a permanent relationship, for it is only then that he will feel complete. If he meets a Cancerian, chances are that they will get along well as their goals are often similar. The earlier they deal with any indecisiveness, a typical Libran trait, or caution, a typical Cancerian trait, the happier they will be. The Libran will soon realize that a Cancerian is highly emotional, and, as a result, her moods will change quickly. Fortunately, he has the ability and temperament to cope with them. But there are times when she can make some cutting, harsh remarks, which he will not be able to accept in silence. Then a quarrel ensues. Although this partnership is not too easy in some respects, it is worth developing slowly. She will feel more emotionally secure and ready for a relationship if she has Cancer rising. Their relationship will be more fun for him if she has Venus in Leo. They should readily develop joint interests.

The Libra Man in Love...

with Leo

This is one of the most glamorous, romantic, generous and fun-filled partnerships in the Zodiac. Frequently, there is natural rapport and sympathy between this pair. He will find her loving and sexually enthusiastic. Either they will have an extremely enjoyable short affair, or a long, happy one. The Leo woman is known for her firm decisions and good organizing ability; her major weakness is her tendency to be domineering. Therefore, in the early stages of the relationship, her lover would be wise to decide whether to let her make the decisions or to assert himself and share that responsibility. Perhaps the most important aspect of this partnership is that each will enjoy it. He must not forget that she is a strong type, and while she may look at him adoringly, she will certainly have her say. The future bodes well if they have Venus in the same sign at birth. If she has Leo rising, she could be more dominating and expect the unusual from her partner. They both enjoy the luxurious life.

with Virgo

The more slowly and subtly a Libran develops an affair with a Virgoan, the better. She is often shy, especially when young, so she is not likely to be swept off her feet. The Virgo-born have few affairs, but once they fall in love they make faithful, endearing partners. The sign Venus was in at the time of Virgo's birth is extremely important in this partnership, and needs to be carefully considered. If it was in Libra or Leo, she will be well-disposed towards the Libran man. However, if it was in Virgo with her Sun, then he will need to show a great deal of tact and consideration. Interestingly, if he should have Venus in Virgo near her Sun, he will be more sympathetic towards her, and will find it easier to understand her point of view. She is fussy, critical and analytical—traits that he could find annoying. Since they are neighbours along the Zodiac, there are also temperamental differences, but Venus could have an important influence. Expectations for a future together are higher if she has Virgo rising.

with Libra

The Libran man who wants to develop a relationship with a Libran woman may find himself tasting his own medicine! Often when a woman makes the first advances, he keeps his distance until he finds out more about her through mutual friends. Consequently, he must expect the same treatment when he finds a Libran girl to whom he is attracted. In this case, the relationship would develop faster if he were to assert himself more than usual. When two people of the same sign become involved, the most interesting thing to discover is how they differ. Although they will be closer to each other in temperament and behaviour if they both have Venus in the same sign, this planet will be responsible for their different attitudes towards love and sex if it falls in different signs. In general, they are compatible, needing love, affection and harmony in their lives. But when upsets occur, they will be quite severe. She could be rather selfish towards him if she has Libra rising. Joint decision-making is necessary.

with Scorpio

The Libran man who is as easy-going as his Sun sign is supposed to be will not be disturbed by the differing characteristics of his Scorpio partner. She is highly sexed, emotional and introspective. Most of the time they can be very happy together, but occasionally the strength and depth of her personality will overwhelm him. If he is handsome and women find him attractive, she may well exhibit a jealous streak. Sexually, the Libran man will find her a demanding and possibly exhausting partner, particularly if he prefers a tender, romantic sex life to a hectic one. The position of Mars will be a guide to her sexual nature, as this planet is her part ruler. Their relationship will be strengthened if they have Venus in the same sign, although temperamental differences will occur. She could be gentler if Scorpio is rising in her birth chart, but he must remember that this is one of the strongest signs, and, thus, she may become the dominant partner. His indecisiveness will force her to make the decisions.

with Sagittarius

The Libran man will find his Sagittarian woman fun-loving, challenging and refreshing, but he will have to use all his charm and resourcefulness if he is to catch her. She loves freedom and may not want to be caught, or, at least, to stay caught for long. They will enjoy their affair, but he must expect that he will have rivals. Intellectually, this is a sound relationship. Both enjoy exchanging ideas and discussing viewpoints. Sexually, he may find her overly enthusiastic and, perhaps, in too much of a hurry. However, she will respond well to him, and he will not have to put up with any indecisiveness from her. Her experience and avid interest in sports and the outdoor life could cause some practical difficulties; he may feel like a lazy evening at home listening to records while she wants to go ice skating. But she is warm and enthusiastic whether Sagittarius is her Sun or ruling sign. The partnership will never be dull for him with her tremendous energy and constant encouragement behind it.

with Capricorn

When a Libran man is attracted to a Capricorn woman, he will have to resign himself to the fact that she will be demanding, but not in a sexual or emotional sense. She takes life seriously and is extremely ambitious, doing everything within her power to spur her loved one into whatever action is necessary for him to reach the top of his career or profession. In turn, he can depend on her to organize dinner parties for his business associates and to be a gracious hostess. They may have minor disagreements about money, as she is inclined to be economical and he tends to be extravagant. Although the Capricorn woman is not a particularly demonstrative or passionate partner, a strong bond of affection should develop between them if his Venus falls in Aquarius. In addition, the outlook seems favourable for a happy life together. If, however, she has Capricorn rising, she is likely to have a motherly attitude towards permanent relationships, and her Libran lover could find this inhibiting.

with Aquarius

If a Libran is attracted to an Aquarian, he should initially think in terms of friendship and intellectual stimulation. Aquarius has the reputation of being the friendliest sign of the Zodiac, and also has a low emotional level. He would be wise, therefore, to concentrate on less sensual matters until she feels romantically inclined. He will admire, but perhaps not entirely approve of, her self-containment. While the ties between them will gradually strengthen, she can remain a loner, especially if she has Venus in Capricorn. This aspect of her personality will puzzle Libra, who is so communicative. Once Aquarius is won, however, she will be faithful. He may be astonished at her progressive ideas, especially about sexual matters, but she will be good for him. He could find her stubborn and may find himself yielding more than he anticipated. Uranus is her ruling planet, and the sign that it was in at the time of her birth has considerable relevance to understanding the Aquarian woman.

with Pisces

On the credit side of this combination, Libra will find his Piscean woman an easy-going and willing partner. She is sensitive and emotional, but occasionally she becomes confused about what she wants in life. At these times, it is difficult for her to channel her energies in a positive, creative manner. Then, it will be essential for her Libran lover to assume a more dominant, guiding role; he will not find this easy to do as it runs contrary to his nature. On the other hand, if he remains his sympathetic, adaptable self, she may become too dependent on him. It is important for the Libran man to think consciously about the direction and shape of their relationship. If he does not, it could drift aimlessly. If she has Venus in Aries, it will make her a more enthusiastic partner for Libra. Should she have Pisces rising, she will be more critical towards him. The sign Neptune was in at the time of her birth should be carefully noted as this is her ruling planet. Both appreciate the other's good qualities and artistic potential.

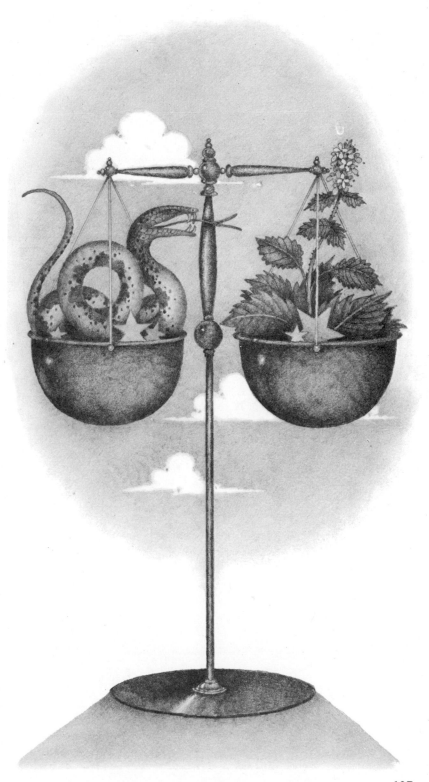

The Way to the Libra Heart

Although Librans are romantics, and are often accused of being in love with love, it would not be unusual for them to be in a quandary at the same time. They either waver at the prospect of total commitment or rush into a relationship because they need an emotional attachment. For them, it seems that there is no middle ground; it is a case of one extreme or the other. Sometimes, Librans want romance without sex. At other times, despite the fact that the sexual side is progressing nicely, they would recoil at the mere mention of marriage. Consequently, they are inclined to keep their lovers waiting indefinitely for an answer.

What must be understood, however, is that if Libra is the rising sign, marriage or a permanent relationship will often bring psychological wholeness to the Libran-born. Moreover, once they make a permanent commitment, they will do everything to ensure that harmony prevails. To bring out the best in them, the Scales, which are the symbol of Libra, have to be balanced.

The male Libran usually makes an excellent husband; he is affectionate, easy to live with and not too demanding. The female Libran makes an ideal wife, whose every thought revolves around her mate. She will entertain well and help her husband make progress in his career.

Librans are kind and extremely generous, but they like to hear profuse thanks for their gifts and to receive recognition and affection for any good deeds they do. So when friends or family members are not as responsive as they expect, Librans become upset, and, at worst, show resentment. Less florid types, such as Virgos and Capricorns, will need to express themselves more fully if they want their affairs with these zodiacal partners to thrive.

The Libran-born are uncomplicated and amiable types. Well-liked and considerate of others, they make every effort to see that friends feel comfortable and are treated fairly.

Whatever the setting, it is characteristic of Librans to enjoy the good things in life. Usually they have hearty appetites, downing huge portions of the richest food and drink. As might be expected, excess poundage is frequently a problem for many of them.

Obviously, one way to the Libran heart is through the stomach. So if you are trying to attract a Libran-born, extend an invitation for a home-cooked dinner and make the setting as romantic as possible. Place a bowl of fresh flowers on the table, dim the dining-room lights and have quiet lyrical music playing in the background. When you plan the menu do not forget that quantity is as important as quality in this case. Home-made tomato soup and roast turkey are certain to please. And for the appetizer, serve avocado filled with small shrimp. The dessert should be sweet-tasting and topped with strawberries, but anything that has a delicate flavour and colour will be appealing to the Libran. Wines should not be too dry; a Sauterne would be a good choice.

Librans enjoy receiving gifts and are so impressed by them that it is not too difficult to find things which are certain to give them pleasure. The label from an exclusive shop may please the Libran-born more than they would care to admit. For the women of this sign, choose particularly feminine items—floral-scented perfume or toilet water, flowers, chocolates. Should you consider buying your loved one clothes, remember that Librans are particularly fond of shades of blue and pink.

As for the men, you cannot go wrong if you buy presents that appeal to their romantic nature. Select an exotic-smelling aftershave lotion, a silk dressing-gown or perhaps a kaftan. The last item would be most appropriate if he has Venus in Scorpio or Leo. If you feel inclined to focus on his athletic interests, what about golf clubs? The game, quiet and gentlemanly enough to suit every Libran, frequently becomes competitive. Then you may see your man's love of peace and tranquillity put to the test. Of course, records are always popular.

Since comfort is vitally important to all Librans, make sure your home is warm, as they are sensitive to draughts, and that you have soft chairs or couches which would be suitable to relax in after the meal. Play some romantic music.

The Scorpio Woman

October 23rd – November 22nd

Ruling Planets: Pluto ✳ Mars
Triplicity: Water
Keywords: Emotional ✳ Intuitive
Jewel: Opal
Flowers: Red Flowers ✳ Geranium
Trees: Bushy Trees ✳ Blackthorn
Cities: Liverpool ✳ Washington D.C.

The Scorpio Woman in Love...

Although the Scorpio woman will not hesitate to make her prospective lover aware of how she feels, she will not act without caution. More than likely, she will also have decided what approach to use. The Scorpio-born is known for her intensity and sense of purpose; she lives life on a high emotional level. In love, she is interested in the fullest development of a relationship. The Scorpio woman will be generous to her partner in every respect, and her loved one will derive a great deal of pleasure from an affair with her.

It is likely, however, that at some time her partner will also feel her jealousy, which is the worst Scorpio fault. Should she suspect that her man is attracted to another woman, she will certainly let him know how she feels. There are two main reasons that she needs to be extremely careful in this respect. Many times she may have no reason to be jealous. She may perhaps have seen her lover innocently talking to another woman, but immediately Scorpio jumps to conclusions and thinks they have been planning a secret weekend. It

is also possible that Scorpio may have a relationship with a partner who needs a certain amount of freedom of expression, and who will not want to be too tied down to one woman. So if she feels herself getting jealous, she should consider this possibility before confronting him. Otherwise, she may lose him completely. Frequently, jealousy goes hand in hand with possessiveness, so the Scorpio woman would do well not to think of any lover as solely hers. Many men will not appreciate this trait and, as a result, would be

inclined to break off the relationship.

In general, men are attracted to Scorpio's great capacity to enjoy life. Everyone born under this sign has a tendency to do things to excess, and when a Scorpio woman is in love, this trait is even more apparent. She is the most highly sexed type in the Zodiac and loves deeply. At times her lover may find she is taking up too much of his time and energy. The Scorpio woman should think about this possibility, particularly if he has a demanding and worthwhile career.

with Aries

The true Arien man is basically straightforward and uncomplicated, so the Scorpio woman should have no difficulty attracting his attention. There is no need for her to make elaborate seduction arrangements; she should telephone him and suggest going out for a beer. He will be as highly sexed as she, and from that point of view will be the most satisfying partner in the Zodiac. The Arien man is often selfish and likes to feel free. In general, he will not allow himself to be bogged down by his relationships; she should bear this in mind if she begins to feel jealous. They can have a lot of fun together, but their emotions are completely different: hers are intense and extremely passionate; his lively and enthusiastic. Quarrels are inevitable, as both have such powerful drives. They would benefit enormously by developing joint interests. Overall, theirs will be a high-powered partnership. He will be more affectionate towards his loved one if he has Venus in Pisces or Taurus.

with Taurus

Sympathy and considerable rapport should emerge as the relationship develops between these two polar signs of the Zodiac. Initially, the Scorpio woman could find her Taurean partner slow in responding to her sexually, but if she is patient, she will eventually discover a wonderfully passionate and sensuous lover, who will not disappoint her. It is possible that her handsome Taurean man will be possessive or else he may have a string of admirers. Should Venus, his ruling planet, be in Gemini, he could have a surprisingly flirtatious streak, which she will have to tolerate. This will not be easy for her, as jealousy is Scorpio's worst fault. Although there are differences between the two types, their relationship has the potential to become permanent; each partner can be psychologically, emotionally and sexually satisfying for the other. If he has Taurus rising, the Scorpio woman should find her lover more intense and emotional. Both have excellent business sense.

with Gemini

The Scorpio woman will probably be first attracted to the Gemini man's slim, active body and quick movements. In addition, she will like the way he talks freely to her about a variety of subjects. The Gemini man can be evasive, however, whenever she mentions the possibility of developing their relationship. They should have a lot of fun together, but she must remember that he does not take his love life as seriously as she. His flirtatious nature will be one manifestation of his inherent duality, and the Scorpio woman should therefore not be surprised if she discovers that he is having affairs with other women. Jealousy is likely to be her immediate and natural reaction, but when she confronts him with her knowledge, he will probably tell her that his other loves are not important. Allowances will have to be made for their temperamental differences. Should he have Venus in Taurus or possibly Cancer, she should be able to meet the challenge of the partnership.

with Cancer

If a Scorpio woman has decided that she wants to get involved in a permanent relationship, a man born under the sign of the Crab might prove the perfect partner. He will be kind and sympathetic; sexually, she will find him a rewarding lover. The Cancerian man has a high emotional level that will harmonize with her passionate nature. She will soon learn that he can occasionally be harsh and very moody, but she should be able to cope with these abrupt changes. From a practical point of view, both are hard workers, so if they begin a joint business undertaking, for example, the Scorpio flair for finance combined with the Cancerian natural shrewdness should ensure success. Should he have Venus in Taurus, Scorpio will find him more sensual. They should thoroughly enjoy their affair if it is in Leo. But if he has Cancer rising he will probably be less emotional and perhaps sharper towards her. His practical streak, however, will be emphasized.

The Scorpio Woman in Love...

with Leo

Basically, this is a pairing of two strong astrological types; their character traits are so different that the Scorpio woman and the Leo man are likely to encounter some problems should they begin an affair. She will certainly enjoy being with him and will soon discover that he loves doing things in grand style. Together they should see and experience a lot in life. The Leo man is an enthusiastic, emotional type, and although he has strong feelings, they are more open and less complex than hers. Sexually, he is passionate, but it will be his enthusiasm rather than a deeply smouldering intensity that will drive him. Scorpio and Leo will differ considerably in this respect. While he may seem more domineering, any jealousy that she tries to express will not be well received. The Leo man will not allow himself to be possessed. There could be rivalry if he has Leo rising. Since both are stubborn individuals, compromises need to be reached for a relationship to mature.

with Virgo

When a Scorpio woman is attracted to a Virgoan man, she should proceed with care, for he is often genuinely shy and modest. He will not appreciate a seductive approach, so regardless of how passionate the Scorpio woman may be feeling, she would be wise not to make her intentions too obvious. The best way to cultivate a relationship with the Virgoan man is to discover his hobbies, and then develop an interest in one or two of them. The friendship stage of any affair is important to the Virgoan-born. The Scorpio woman will quickly realize that his emotional level is lower than hers, and that he has a clinical attitude towards sex, which she will not share. Although there are striking differences between them, Virgo's critical, analytical side can blend well with Scorpio's inquisitive, searching nature. If both partners have Venus in Libra, it will help bridge the major differences between them. Should he have Virgo rising, he will be less critical.

with Libra

The Libran man is easygoing, kind and romantic, but he will probably not be as highly sexed as she; this may become an eventual source of disappointment to the Scorpio-born woman. In general, she may find herself faced with making the decisions for the both of them, and although she is likely to enjoy this role, the Scorpio woman should ask herself whether the Libran partner is not drawing too freely on her abundant emotional and psychological strength. Consequently, problems of this nature should definitely be discussed at an early stage in the relationship and not shelved. Although the Scorpio woman is born under one of the strongest signs, and frequently has enough energy for two, it is not difficult for a lover to take advantage of her. Libra and Scorpio are neighbouring signs of the Zodiac, and while they can share the position of Venus or have that planet in their respective Sun signs, there will be psychological differences.

with Scorpio

If a Scorpio woman and man fall in love with each other, it will be important for them to recognize their different personality characteristics rather than concentrate on the similar ones. Allowances will have to be made for these opposing traits, as they are bound to have a powerful effect on their relationship. As soon as possible, they should find out where Mars, the co-ruling planet, was when both of them were born, for it can either increase their joint sexual and emotional energies, or restrain them. The partnership will work out very well, or not at all. If the Scorpio woman feels that the affair is beginning to deteriorate, she would be wise to break away, for deep within the Scorpio-born is a powerful force that can become destructive and negative under certain conditions. It is even possible for a love-hate situation to develop. But should he have Scorpio rising, circumstances will be the most favourable for them to make a long-lasting commitment.

with Sagittarius

Their Sun signs alone indicate that they are strikingly dissimilar in many respects. The open, freedom-loving, uncomplicated Sagittarian man will show his Scorpio partner some completely different ways of approaching life and love. It will not take her long to realize that he cannot tolerate jealousy, for he will respond most sharply to any display of it on her part. He needs his freedom, whether it is in a brief liaison or in a permanent commitment; he both enjoys and thrives on the challenge of a new conquest. The Sagittarian partner also likes to enjoy life, particularly outdoors. He loves food and will relish an expensive meal in a good restaurant as much as she will. Although the Scorpio woman should not have any difficulty attracting him, she may have to expend a great deal of effort to keep him interested. Should he want to end the affair, however, no amount of emotional argument will sway him. Fortunately, they will share an enthusiasm for sex.

with Capricorn

The Scorpio woman must remember that the Capricorn man has a low emotional level and is often considered to be a loner, both in the physical and emotional sense. Consequently, she should be prepared to meet some resistance in her efforts to attract his attention. But if a liaison does develop, she may discover that he is not as demanding sexually as she; he is energetic, however, and will work hard for her and their relationship. Although they may be able to reach a sympathetic understanding, they will have to make provisions for the vast differences between them. Unfortunately, if the negative factors outweigh the positive, these two have a tendency to stay together, possibly injuring each other by the very tenacity with which they cling to each other. If they decide to make the relationship permanent, it is quite likely that they will be able to fulfil all their ambitions and achieve material progess. In addition, the Scorpio woman will find her Capricorn partner extremely faithful.

with Aquarius

This could become a tense and edgy partnership, though it will probably be an exciting one. There is no doubt that even in the early stages of their affair, the differences between the two will become readily apparent. Emotionally, the Aquarian man is cool and may be happiest when involved in a sexual partnership without any strings attached. If the Scorpio woman can accept this, she should enjoy the liaison, for sexually he is often the type to experiment and indulge in advanced techniques. Moreover, she may find that they are on different psychological wavelengths, and that he can occasionally be as stubborn as she. Despite the Aquarian man's advanced opinions, he has a tendency to be rigid in his beliefs; however, the Scorpio woman is likely to challenge many of these. If he has Aquarius rising, it is possible that he may want to dominate, especially if he has made a permanent commitment. Uranus, his ruling planet, will have an important effect on this pairing.

with Pisces

It is with a Piscean man that a Scorpio woman can express herself most satisfactorily and positively. But she must be careful not to make it too apparent that she is the dominant partner, accepting total responsibility for any decision-making; he will cheerfully acquiesce to the role reversal. He could, however, become weak-willed, so she needs to handle the situation tactfully. Usually, the Piscean-born needs someone to give him a sense of direction in life, for he is often extremely clever and is creatively and artistically talented. It is mainly a question of helping him develop his potential to the fullest. The Scorpio woman has the ability to successfully bring out the best in her Piscean partner. Sexually, she should find him satisfying, but he may have less stamina than she. The Piscean man will react more critically towards her if he has Pisces rising, and more passionately if he has Venus in Aries. The sign Neptune, his ruling planet, was in when he was born is important.

Making the Most of Scorpio

Scorpios have a hypnotic and penetrating expression that is one of their most powerful assets. Regardless of whether or not it is consciously employed, the Scorpio-born seem to have no difficulty attracting anyone's attention, be it in a roomful of people or on a busy street. The overwhelming characteristic of those born under the eighth sign is their smouldering intensity.

Scorpio, as a sign, does rule the genitals, and, therefore, it is not surprising to learn that sexuality forms an integral part of the Scorpio image. The clothes that both sexes typically wear, for example, emphasize this aspect, although they do enjoy experimenting with a variety of styles. Many Scorpio women own high, shiny black leather boots and at least one slinky black dress. The men often appear dressed in some item of leather clothing. Of all the zodiacal types, Scorpios seem to be best able to carry off this look. There are times, of course, when the women want to accentuate their femininity. Gypsy-style dresses with deep scooped necklines would be perfect for this purpose. And Scorpio men can make an ordinary three-piece suit look striking. Both take their image seriously and consciously develop it.

Voluptuous could rightly be used to describe the figures of the Scorpio-born. They are naturals at making the most of themselves under any circumstances; they never miss an opportunity for fun and enjoyment. Since they find restraint difficult, over-indulgence often results. If it is true that Scorpios work hard, it is equally certain that they play hard. They have enormous appetites, not only sexually, but also gastronomically. Physically, there are two distinct types of Scorpio: one is wiry and lean with a high metabolism; the other, who make up the majority, is rounder in build and has a tendency to put on a great deal of weight. Scorpios who fall in the latter category can, however, adhere faithfully to a diet for a few weeks. But once they have shed the excess pounds, they frequently decide to celebrate the loss by asking their friends to a dinner of rich food, good wines and spirits. They are likely to continue their eating binge, and within a few weeks regain whatever they lost, and perhaps even more.

Friends would be wasting their time if they tried to tell the Scorpio-born to cut down on food or, indeed, sex; they cannot live under constraints for they get bored too easily. The best approach is to tell them how tremendous they look when they are slim. Hopefully, the compliments will encourage them to keep a careful watch on their weight.

Much of the strength and some of the weaknesses of the Scorpios come from the influence of their ruling planet, Mars. They have powerful feelings and must live life at a high emotional level. Scorpios need sexual fulfilment, and if they are not totally satisfied their energy can become a destructive force. In love and friendship, they are passionate, but find it difficult to make allowances for the failings of partners. They are inclined to be critical of others, but resent criticism of themselves. Brooding and resentful feelings are common manifestations of their dissatisfaction.

The emotions of the Scorpio-born, however, can be channelled positively, perhaps in advancing their careers or in fighting for important social causes such as the improvement of housing conditions or the end of financial exploitation. Whatever they do, they need to feel that their work is important. They cannot function well when faced with trivial matters. Those born under the eighth sign of the Zodiac try to establish a pattern to their lives.

Jealousy is the overriding weakness of Scorpios. They must do everything in their power to curb it, particularly in their love relationships. Most partners will not tolerate displays of it, for in many cases the jealousy is unwarranted. Unfortunately, in these situations the vivid imaginations of the Scorpio-born have been working overtime.

On the credit side, Scorpios have many positive qualities, such as abundant emotional strength and courage. These they readily show to friends and lovers. Moreover, they are extremely generous and delight in giving gifts. They do this primarily because they love life and want others to enjoy it too, not because they are trying to buy popularity.

The Scorpio Man

October 23rd – November 22nd

Ruling Planets: Pluto ✳ Mars
Quadruplicity: Fixed
Keyword: Resistant to change
Metal: Iron
Countries: Norway ✳ Morocco ✳ Paraguay
Animals: Crustaceans ✳ Insects
Colours: Deep Red ✳ Maroon ✳ Burgundy

The Scorpio Man in Love...

Strategy must be the Scorpio man's keyword when he is about to embark on a new affair. He should plan his moves carefully and consider an alternative course of action, should one fail or not seem suitable or advantageous under a particular set of circumstances. Because he is energetic, he will not waste any time. But the Scorpio man will not act hastily, proceeding gradually and determinedly towards his objective.

He will treat his girlfriend generously and make certain that she thoroughly enjoys the affair. But there is no doubt that he is extremely demanding, sexually; he must accept the possibility that his lover may be less forthcoming or passionate than he. In addition, the Scorpio man must remember that he is highly emotional, and, consequently, when he is in love, the intensity of feeling he experiences may be too much for a partner to deal with, especially if, for example, her sign falls into the air triplicity.

The Scorpio man would fare better in his love relationships if he could permit his partner to continue her former friendships, perhaps even other liaisons, until she feels ready to commit herself wholly to him. Of course, this will be extremely difficult for him, as he has an inordinate capacity to feel jealousy. But he must remember that she will have her own approach to love and sexual involvements, which may not be identical with his. In addition, she will probably not have the patience and fortitude to cope with this negative trait of his.

In general, the Scorpio man frequently takes his love life too seriously. He will certainly enjoy it, but the depth of his feelings can sometimes overwhelm him. He may refuse to take no for an answer, although he can be quite ruthless about ending an affair or even a marriage if he feels he must. Pluto, his ruling planet, governs "beginnings and ends", and Scorpio himself has a powerfully destructive force which, if he cares to

use it, can in extreme cases be psychologically or even physically dangerous. Such characteristics make other, less complicated types reject any partnership with those born under the sign of the Scorpion.

It seems to be psychologically necessary for most Scorpios to make abrupt changes during their lives, but after ending a long-lasting commitment or giving up a promising career, they frequently find themselves in worse situations, with even less sympathetic partners. Perhaps their intensity causes this.

with Aries

These two are highly sexed and should complement each other well, but the Scorpio man will quickly discover that his partner is usually quite independent. While he will admire and respect that quality, he must also accept a concomitant love of freedom. If the Arien woman has a successful career or one that requires her to travel a lot, she may be reluctant to give it up when she marries. If this should happen, he could become extremely jealous, and should a quarrel ensue between these individually powerful personalities, it will probably be fierce and stormy. But these two can share many fun-filled moments together if they are willing to accept mutual differences in emotional level. The sign Mars was in when they were both born is important, for it rules Aries and is a co-ruler of Scorpio. The Scorpio man must beware of her selfishness, which will be even more apparent if she has Aries rising. At the same time, she may operate on a higher emotional level.

with Taurus

Opposite signs of the Zodiac are involved in this coupling, which seems to indicate that there will be a natural rapport between Scorpio and Taurus. He will find her practical, steady, secure, but possibly possessive. In addition, the Taurean lover is likely to be beautiful, passionate and sensuous. Sexually, the Scorpio partner should be fulfilled, but he will not find her too eager to develop the relationship quickly, nor too easy to arouse. The powerful psychological bond between them should make it relatively simple, however, for them to accept this difference. This partnership has an excellent chance to become permanent, as long as they are aware of and can cope with each other's major weakness: the jealous streak of the Scorpio man and the possessive nature of the Taurean woman. If they were to get involved in a joint business undertaking, their combined practical qualities should guarantee its success. The Scorpio man should check her Venus sign.

with Gemini

The Gemini woman's attitude towards love and sex is quite unlike the Scorpio man's, but he will have ample opportunity to discover just how they differ. As the liaison deepens, she will discuss this at great length, and will answer in her own lively and individual way the many incisive questions he asks. What she says, however, may not be what she is actually thinking; she will either respond in an outrageous fashion to provoke him, or express what she thinks he wants to hear depending on her mood or how much she wants to please him. The Scorpio man must recognize her duality, which may mean that she will not be a faithful partner. Moreover, there is a distinct possibility that she may not want a deep emotional involvement, particularly if her career is rewarding. But fortunately for him, the Gemini woman enjoys sexual experimentation. An affair with her will be fun-filled and lively, as the Gemini lover is not intense and has a low emotional level.

The Scorpio Man in Love ...

with Cancer

This is basically an excellent partnership, although it can occasionally become too emotional. And should a sensitive Cancerian woman be upset or made unhappy by a passionate and perhaps jealous Scorpio lover, they will have to work extremely hard to get their relationship back on an even keel. It will not take the Scorpio man long to find out that his Cancerian woman has an individual and instinctive protective system, for it becomes immediately apparent the moment she is challenged; she can look after herself very well. Underneath her shell, she is, however, kind and definitely not as harsh as she may sometimes appear. In fact, the Cancerian woman has a decidedly romantic streak and may even be too sentimental. The relationship could work out extremely well if the two concerned decide to make it permanent. He must expect his loved one to have sudden changes of mood, as this is a powerful characteristic that she cannot completely control.

with Leo

The potentially serious difficulty in this combination of two of the most powerful signs in the Zodiac is that neither may want to give way to the other on important issues. Consequently, stalemates are likely to occur between a Scorpio man and a Leo woman. She will still be a strong, fiery, emotional type who always wants to lead, and therefore will try to dominate her Scorpio man. In fact, she may well drive him crazy by her attempts to do so. But if they can successfully curb their stubborn natures and are open to compromise, they can share many happy moments together. The Leo woman lives life to the fullest emotionally, sexually, and socially, so her Scorpio partner will certainly not be bored. Together they should enjoy doing things in grand style. Considerable thought must be given to a permanent commitment, especially if she has Leo rising. Should she have Venus in Cancer, the Scorpio man will find her more tender and affectionate.

with Virgo

The Scorpio man who is considering a love affair with a Virgoan woman will need to refrain from his usual direct and passionate approach. Since she is genuinely shy and retiring, he would do well to focus his efforts on a friendship with her. If the Scorpio man is willing to be patient and persevere, chances are excellent that he can win her heart. Gradually a basic sympathy will develop between them. Despite their different emotional and sexual needs, these two do have a great deal in common. Mutual involvement in some hobby or work project will help them discover similarities. She has an analytical mind and is fascinated by detail, while he likes research and study in depth. Both are extremely careful in whatever they undertake and are hard workers. If Venus was either in Libra or Scorpio, their future together will look more promising, for she will be more romantic towards him. And should she have a Virgo ascendant, her emotional level will be higher.

with Libra

It will not take the Scorpio man long to discover that the Libran woman is charming, relaxed and romantic. When he arrives at her place after a hard day's work, she will look her best, have a gin-and-tonic ready to help him unwind and a delicious dinner waiting in the oven. But as the evening passes and his thoughts turn to a different kind of relaxation, he should not be too surprised if she complains about having a headache or a similar malady that is so painful she cannot think about sex. He will have to come to terms with this Libran trait: she may be too languid for him sexually and too infatuted with the idea of love. If Venus was in Scorpio, near his Sun, when she was born, her passionate nature will be revealed; if she has Libra rising, he can expect a more ardent partner. Should this couple contemplate marriage, however, allowances will have to be made for Libra's tendency to resentfulness and Scorpio's to jealousy.

with Scorpio

Both should find out their respective rising signs, so that they can judge whether they have sufficiently different character traits to balance the powerful combination of emotional and sexual forces. The sign Mars was in when each was born will add important dimensions to their respective personalities. They could easily nurture a love-hate relationship, but are best equipped of all the zodiacal pairings to handle such a situation. A strong sense of sympathy and understanding will help unite them; they share many virtues and failings, and, consequently, should be able to recognize and deal effectively with problems. Jealousy will undoubtedly cause many stormy scenes. The Scorpio man, in particular, should accept the responsibility of realizing the importance of equality in the home. Both have the ability to work hard for the relationship; sexually, they should complement each other well, as both are highly sexed and are likely to have had other liaisons.

with Sagittarius

A Sagittarian woman has an enthusiastic attitude towards love and sex, but has also an inherent duality that manifests itself in most spheres of her life. Her Scorpio lover will soon discover that although she is emotional, she does not take her relationships too seriously. Their liaison may be progressing nicely, but she is likely to be involved in another affair at the same time. The Scorpio partner must try hard not to show his jealousy, for she cannot tolerate displays of it. In her eyes, it is a wasteful emotion. Moreover, the Sagittarian woman refuses to feel too tied down; she likes her freedom. Since their psychological motivations are so dissimilar, they will have to make a thorough attempt to understand the complexities of their respective natures, and work out some compromises should they consider a permanent union. If Venus is in the same sign in both their birth charts, theirs will be an extremely passionate involvement. His problems may increase if she has Sagittarius rising.

with Capricorn

From the material point of view, the keyword in the partnership between a Scorpio man and a Capricorn woman is success. He will find that unless she constantly complains about her responsibilities and problems, the Capricorn partner will be eager to help him achieve his ambitions and get to the top of his particular career or profession. Emotionally, however, she is frequently cool and not likely to make many demands in their physical relationship. He would do well to note the position that Mars occupied at the time of her birth, as it could increase her sexuality. Once she has made a permanent commitment, the Capricorn woman is extremely faithful, and of all zodiacal signs is the least likely to give her Scorpio partner a genuine reason to display his well-known jealous streak. It is possible for them to share the same Venus sign; if her Venus is in Scorpio, he should find her a more responsive partner. She will react more sensitively and tenderly towards him if she has Scorpio rising.

with Aquarius

Exciting, fun, tricky, and possibly demanding—these words could all be used to describe an affair between a Scorpio man and his Aquarian partner. Both can be stubborn, although it is a surprising trait to find in the forward-looking, modern Aquarian woman; both can have definite life-styles which neither will want to change. The Aquarian woman may want a physical relationship without deep emotional involvement, and if she has Venus in Aquarius or Capricorn, she will prefer ties of friendship. These two could have an active and rewarding sexual relationship, for they both enjoy experimentation. Since both signs are of the fixed group, whenever they clash it will be difficult for either to give way. This is a partnership that needs a great deal of careful thought and planning. They must both accept and respect their differences if they want the liaison to deepen. She will react more warmly towards her Scorpio lover if she has Aquarius rising.

with Pisces

A Scorpio man may be precisely what a Piscean woman needs, for he will do a great deal to strengthen her psychological and emotional faculties, helping to shape her life, offering practical advice about her career and bringing out her best qualities. Sexually, they should have a mutually rewarding relationship. He could find her lack of self-confidence and assurance trying at times, but can successfully boost her ego and encourage her to develop these qualities. Long-term prospects for the partnership are excellent, although his patience will be severely taxed while the affair is developing. If she has Pisces rising, his problems will be fewer; the sign Neptune, her ruling planet, was in at the time of her birth is important, as it will have a significant effect on her personality. Should she have Venus in Aries, her Scorpio partner will be delighted for she will have a more positive and lively attitude towards her love life. The position of Mars will determine how energetic she will feel.

The Way to the Scorpio Heart

Before considering the best way to reach the Scorpio heart, it might be worthwhile to stop and think for a moment about the pros and cons of such an involvement. On the positive side, you will certainly have a great deal of fun with the Scorpio-born, attending sporting events, sailing, going to the theatre and cinema. Affairs with them are not easily forgotten, for they do not enter into anything half-heartedly. Scorpios have powerful feelings and express themselves passionately in whatever they undertake. Moreover, they are generous and enjoy buying presents for others as well as taking them to the finest restaurants. Loved ones are bound to put on a few extra pounds while being lavishly entertained by their Scorpio admirers.

The negative side must, however, be mentioned. Scorpios are extremely demanding both emotionally and sexually. This may prove exhausting for their partners. In addition, the Scorpio-born are unbelievably jealous of either real or imaginary rivals. It is this trait above all that is responsible for wrecking so many potentially dynamic partnerships, for most people do not have the degree of inner strength necessary to cope with this destructive force. Unfortunately, the majority of Scorpios do not realize how potent and negative their jealousy can be; they must learn to make a deliberate effort to suppress it whenever they find such feelings beginning to erupt.

Scorpios of both sexes are generally good looking, sometimes in a sultry, dark way. Their penetrating, almost hypnotic deep-set eyes reflect a smouldering intensity that will be extremely difficult to resist. Remember that they work hard and play hard, and find restraint difficult. Scorpios can, however, be relied upon to give a great deal in emotional and sexual relationships, with the accent on enjoyment.

If you wish to attract the attentions of a Scorpio man, you would do well to wear a dress with a plunging neckline and douse yourself with some expensive French perfume. He will probably respond more enthusiastically than you expected. Alterna-tively, you can always ask him to dinner, and he will almost invariably accept. Unless you are a good cook or have access to a restaurant that prepares excellent take-away meals, this approach is not recommended. But if you do invite him, he will probably arrive carrying a splendid bottle of wine, perhaps a Burgundy. Serve him courses that are hearty as well as delicious-tasting. The Scorpio man is certain to enjoy clam chowder followed by *filet de bœuf en croûte*. For dessert, either black-currant pie, rich with vitamin C, or prunes in sherry, which are excellent for the digestion, would tempt his palate.

After you have eaten and retired to the living room, strive to make the atmosphere as seductive as possible. Dim the lights, scatter soft, comfortable floor cushions on the carpet, burn some incense and have one of the more romantic Ella Fitzgerald or Frank Sinatra records playing in the background. Of course, if the object of your affections has Scorpio as her or his ascendant and Sun sign, sensual feelings will be so powerful that the setting may actually go unnoticed.

Since Scorpios are born under the most highly sexed and passionate sign of the Zodiac, they will demand a great deal from their partners and will waste no time in developing a physical relationship. They live their lives on a high emotional level and will expect lovers to do likewise. Should you be involved with the Scorpio-born but attracted to another, only two courses of action are possible. Either forget this new prospect and turn your attention back to Scorpio, or finish completely with the latter. Scorpios are the detectives of the Zodiac, and the chances of deceiving them are very slim.

You will not go wrong if you give a body lotion with a heavy, dusky, interesting scent to either male or female Scorpios. And since both are attracted to the sea, a bathing suit or appropriate paraphernalia for a particular water sport is certain to please. The men of this sign like fashionable belts and jewellery of modern design. They are particularly fond of the opal, the gem associated with the Scorpio-born. Both sexes will enjoy reading books which explore subjects in depth.

The Sagittarius Woman

November 23rd – December 20th

Ruling Planet: *Jupiter*
Triplicity: *Fire*
Keyword: *Enthusiastic*
Jewel: *Topaz*
Flower: *Pinks*
Trees: *Lime * Birch * Oak * Ash * Chestnut*
Cities: *Toledo * Stuttgart * Budapest * Cologne*

The Sagittarius Woman in Love...

The Sagittarian approach to life is enthusiastic and positive, and when the woman born under the sign of the Archer falls in love, she will radiate happiness. Rather than appear to be in a dazed dream-like state, she will probably glow and, at the same time, be more lively. Everyone she knows will quickly realize that love has entered her life. Since the Sagittarian woman is quite open and frank, she will probably make a point of telling friends about her loved one and his virtues.

Unfortunately, there are times when her optimism knows no bounds, and, consequently, she can experience considerable disappointment in her love life. She has tremendous resilience, however, which is part of her natural defence system. But it must be said that the Sagittarian woman does not take love and sex too seriously; she will be the first to admit this. Consequently, if she is hurt, she does not find it difficult to move on to the next relationship.

The Sagittarian woman is basically freedom-loving, and the prospects of

marriage and motherhood present serious problems to her. Furthermore, if she holds a university degree and has an interesting job, she will be reluctant to sacrifice a career. The Sagittarian-born generally have enquiring minds, and need considerable intellectual stimulation. When she does decide to settle down and have a family, she will enthusiastically accept the challenge. Her children should benefit immeasurably from her intellectual qualities. When they are young, she will undoubtedly try to continue to do some part-time work or, perhaps, to attend an adult education class. She needs a project outside the home to offset the drudgery and boredom of domestic chores. A woman who is born under the ninth sign of the Zodiac, or who has Sagittarius as her ascendant, may find that the demands of domesticity will disturb her throughout her life.

It is equally important for the Sagittarian woman to have a satisfying sexual partnership, if she is to keep her natural duality under control. Frequently, she is involved in more than one liaison at a time.

with Aries

In the early stages of their affair, both the Sagittarian woman and the Arien man will discover that they have a great deal in common. Both are informal, freedom-loving and passionate, and enjoy the outdoors. It is possible, however, that the Sagittarian woman may find her lover moving at too quick a pace, even for her. If she is looking for a relationship with no strings attached, then she has chosen an excellent partner. Although he can be intolerably selfish at times, she should have little difficulty coping with this character trait. Since these two are basically forthright individuals, any problems that arise between them will be discussed openly and resolved without complications. If they decide to make the relationship permanent, both will work hard for its success and each will encourage the other. He will be more romantically inclined if Aries is rising. The sign Mars, his ruling planet, was in at the time of his birth should be carefully studied.

with Taurus

Although the Taurean partner has the ability to make the Sagittarian woman feel secure, which she will particularly appreciate after terminating a more tempestuous affair, inevitably there will be vast differences in opinion and temperament between them. She will find him a rather slow but sensuous and passionate lover; it will not be easy for her to come to terms with his possessiveness, his fixed opinions and his conventional outlook. The Sagittarian woman could certainly help him keep abreast of new ideas, but should she marry him, challenges and problems will constantly face her. On the positive side, however, a partnership with the Taurean man will probably solve her greatest problem, restlessness. A relationship between these two will have obvious pitfalls, but they can learn a great deal from one another. If he has Venus in Aries or Gemini, she can expect him to be highly emotional. They would do well to cultivate a common interest.

with Gemini

The polarity between signs of the Zodiac works to their advantage. The Sagittarian woman will find that her Gemini man is eager to spend hours with her chatting about a variety of subjects. Although her deeper and broader outlook will enable her to sum up his endless ramblings in one succinct sentence, this should nevertheless, from an intellectual point of view, be a stimulating partnership. In the sexual sphere, however, the Sagittarian woman will quickly learn that her lover is not as passionate as she, and that he is often reluctant to fully trust his emotions. In addition, both are prone to be restless, and because of their natural duality are likely to be involved with other people while continuing their relationship. She is perhaps less under the influence of this inherent trait than he. If both can channel their abundant energies into intellectual pursuits, such as creative writing, the relationship will have an excellent chance of success.

with Cancer

The Sagittarian woman may have difficulty understanding the complicated motivations of the Cancerian-born. She is optimistic and direct like the Archer which is the symbol of her sign; he is prone to worry and is evasive. In addition, she is energetic, extroverted and inclined not to take life and love too seriously. He, however, is quiet, often inhibited and eager to cherish and protect a loved one. Sexually, there should be no problems; the Sagittarian woman will respond well to the sensitive and extremely sensual Cancerian approach. But she will be distressed by his abrupt changes of mood; he, in turn, will be perplexed by her constantly cheerful, straightforward attitude towards life and her genuine disinclination to worry. They are both sensible, however, and could strengthen their relationship through joint academic interests, perhaps relating to history. If he has a lively Venus in Gemini, she should find him less clinging and more light-hearted in his attitude towards her.

The Sagittarius Woman in Love ...

with Leo

Since the ruling planet of Sagittarius is Jupiter, king of the Gods, it is not unusual for a woman born under the sign of the Archer to identify with the regal Leo man. At first, he may not appreciate her informal ways, as he has a tendency to be pompous, but as the affair deepens, they should be able to combine successfully their optimism and enthusiasm for life with their mutual desire for sexual fulfilment. Their general outlook on life is fairly similar, but he is much more conservative and, at times, could be somewhat shocked by her unconventionality. The Leo man will have to accept his Sagittarian lover's need for freedom. It will not take her long to adjust to his extravagant tastes, and she will enjoy the elegant and dignified way in which he carries off every occasion. He will admire her organizing ability, but if their relationship becomes permanent, they would be wise to agree on joint rulership. Unfortunately, her partner will be even more pompous if he has a Leo ascendant.

with Virgo

Although the Sagittarian woman will be attracted to her Virgoan lover's sharp analytical mind, and will find it relatively simple to develop a stimulating intellectual friendship with him, she will soon learn that patience is necessary in the sexual sphere. Generally, Virgo is not highly sexed and is conventional in outlook. As a consequence, if she makes her usual honest, direct sexual approach he may be put off. Besides, he is probably shy and could be genuinely embarrassed by this type of advance. More than likely, there will be a compelling hobby, an enthusiasm for sporting events or a literary interest that both can share. The Sagittarian woman would do well to impress her Virgoan partner with her mental faculties. He will certainly respond more warmly towards her if he has Virgo as his ascendant rather than as his Sun sign. The position of Venus can also be helpful; the Virgoan partner will be more affectionate if Venus was in Leo or in Libra at the time of his birth.

with Libra

The Sagittarian woman and the Libran man function at vastly different energy levels. In general, she will be extremely active, aware that she will only be at her intellectual and physical best if she does some form of demanding regular exercise; he, however, flourishes in a relaxed state. But both can gain a great deal from a partnership. She should find his natural charm and romantic nature most appealing; he will probably be infected with her enthusiasm for life and admire her excellent mind. Their affair may not progress too quickly at the beginning, as he tends to be indecisive. Probably, the Sagittarian woman will have and will enjoy the responsibility of making the major decisions for both of them, although she should try to encourage him to share some of the burden. In his worst moods, the Libran partner can be resentful. As a result, she will have to be quite tactful if she is also involved in other liaisons. This can be an excellent pairing.

with Scorpio

Both partners are emotional, energetic and highly sexed, but their psychological motivations could not be more different. The Scorpio man's emotions are deep and intense; the Sagittarian woman's are fiery and enthusiastic. He is jealous, she could not be less so; he is secretive, she is quite candid and often tactless. But they both get a great deal of fun out of life and could have a dynamic partnership. There will be a special attraction and harmony between them if they share Venus in the same sign. In fact, depending on its position, that planet could exert a strong, positive influence on the relationship should they make it permanent. Before doing so, however, they must recognize and accept each other's differences. Although they have many objectives in common, their methods of achieving them are totally dissimilar. If they are able to come to terms with this, together they will enrich their lives materially and socially. Problems will arise if he has a Scorpio ascendant.

with Sagittarius

In general, when two people born under the same sign fall in love, their positive and negative personality traits are emphasized. Consequently, the Sagittarian couple would do well to check their rising signs to discover how they differ. Since Sagittarians are open, broad-minded and fair, they should find it easier than most other zodiacal types to resolve problems that arise. Fortunately, they will understand and accept each other's need for freedom of expression. The natural communication between Sagittarians is often uncannily good; sometimes words need not be exchanged for thoughts to be shared. Their sex life should be mutually rewarding, and the position of Venus in their respective birth charts will determine each partner's emotional level. Hopefully, at least one partner will have Sagittarius rising. They should derive a great deal of pleasure and satisfaction if they can find an intellectually demanding project to work on together. Compromises are easily reached.

with Capricorn

If the Sagittarian woman has just gone through a particularly chaotic period, the practical, industrious, possibly pessimistic Capricorn man could be precisely the partner she needs. But temperamentally they are very different: the Capricorn lover can be emotionally cool and possibly remote; the Sagittarian woman is passionate and will not take her love life as seriously as he. But he is a faithful partner, and may have difficulty accepting her need for freedom. Each will appreciate the other's sense of humour, and this may help surmount some of their difficulties. His ambitious nature should ensure material success. Since they are neighbours in the Zodiac, they could share the same Venus sign, which will undoubtedly benefit the partnership. Should they consider a permanent relationship, careful examination must be given to Capricorn's rising sign. If it is in a fire or an air sign, their future will be more promising. He will be warmer if he has Capricorn rising.

with Aquarius

A relationship with an Aquarian man should satisfy the truly liberated Sagittarian woman. Admittedly, he is modern in outlook, can be unconventional and is favourably disposed to sexual experimentation. But the Aquarian man may simply not want a relationship with emotional ties. If she can accept this, theirs can be an intellectually satisfying partnership. They will be stimulated by each other's opinions, outlook and attitude towards life. Once the Aquarian man has made up his mind about anything, he will be reluctant to change it. His stubbornness may be challenging for her. There is a good chance that the Aquarian man will prove to be too remote and cool for the warm Sagittarian woman. A friendship, however, will be easy to cement, for they respect each other and are both proud of their independent ways. It is important for the Sagittarian woman to find out her partner's ascendant, as well as the sign his ruling planet, Uranus, was in when he was born.

with Pisces

It is not surprising if a Sagittarian woman finds herself attracted to a Piscean man; there should be a natural sympathy between them which will help them develop their relationship. Of the two, she has the stronger personality, and, therefore, the Sagittarian woman must try to quell her natural restlessness; he could be easily influenced by it, and, as a result, their partnership could lose its direction and their respective careers could even be adversely affected. Since the Piscean man is highly emotional and sensitive, he may have difficulty accepting her freedom-loving ways. Her inborn duality could hurt him deeply because he could not be anything but subjective about it. She may need to encourage her partner to develop his creative or literary potential, for he tends to be a dreamer and is frequently swayed by opposing forces. The easygoing characteristics of both, as well as their sense of humour should make it relatively simple for them to resolve any superficial problems.

Making the Most of Sagittarius

Most Sagittarians, it often seems, do not make the most of themselves. The majority are preoccupied with their studies or sporting activities, and, consequently, are not particularly concerned with the way they look or how they appear to others. They tend to cling to one style of dress, with the accent on comfort rather than on fashion. They feel happiest in jeans or slacks, shirts or turtleneck sweaters and scarves, looking very much as they did in their student days. In fact, Sagittarians, regardless of age, generally have a great appetite for knowledge and enjoy the challenge of studying in depth any subject that fascinates them.

Clothes, then, tend to be low on the list of interests for Sagittarians of either sex. Conversely, there are individuals born under this sign who appear very casual in dress, but who have actually given considerable thought and time to attaining that look. They manage to look marvellous in their own way, provided the tendency to simple carelessness is deliberate. These Sagittarians, for example, would be the type to add scarves to their open collars. Most Sagittarian men only wear ties under protest; once the working day is over, they will be discarded with a sigh of relief. An increasing number of Sagittarian men find casual business dress extremely appealing and highly practical.

Both sexes often favour shades of golden-brown, red and dark blue. But for a touch of drama, dark purple, the Sagittarian colour, can be effective and very flattering. The influence of Jupiter, their ruling planet, is obvious in the choice of clothes for glamorous occasions. The men frequently wear purple shirts; the women are partial to purple dresses or long, flowing, purple velvet cloaks.

Sagittarians are known for their breadth of vision. They have the ability to grasp the essentials of an idea quickly and assess its possibilities. Unfortunately, they are prone to dismiss the details of a situation and can become quite annoyed if minor obstacles are put in their way.

Sagittarius, together with Gemini and Pisces, is a dual sign of the Zodiac. As a result, it is common for those born under the sign of the Archer to work on more than one project at a time, have more than one hobby and more than one mistress or lover. It is the challenge that attracts the Sagittarians as well as their desire for new experiences. They are extremely versatile and have high energy levels, which need both physical and mental exercise.

Like the symbol of their sign, Sagittarians have a constant tendency to shoot off psychological arrows in all directions, but, unfortunately, restlessness usually sets in. The Sagittarian-born should think carefully about this aspect of their personalities; if they cannot curb it, they will never be at peace with themselves. Furthermore, they are likely to miss out on the opportunities to develop fully their best potentialities, simply because they want to get involved in another conquest. Once Sagittarians can find a group of interests that can absorb their attention, they are usually able to come to terms with themselves.

There are two types of Sagittarians,

each thriving in distinctly different atmospheres. One type loves the fresh air, mountains, open countryside and sweeping landscapes; the other prefers libraries, bookstores, or any place that is suitable for an academic discussion. Both types dislike small rooms; they generally have a preference for open-plan living in their homes, disdaining anything which resembles a warren of tiny rooms with interconnecting passages.

Their life-style is basically informal. When entertaining, the Sagittarian-born are more likely to invite several friends and set out a simple buffet than to arrange a formal dinner for six or eight. Their furniture will be comfortable, but, as might be expected, Sagittarians are not overly concerned about appearances. The rooms in their homes will definitely have character: books, papers and magazines of specialized interest will probably be piled or scattered throughout, for it is against this background that they thrive. Those born under the ninth sign of the Zodiac depend on their open and unaffected charm to serve them in good stead.

The Sagittarius Man
November 23rd – December 20th

Ruling Planet: *Jupiter*
Quadruplicity: *Mutable*
Keywords: *Adaptable* ✳ *Changing*
Metal: *Tin*
Countries: *Spain* ✳ *Australia* ✳ *Hungary* ✳ *Madagascar*
Animals: *The Horse* ✳ *Animals That Can Be Hunted*
Colours: *Deep Blue* ✳ *Royal Purple*

The Sagittarius Man in Love...

The Sagittarian man will use a casual, easygoing approach to attract the object of his affections. He is more likely to ask her for an informal lunch date than to a grand dinner at some exclusive restaurant. It is not a question of his being miserly, it is simply that he is not impressed by surroundings and particularly loathes those that are affected or artificial.

As the symbol of his sign suggests, the Sagittarian is a hunter and will not want to waste a minute when he finds a particular woman appealing. Actually, he functions best when he is in full pursuit. It is quite possible that he may be involved in more than one relationship at the same time, for he generally does not take his love life too seriously. This does not stem from lack of concern about his partners, but is due to a great fear of feeling hemmed in, and he certainly cannot cope with it in emotional entanglements. Should he marry, his wife will inevitably have to make allowances for this overriding need for a sense of freedom. To prevent it from becoming a source of great conflict between them, she must learn not to get annoyed or show jealousy, for he will not tolerate any expressions of possessiveness.

Sexually, he is passionate, but not in an intense way. His love is lively and enthusiastic; enjoyment is one of his basic motivations. Although the physical element is important to him, he will not feel fulfilled if his partner is unable to match him intellectually. As a result, he often becomes restless and dissatisfied in his emotional relationships. It is also true that the need to take up a new challenge can sometimes be more important to him than nurturing and sustaining the actual relationship. This preoccupation with conquest can be unsettling for everyone. In addition, the Sagittarian man has a tendency to become overly concerned with his career or with study, and this can also have a negative effect on any emotional partnership, be it a brief affair or a permanent commitment. Neither his girlfriend nor his wife can be

expected to endure his neglect in silence.

In the past, astrologers talked about the undeveloped and the evolved personality types. Although today most tend to disregard these broad descriptions, Sagittarians could to some extent be loosely categorized as one or the other. Sagittarians who are blindly optimistic, overly enthusiastic, and who drive their cars too fast and are frantically involved in sports of every kind represent the undeveloped type. The evolved Sagittarians are broadminded, fair and lots of fun. They have profited from past experiences, come to terms with their restlessness and have not neglected their intellect.

with Aries

A Sagittarian man who is attracted to an Arien woman will soon realize that she has an approach to love and sex not unlike his own. Since she is freedom-loving, she will probably not want to become seriously involved in an affair. In addition, her love of the outdoors and her enthusiasm for sex should make her an eminently suitable partner for the Sagittarian man. As both these signs fall into the fire grouping, there should be a natural harmony between them. It is quite likely that their outlook and opinions on important issues will be similar, although his may tend to be more philosophical than hers. They can expect to have many fun-filled, memorable times together if they decide to make their relationship permanent. No major complications should arise, although he will have to devise an attitude to cope with her selfish streak. If she has Venus in Aries with the Sun, or Aries rising, she will respond to him in a more ardent manner.

with Taurus

The success or failure of an affair between a Sagittarian man and a Taurean woman will depend to a large extent on the couple's respective rising signs, and on the sign that Venus was in when each was born. Basically, Taureans are possessive while Sagittarians need their freedom. If they have other characteristics which will help counter these strong opposing traits, they will have a better chance to develop a lasting relationship. Sexually, the Sagittarian man will find his Taurean woman passionate, although perhaps rather slow to arouse. Temperamental differences between them are inevitable. The Sagittarian man was born under an adventurous sign and, therefore, finds change both challenging and exciting, but the Taurean woman likes a set routine and adheres faithfully to it. She will be more intense in her emotional relationships if she has Taurus rising. Should Venus fall in Aries or Gemini, many positive factors will be working in their favour.

with Gemini

In this pairing, opposite signs of the Zodiac are involved which indicate that there will be a natural rapport between them. But both the Sagittarian man and the Gemini woman are restless and could easily become discontent. The Gemini woman, for example, might feel that her intellectual powers are not as comprehensive as those of the Sagittarian-born, and she may find herself caught up in a battle of wits which could be exhausting for both of them. Her partner should make allowances for this difference and try to help her broaden and deepen her intellectual interests. Both have a strong element of duality in their natures, and thrive on involvement in more than one project and relationship at a time. Sexually, they are mutually compatible, although she will probably be less passionate than he. Basically, this partnership has an excellent chance to succeed. Communication will never be a problem for them. If she has Gemini rising, she will be more tender.

with Cancer

The Sagittarian man often makes an excellent father, for he has the natural ability to teach, to guide and to develop the minds of children, and he has the right philosophical attitude towards parenthood. So if he has reached the point in his life where he is seriously contemplating marriage, he is likely to find the Cancerian woman on the same wavelength. If he only wants another light-hearted, fun-loving affair, he should think again before getting too involved, for Cancerians tend to take love seriously, and most females of the sign seem to view each man they date as a potential husband and father of their children. Consequently, he must make it clear to her if he is not serious, or be prepared to cope with some fairly emotional scenes. Their sexual relationship should be rewarding, as he will find her a sensuous lover. If she has Venus in Leo, her affection will be expressed more overtly; should she have a Cancer ascendant, she is likely to be cooler towards him.

The Sagittarius Man in Love...

with Leo

Although a Sagittarian man might find a Leo woman attractive at first sight, he might also be slightly put off by her rather showy, even pompous manner. As he gets to know her better, however, he will realize that while she certainly enjoys glamour, she has a realistic as well as optimistic outlook on life and a natural sense of fun. He will appreciate her exuberant and enthusiastic attitude towards sex and will revel in her attentions. The Leo woman has a tendency to put the lovers she admires on a symbolic pedestal. If the Sagittarian man is preoccupied with his career, she will probably take charge of the routine matters in their daily lives; he will not protest because he excels at organization. Should they make their relationship permanent, undoubtedly, they will decide on a joint rulership. This is basically an excellent combination for there is genuine sympathy between them. She can be demanding in marriage if she has Leo rising.

with Virgo

If the intellectually well-endowed Sagittarian man finds himself attracted to a Virgoan woman, he would do well to engage her in complicated discussion or provoke a stimulating argument. As he begins to know her, he can assess whether she is shy and reticent, or has matured through other experiences, and is now ready for a deep emotional and sexual relationship. The Sagittarian man will not find it difficult to develop a common interest, such as cycling, walking or any outdoor sporting activity, with her. From a psychological point of view, he should be able to soothe her when she is worried or nervous. The relationship could be marred by restlessness, and both partners must be aware of this possibility. If she has Virgo rising, she will respond more warmly towards him. It is possible that they could either share the same sign for Venus, either in Scorpio or in Libra, which would bode extremely well for their long-term happiness.

with Libra

The Libran woman needs plenty of time to relax and enjoy life during a romance. So if a Sagittarian man is attracted to her, he will not only have to slow down the pace of his life to match hers, but he will also have to become thoroughly involved in the romantic side of love. The Libran woman is no fool, and she will realize that underneath his sometimes brash exterior there is a touch of romanticism which she may be able to bring to the surface. In a more serious vein, however, there are bound to be some differences between them that cannot be so easily resolved. The Sagittarian man could find her indecisiveness irritating, and sexually she may well be less passionate and demanding than he had at first thought. Much can be said, however, in favour of the partnership, and should they share the same sign for Venus, her ruling planet, the couple should enjoy a mutually satisfying life together. She may be more emotional if she has Libra rising.

with Scorpio

When a Sagittarian man becomes involved with a Scorpio woman, there are likely to be clashes, mainly revolving around his need for a certain amount of freedom and her inability to accept it. In this case, these two powerful types may not want to give way; it is very hard for the Scorpio woman to cope with rivals or even innocent flirtations. She cannot stifle any pangs of jealousy, while it is equally impossible for the Sagittarian man, partly because of his inherent duality, to give up his freedom. They both, however, share the capacity to enjoy life. Together they can progress materially and socially, and should have no problems in their physical relationship. They are both energetic, dynamic personalities and would do well to cultivate a joint interest, perhaps involvement in a community project. The Sagittarian lover will be better able to understand his partner if he learns which sign Mars was in at the time of her birth, as well as that of Venus.

with Sagittarius

In general, the Sagittarian man will find a natural sympathy existing between his female counterpart and himself. In many respects, they are quite similar, although she occasionally does approach a problem in a slightly unexpected or unusual way. In addition, he may be slightly surprised when he hears her verbalizing his own pet theory on a particular subject. The female Sagittarian has a rather strong, positive outlook on life, which he will respect. Intellectually, they may enjoy challenging one another, as they are likely to be equally matched. They will have fun discovering how they differ and would do well to check their respective rising signs. Sexually, for example, their attitudes should be similar. A Sagittarian woman, like the man of that sign, needs her freedom and cannot bear to be possessed. They will quickly reach mutual understanding on this issue. If she has a Sagittarius ascendant, theirs will be an eminently successful, and fulfilling coupling.

with Capricorn

A Capricorn woman could do a great deal for a Sagittarian man. From a practical point of view, she is ambitious and could help him by entertaining professional associates as he strives towards a top position in his work. Furthermore, she can make certain that he is free of domestic cares and worries which might preoccupy him during times of strain in his job or studies. Although she may have the superb offbeat sense of humour that will endear her to a warm-hearted Sagittarian, he must remember that she has a lower emotional level than he, and occasionally is even aloof. The signs Mars and Venus were in at the time of her birth will be revealing. Temperamentally, these two are totally different. She is formal, often worldly and has a tendency to complain about the responsibility and worry attached to being his partner. He will not tolerate this kind of nagging, so care is needed. The Sagittarian man is informal, affectionate and likes to enjoy life.

with Aquarius

The Aquarian woman has many qualities, including independence and individuality, that will appeal strongly to the Sagittarian man. She does not worry about what others think or do. Although he may be physically attracted to her, the sexual part of the relationship may be slow to develop. She frequently prefers bonds of friendship or partnerships without emotional ties. Should they become lovers, however, she may still be reluctant to give up her way of life. The Aquarian woman is the least possessive of all the zodiacal types, which will certainly please him. This could be a partnership of two individuals which will work well but will sometimes be rather distant. They should be stimulated by each other's opinions and outlook on life. The Sagittarian mind is more traditional than the modern, unconventional Aquarian's. The sign in which her ruling planet, Uranus, was at the time of her birth will be revealing. She will respond more warmly towards him if Aquarius is rising.

with Pisces

While there is a great deal of empathy between Sagittarius and Pisces, the Sagittarian man will soon realize that a relationship with a Piscean woman could have a disastrous influence on him because he could easily permit his life to become as disorganized and chaotic as hers. If he recognizes that this may happen, and, as a result, is on his guard, their relationship will have a better chance of success. The Piscean woman is not a strong type. She is highly emotional, and may draw heavily upon his psychological resources to bolster her. He will readily offer encouragement and support, but there could be an element of restlessness in the partnership. Their combined senses of humour and easygoing natures should help them overcome any difficulties. Neptune is the ruling planet of Pisces, so the Sagittarian lover should find out its position in her birth chart, for it will reveal additional elements of her character and he will better understand her.

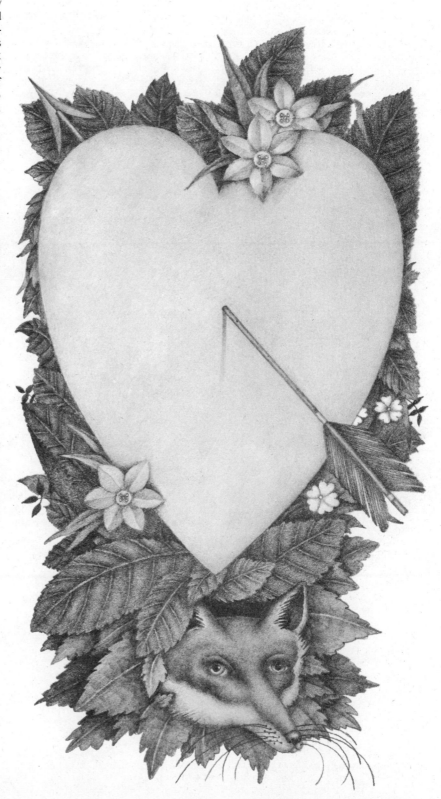

The Way to the Sagittarius Heart

The Sagittarian-born are not difficult to please. They are enthusiastic in love and in their attitude to life in general. But they need partners who are not clinging or possessive. Freedom is of the utmost importance to them and, therefore, loved ones will need to be extremely considerate and broadminded.

Those born under the sign of the Archer fall into one of two categories. First, there are those less mature Sagittarians, who are usually less likable, and, fortunately, in the minority. They are very sporty, love travel and speed, and tend to emphasize this aspect of their personalities. They can be boisterous, overpowering and overly optimistic, but they are always fun and make certain that their partners enjoy life as much as they do. Unfortunately, their devil-may-care attitude towards life can prove exhausting and irritating to their loved ones. In general, as these racy Sagittarians mature, they take on the more intellectual attributes of the other type and they profit from past mistakes.

The second type are often academically-orientated and extremely well-versed in a variety of subjects which are often unrelated. They are constantly searching for greater knowledge. They have excellent judgement and others will come to them for counsel. Their advice will undoubtedly be laden with good sense and perhaps a touch of inspiration. They have the ability to encourage those who are less confident to make the most of themselves.

If you feel that your Sagittarian lover is too bogged down in study, encourage her or him to take some form of physical exercise, for those born under this sign need it more than any other zodiacal type. The Sagittarian's love of good food and wine also encourages weight problems. Perhaps you could both join a club that has fencing, archery or tennis facilities. Or consider horseback-riding or ice-skating. More than likely, Sagittarians will prefer to exercise in the open air, as they love the countryside. But for the strictly academic type who spend a lot of time in libraries and stuffy bookstores, plan a camping trip that ensures lots of fresh air, sunshine and activity. Sagittarians will be extremely grateful for this kind of consideration and treatment.

In terms of food, Sagittarians have a hearty appetite and seldom refuse a second helping. If you are planning a special dinner, serve poultry, game or trout if you can manage it, preceded by a light, cold first course such as cucumber soup and followed by a steaming hot pudding. They will particularly appreciate this type of meal if they have been outdoors most of the day. As for the wines, Sagittarians are associated with Spain and Hungary so consider one of the Spanish reds or Hungarian Tokay.

At Christmas or on special occasions, you cannot go wrong if you give the Sagittarius-born a book. But do find out whether they already have a copy, for they generally have a well-stocked home library. Women of the sign would enjoy receiving luggage or would probably love to own a guitar. Males favour casual clothes. A sweater would be a most appropriate gift. Remember that simple presents also please both sexes, and if it is something you have made yourself, he or she will respond most enthusiastically to the gift and to the time spent.

It is not difficult to find the way to the Sagittarian heart, so it is not necessary to devise a variety of complicated plans to attract their attention. They are frequently first drawn physically to members of the opposite sex, and although Sagittarians are demanding in love, they need partners to match them intellectually. There are a few golden rules which may be useful to sustain their interest: do not be too formal, be friendly, natural and casual. Never try to put on an act as he or she will see through it instantly and let you know. It will be to your advantage if you can intelligently discuss a favourite subject, but do not attempt to bluff your way through any topic, as the Sagittarian is bound to realize what you are doing and undoubtedly will have less respect for you. It is much better to admit honestly that you do not know anything about the subject and ask for an explanation, then follow up with a few pertinent questions. A straightforward approach is called for with Sagittarians.

The Capricorn Woman

December 21st –January 19th

Ruling Planet: Saturn
Triplicity: Earth
*Keywords: Practical * Stable*
Jewel: Turquoise
*Flowers: Ivy * Pansy*
*Trees: Pine * Yew * Elm * Poplar*
*Cities: Oxford * Brussels * Port Said * Mexico City*

The Capricorn Woman in Love ...

Capricornians are generally serious-minded people, and when a female of the sign realizes she is in love, she will consider the implications and her future objectives very carefully. She may feel that it would be wise for her to experience more of life and love, or, if she is ambitious, perhaps she will regard her own career as more important than an emotional involvement. But the Capricorn woman could opt for marriage and the opportunity to help the man she loves advance in his profession. Once she has made up her mind, she will adhere faithfully to her decision.

The Capricorn-born is not a person of many words and, consequently, what she says she sincerely means. Basically, she is not a romantic, but rather a woman with a clear, cool ánd calculating mind. Any man who lives with a Capricorn woman must realize that the moral support she gives him, as he works to enrich their lives and to progress in his career, is her way of expending emotional energy. And he will undoubtedly do well, partly because of her constant encouragement.

It is not always easy for the Capricorn woman to relax fully in a sexual relationship, and it may take her time to settle into one. Perhaps she has isolated herself too much while concentrating all her efforts and attention on fulfilling her ambitions, be it in a career or in her studies. And sometimes a pessimistic attitude towards life will hold her back. When a man suggests an evening out, or she is in a good position to develop a relationship, she may feel that other commitments prevent her from doing so. If she frequently finds herself in such situations, it is vitally important that she honestly ask herself whether

with Aries

Before getting involved with an Arien man, the Capricorn woman must accept that he is highly sexed and, therefore, not likely to appreciate her typically slow and formal responses. She must be prepared for the physical side of the relationship to develop quickly should she express the slightest interest in him. The Capricorn woman will admire his energy and vitality and will share his love of the outdoors. Temperamentally, however, there are vast differences between them. She will probably find that he often puts himself first, and he may feel that she is too remote and chilly. They would be wise to cultivate a joint interest which will strengthen the relationship. Theirs can be a mutually rewarding pairing if they can blend his enthusiasm and zest for life with her cautious and practical outlook. She should find out the sign Mars, his ruling planet, was in at the time of his birth, as it will have the greatest influence on the development of his character traits.

with Taurus

As they get to know each other, both will realize that they complement each other well. The Capricorn woman will find her Taurean partner as practical and as dependable as she, and there should be a natural sympathy between them. Although he is passionate and sensuous, he is also considerate and will not try to rush the sexual side of the relationship too quickly. The Taurean man usually sets high standards for himself; he likes comfort and luxury and is eager to earn a lot of money so that he can buy fine quality items. Possessions are extremely important to him. She is also ambitious and will certainly encourage his efforts to advance his career, They may clash, however, for he has a tendency to be more extravagant than she. Basically, this is an excellent combination. If he has Taurus rising, she must expect him to be more sexually demanding. The sign his ruling planet, Venus, was in when he was born will influence the extent of his ability to be tender and affectionate.

with Gemini

If a Capricorn woman should decide that she wants a relationship with someone who will not take her too seriously, or will not want a deep emotional involvement, then a Gemini man will probably be the right partner for her. He tends to be one of the emotional lightweights of the Zodiac and frequently is involved in more than one affair at a time, for he has a natural duality which permeates every sphere of his life. Sexually, these two can have a great deal of fun, but when it comes to friendship, she may find him too superficial and inconsistent for her. They will appreciate each other's sense of humour: hers is dry and offbeat; his is cynical or satirical. If they can cultivate a joint interest, their relationship will be strengthened. If they are considering a permanent relationship, it is essential that they recognize their differences and make allowances for them. He will respond well to her ambitious nature, and she will gain from his versatility and agility.

with Cancer

Since polar signs of the Zodiac are involved in this pairing, there will be a natural rapport between these two. The Capricorn woman must be prepared, however, to deal with her Cancerian partner's sudden changes of mood and his high emotional level. He is a passionate and sensual lover, but will also be very considerate of her feelings. There is a distinct possibility that he will get angry and be somewhat snappy at times, but she should be able to cope with these negative traits. If he has Cancer rising, or if his Venus is in Cancer with the Sun, he will be more tender towards her as well as eager to look after her. The Capricorn woman should think seriously if she gets a proposal of marriage from him, for the Cancerian man makes an excellent husband and father. Should she want to continue her career, he will be willing to help with the children and perhaps do some of the cooking. Her practicality and his shrewdness will prove to be assets in joint financial matters.

her responsibilities are hampering her from physical involvement or whether she is using obligations, real or imagined, as a convenient excuse to avoid such entanglements.

There are many Capricorn women, however, who do not have such difficulties. They have come to terms with their personality traits and needs. In marriage, they make faithful partners, although Capricorns will never be highly emotional or passionate lovers. Their offbeat, dry sense of humour can be relied upon to brighten the lives of all those close to them.

135

The Capricorn Woman in Love ...

with Leo

The leonine way of life will both delight and horrify the careful Capricorn woman. She will be impressed by his ambition and desire to get to the top of his profession so that he can enjoy a comfortable and luxurious life-style. But she may well be shocked when she learns just how extravagant he is, and how much he enjoys being so. When she spends a lot of money, it is usually for a practical reason. He, however, will spend money on friends primarily because he derives great satisfaction from making other people happy. The Capricorn woman has an earnest and sensible outlook on life, and Leo has a cheerful and positive one. If they can reconcile their points of view, theirs can be a happy and rewarding relationship. He is usually highly sexed and may occasionally be too demanding for her. He could be more self-assertive if Leo is rising. Should he have Venus in Cancer, his warmth and enthusiasm will prevent her from becoming too serious.

with Virgo

The Capricorn woman must use considerable care and tact if she wants to attract a Virgoan man. She should have no difficulty cultivating a friendship with him, as they have many interests in common—a love of gardening, music, books and the theatre. But she will soon discover that he is genuinely shy and reticent about developing an emotional relationship. This will not distress her too much, for she is generally cautious and prefers affairs that progress slowly. Both were born under signs belonging to the earth group, which indicates that there will be a certain amount of sympathy between them. The Capricorn woman must remember that he can be extremely restless, but she should be able to soothe his nerves and offer practical suggestions to ease any strain. If he has Virgo rising, he is likely to be a more responsive partner. Unfortunately, the Virgoan man has a tendency to be critical, but she must not let his criticism depress her.

with Libra

The Capricorn woman will soon realize that her Libran man is a pure romantic. He will probably not take life as seriously as she and can sometimes be lackadaisical. Since he is so easygoing, she may well be able to exert a practical influence on him. If she succeeds, he could adopt a more ambitious and progressive attitude towards his career. More than likely, the Capricorn woman will find that her Libran lover tends to rely on her for decision-making, particularly if they make their relationship permanent; she can usually cope well with this responsibility. He will help her relax and enjoy herself more. Undoubtedly, he will also encourage her dry sense of humour. A mutual interest in music should bring these two even closer. Sexually, he is not too demanding; if he has Venus in Scorpio, however, she can expect him to be more passionate. Every so often, tensions could arise, but if both partners are sensible, they should be able to work out any problems.

with Scorpio

Even the coolest and most cautious woman may have difficulty resisting the advances of a Scorpio man. Although he was born under the most emotional and sexually demanding sign of the Zodiac, he will not try to suddenly sweep his Capricorn woman off her feet. Instead, Scorpio will take his time, carefully plotting every move in advance. His slow approach will give her the opportunity of adjusting to him and to his views on love and sex. If she decides to become totally involved with him, she is bound to enjoy life and may possibly gain some weight, for Scorpios treat their loved ones generously, taking them to the finest hotels and restaurants. They should develop joint business interests, as Scorpio has an aptitude for finance, and Capricorn is ambitious. Emotionally these two could not be more dissimilar, but if they are able to accept each other's character traits they can have an excellent relationship, particularly if he has Scorpio rising.

with Sagittarius

Capricorn will tend to take everything too seriously, Sagittarius too casually. She is usually chilly and ambitious; he is affectionate and eager to enjoy life. But should these two be mutually attracted, they could have a lot of fun together. Each will appreciate the other's sense of humour, and if the Sagittarian man is the studious type, they will probably spend hours together discussing various books. Since both are strong types, they must expect to have some temperamental clashes. Sexually, the Capricorn woman may find her Sagittarian lover passionate, somewhat boisterous and perhaps even nonchalant. He is a freedom-loving individual, and if she wants their liaison to deepen, she will have to accept this aspect of his character. He will not tolerate possessiveness or jealousy. His attitude towards her could be too light-hearted if he has Sagittarius rising. They should compare the sign Venus was in when each was born, as this could form an excellent link between them.

with Capricorn

Cold, remote Saturn is Capricorn's ruling planet, but it is also associated with the winter feast of Saturnalia, which precedes Christmas, and is a time of fun and games. So if the Capricorn man and woman can relax and stop thinking about their respective careers for a while, they could really enjoy life together. There will be a natural rapport between them, and they should recognize and identify with each other's character traits. They must guard against becoming too materialistic and concentrating their efforts on climbing the social ladder, forgetting who their real friends are, and entertaining only those people who can help them reach their goals. In a sexual relationship, the Capricorn woman should find that her partner will not make unreasonable demands upon her. They will have a better understanding of one another if they check the signs Venus, which determines level of affection, and Mars, which influences sexual energy, were in when each was born.

with Aquarius

There is a definite affinity between a Capricorn woman and an Aquarian man. These are the only neighbouring signs in the Zodiac that do not have an edgy tension or at least a temperamental difference between them. The Capricorn woman will find the Aquarian man friendly and modern in outlook, but not very emotional. It is possible that his opinions and view of life may be too unconventional for her. Differences between them may become more apparent in their sexual relationship. Although the Aquarian lover will enjoy the physical side, he is likely to insist on ties of friendship while she may have contrary desires. He cherishes his independence and individual life-style. But should they eventually marry, they will complement each other well. Both will be faithful partners. A mutual love of the theatre and music will bring them closer together. It is to their advantage to check the position of Mars in their respective birth charts, as it will affect their levels of sexual energy.

with Pisces

The essentially impractical, imaginative Piscean man could learn a great deal from the practical, down-to-earth Capricorn woman. She will readily offer, for example, to put his chaotic collection of books in proper order, catalogue his records or feed his pets while he is on holiday. In addition, she will give him the moral encouragement he needs to develop his creative or artistic potential. As their affair develops, he should be able to channel his energies in a more positive direction. This is not a one-sided partnership, however, as the Piscean man will help the Capricorn woman relax more. Then she will be in a better position to appreciate his romantic and sensual qualities. Fortunately for her, the Piscean lover is not inconsiderate or too demanding sexually. A long-lasting relationship could work out well, but she may be left with the responsibility of decision-making as well as the organization of daily matters. Both types tend to be pessimistic in outlook and worry easily, so care is needed.

Making the Most of Capricorn

There is a quiet elegance about Capricornians that distinguishes them from other zodiacal members. As for physical appearance, the majority of those born under the sign of the Goat seem to be tall and lean. The women frequently have lovely legs; the men have clearly marked lines that run from their noses down to the corners of their mouths. A turned-down smile frequently sets off the Capricorn expression.

In general, the Capricorn image is quiet and unassuming. It is on formal occasions that Capricornians look their most elegant. The men favour well-cut dark suits and rather sombre ties; the women, with their lovely complexions, are likely to wear simple, sophisticated black dresses. Sometimes, however, both sexes are too conservative in their choice of clothes; although each item is of excellent quality, the overall effect can be boring. Perhaps the Capricorn-born should give more thought to accessories. The women could add, for example, an interesting or unusual belt to their black dresses, or possibly a heavy silver pendant. They should also consider buying fine wool dresses in pale grey for evening wear. The men would do well to try somewhat brighter ties or good cashmere sweaters for less formal occasions. For their leisure activities, Capricornians of either sex often choose suède jackets.

Although it is never a good idea to act uncharacteristically, Capricornians should not dismiss the possibility that they may appear unemotional to others. Admittedly, they are people of few words, so that whatever they say is sincerely meant. But there is no doubt that Capricornians do seem distant or cold at times. Consequently, in the early stages of many relationships, they tend to miss out on a lot of affection and fun. Since those born under this sign require so little warmth and attention themselves, they may not realize that their partners need a little more and are likely to feel snubbed if treated in the typical Capricorn manner. Capricornians must make a conscious effort to stimulate their more tender emotions and not be so exacting with their lovers.

The extent to which Capricornians feel free to express their emotions is largely dependent on the position of Venus, the planet of love, in their birth charts. For Sun-sign Capricornians, it can fall in Scorpio, Sagittarius, Capricorn, Aquarius or Pisces. They will be friendlier if Venus was in Capricorn or Aquarius; more warm-hearted if it was in Sagittarius, and more prone to deeper feelings if it was in Scorpio or Pisces.

Should Venus be in a sign that increases their remoteness, however, they should not worry too much, for the recognition of the problem may help them put it into proper perspective and, hopefully, lessen the distance between themselves and potential lovers. The greatest asset of the Capricorn-born is their faithfulness, which can contribute a great deal to the progress and permanence of a liaison or marriage.

Capricornians like peace and quiet, and, therefore, it is not surprising to learn that they generally love the country and, in particular, the mountains. Unfortunately, their jobs frequently tend to keep them in the cities. As they advance in their careers, they should give serious thought to buying either a house or a cottage for weekend retreats in a more rural setting.

It is essential that Capricornians exercise regularly. Some form of sporting activity would be good for either sex. The younger and more adventurous will probably be attracted to rock-climbing or perhaps to athletics. Team games are not usually appealing to Capricornians, who tend to be loners. True to their character, they prefer to rely on their own efforts rather than cooperate with others. Long country walks and skiing are also popular pastimes.

The Capricorn-born are ambitious people who will be successful in whatever they set out to do, provided they do not erect their own complex psychological barriers. Unfortunately, they are prone to worry; if they are constantly thwarted in their attempts to reach certain goals, melancholia may possibly set in. Capricornians must try to concentrate on the positive gains they have made. They work hard both in their careers and in their marriages, and will feel most secure when there is a regular pattern to their lives.

The Capricorn Man

December 21st – January 19th

Ruling Planet: Saturn
Quadruplicity: Cardinal
Keywords: Enterprising ✳ Outgoing
Metal: Lead
Countries: India ✳ Mexico ✳ Afghanistan
Animals: The Goat ✳ Those with Horns and Cloven Hoofs
Colours: Black ✳ Dark Grey ✳ Dark Green

The Capricorn Man in Love...

The "loner" element, which is to be found in all Capricornians, has a powerful psychological effect on their attitude towards love. In his career, the Capricorn man often reaches a position in which he has authority over several other people, and is possibly in charge of a considerable number. As a result, he is accustomed to making final decisions alone and not sharing the responsibility with anyone else. Although he excels in dealing with situations of this nature, he tends to cut himself off to some extent from personal relationships.

It is not unusual for the Capricorn man to sacrifice marriage for the sake of achieving his career objectives. But if he does make a permanent commitment, he is often too self-centred, frequently failing to appreciate his wife's efforts to build a more normal social life for him, as well as her thoughtfulness in arranging their lives so that he has more time for relaxation. It is unfortunate for both when ambition outstrips emotion, for when this does occur, he and his wife are bound to go their own ways. He will regret this separation more than may be apparent on the surface, for he prides himself on being a faithful partner.

The Capricorn man must not neglect the things that make life worthwhile—love, marriage, family life. If this happens, he will miss out on many fun-filled and rewarding experiences. But should he fall in love, he must guard against going to the opposite extreme and trying too hard to do everything properly, as well as insisting that his partner adhere to his high standards. He is the most conventional of all the zodiacal types and generally will not behave in a way which is not absolutely correct. He would do well to relax and let his loved one take the lead sometimes, suggesting dates or casual meetings. If he takes a day off and suggests a drive into the country to

her, he will probably be surprised and delighted to see how a spontaneous act can bring them closer together, emotionally and psychologically.

There are many Capricorn men, however, who are not obsessed with their ambitions and are a lot of fun. They have a dry sense of humour, which is frequently revealed at the most unexpected moments. Although the man born under the sign of the Goat could never be considered highly emotional, he can give a lot of genuine affection and kindness. He will never profess his love, however, unless he is certain his feelings are reciprocated.

with Aries

There are many Arien character traits that the Capricorn man will find appealing. The woman born under the sign of the Ram is industrious, independent and freedom-loving, but her unconventional attitude towards love and sex may surprise him. Consequently, if he expresses an interest in her, he must be prepared for their relationship to develop quickly. The Arien woman may well take the lead sexually. Since he is so accustomed to doing everything properly, he will undoubtedly consider her somewhat unfeminine because of her initiative. But the Capricorn man will have a great deal of fun with his Arien partner; she will help him enjoy his love life, perhaps even more than he has done before. In turn, she can benefit from his naturally cautious and practical outlook. Should they decide to make the partnership permanent, they must make allowances for their basically different motivations. If she has Venus in Taurus, she will be an even more affectionate partner.

with Taurus

There should be a basic sympathy between a Capricorn man and a Taurean woman, as both were born under earth signs. Sexually, he will discover that she will take the lead from him, so their affair should develop steadily, at a pace which is agreeable to both. The Taurean woman is passionate, but slow to arouse. If the Capricorn man is starting to think in terms of a permanent relationship, he would do well to consider his Taurean lover as a potential life partner. She will make a marvellous wife and will certainly help him achieve his ambitions. There does seem to be one area in which they may clash: she loves luxurious comfort and beautiful objects and, consequently, is inclined to be extravagant. This could cause the eminently practical Capricorn man some anxiety. Fortunately, he has the ability to cope with her major weakness—possessiveness. Overall, these two will complement each other well. If she has a Taurus ascendant, she may be more demanding sexually.

with Gemini

Gemini is the most youthful sign of the Zodiac, so a Capricorn man who gets involved with a Gemini woman will undoubtedly feel younger. She may be able to influence him to act more spontaneously, for many Capricorns are overly concerned with doing things according to conventional taste and in the most proper fashion. There are bound to be serious differences between them, for the Gemini woman is restless and will never be the steady, faithful partner that the Capricorn man becomes when he is in love. Her inherent duality will probably affect this area of her life. The Capricorn lover will find that she is not too demanding, emotionally or psychologically, but she does enjoy sexual experimentation. The Capricorn man will benefit from his Gemini partner's approach to life; she, in turn, can profit from his patience and stability. If she has Venus in Cancer, they should be happy together, as she will be affectionate and inclined to look after him.

with Cancer

This partnership's success will depend to a great extent on timing, as both Capricorn and Cancer are basically home- and family-orientated individuals. Once she entertains thoughts of marriage, she views each lover as a potential husband. He frequently does not think about settling down until he has reached certain objectives in his career. Since they were born under opposite signs of the Zodiac, there will probably be a natural rapport between them. It will not take the Capricorn man long to realize his Cancerian partner is emotional, sensitive and moody. But his inner strength and practical nature should help him cope with any difficulties and put them in proper perspective. Sexually, there should be few problems: he will find her romantic, sensuous, and particularly adept at arousing him. They should feel secure with each other, for the Capricorn man is an extremely faithful partner, and the Cancerian woman clings to a loved one and has a strong urge to protect him.

The Capricorn Man in Love...

with Leo

Rivalry will highlight this relationship. Both partners are ambitious, but they differ in their means of reaching objectives. The Leo woman likes luxury and fun; the Capricorn man is more calculating and practical. Before getting too involved, he should consider whether he can cope with the great demands a Leo woman is likely to make on him. She was born under a fire sign, which explains why she does nothing half-heartedly: when she falls in love, it will be passionately. The conservative Capricorn, however, may find her life-style too ostentatious for him. He likes quality too, but expressed in a more dignified manner. As a consequence, both should give considerable thought before committing themselves to a permanent relationship. Admiration rather than love may be the force that attracts them to each other. But there is no doubt that the Leo woman will be able to warm his rather distant and chilly heart. Care is needed, particularly if Leo is her rising sign.

with Virgo

A Capricorn man is one of the best suited zodiacal types to get involved with a Virgoan woman. Both were born under earth signs and, therefore, should find themselves in basic sympathy. She will admire his tact, care and consideration, and he will find her a rewarding partner. The Virgoan woman is often shy, but he is extremely patient and should have no difficulty coping with this aspect of her character. The Capricorn man will be delighted to discover that she is also a hard worker, though she may not be as adept at organizing as he has been led to believe. Should they decide to start a joint business venture, however, it will have an excellent chance to succeed. There are many areas in which they will be able to develop common interests. She is not demanding sexually; fortunately neither of them is highly emotional. The affair is bound to develop slowly and steadily, providing each with much needed stability. If she has Virgo rising, they should have a fulfilling life together.

with Libra

In an affair with a Libran woman, the Capricorn man will find that he has the responsibility for making any major decisions that concern them as a couple. She will support him in such a way, however, that his ego will be bolstered considerably. In addition, the Capricorn man will discover that although she is kind and warm, the Libran woman needs a lot of sympathy and romantic attention. This could present serious problems, for it is not in his nature to give of himself freely or naturally. So if he wants the liaison to deepen, he must learn, for example, to thank her warmly for any presents she chooses for him. This type of consideration and thoughtfulness makes her life worthwhile; she needs to feel appreciated as much as he needs to have moral encouragement in his career and the proper background in which to entertain his business colleagues. The position of Venus, her ruling planet, will have a significant effect on her capacity for giving and receiving love and affection.

with Scorpio

If these two lovers were to begin a joint business endeavour, it would undoubtedly be a success. To a certain extent there is a psychological harmony between them, but the Capricorn man will quickly realize that there are considerable differences between him and his Scorpio partner. She will be sexually demanding and highly emotional; despite his patient, rational outlook, the Capricorn man may have difficulty coping with these traits. In addition, Scorpio is an intense woman who could become as jealous of his constant concern with his career advancement as she might of another woman. A certain amount of frustration may occur on both sides, although it need not be a hopeless situation. Both are strong, energetic types and would do well to cultivate a joint practical interest. If they can learn to respect each other's outlook on life, they have the strength to develop a fulfilling relationship. The Capricorn lover will benefit most if she has Scorpio rising.

with Sagittarius

The Capricorn man should try an informal, casual approach with the Sagittarian woman. More than likely, he will not have to wait long for her to respond. If she is interested in him, she will want to develop the affair quickly. Sexually, they will enjoy each other, but he may find that she is similar to her Arien sisters in her attitude towards love and life in general: the Sagittarian woman is independent, freedom-loving and passionate, yet she will not take her love affairs too seriously. As a result, the Capricorn man is likely to think her somewhat unfeminine. He must expect to have rivals for her affection. On the brighter side, she can help him relax, enjoy life and, hopefully, not take himself too seriously. He is bound to be impressed by her intelligence, and they could well spend hours talking about various literary topics. They both have a lively sense of humour, which may serve them well when confronted with difficulties within the relationship. They may possibly share the Venus sign.

with Capricorn

When two Capricornians fall in love, they should be able to understand and perhaps identify with each other's character traits. There will certainly be a natural rapport between them, but they will also enjoy discovering how they differ. There are usually two distinct types of Capricornians: one is ambitious and lively; the other pessimistic and constantly dissatisfied. It is more common for those with similar personalities to be mutually attracted. Chances for a rewarding relationship to develop occur when one partner has Capricorn as a Sun sign and the other has it as a rising sign. Their emotional levels will probably be similar, as those born under the sign of the Goat do not readily give and receive affection. They should check the positions of Venus, which determines the capacity for love and affection, and of Mars, which influences sexual responses, in their respective birth charts. They must guard against working too hard and taking life much too seriously.

with Aquarius

Contrary to expectation, this is a pairing of zodiacal neighbours who get along fairly well together. The Capricorn man is basically a traditionalist, interested in the past and family trees, while the Aquarian woman is concerned with the future, and may well be living a liberated existence. It is quite possible that he will want to formalize their relationship through marriage, but she will probably disagree. Both are endowed with commonsense and a practical outlook, so they should be able to resolve such differences without too much trouble. She may enjoy sexual experimentation, but is likely to resist any emotional involvement. Should they think in terms of a permanent commitment, then both will be faithful partners. The Capricorn man would do well to check the sign Uranus, her ruling planet, was in at the time of her birth, as it will affect the degree of her unconventionality. She may think more positively about marriage if she has Aquarius as her rising sign.

with Pisces

Once a Capricorn man has begun an affair with a Piscean woman, he will appreciate her tender and loving nature, but will realize that she does not have a great deal of inner strength. His practical, steady manner and his decisiveness are exactly what she needs to help her gain a more clear-cut perspective on her life, as well as to provide her with encouragement to make the most of her excellent creative potentialities. The Capricorn man will have to make allowances for her high emotional level; if she is worried or confused about any problem, he should, however, be able to calm and reassure her. He may well have to be patient with her, as the Piscean woman is likely to have been hurt in other affairs. Since she is very romantic and sensitive, her Capricorn partner must try to express himself as affectionately as he can, if he wants the relationship to deepen. Should she have Pisces rising, she will do everything in her power to assist him in achieving his ambitions.

The Way to the Capricorn Heart

Capricornians do not readily fall in love; they are naturally cautious and reticent. So if you are attracted to someone born under the sign of the Goat, proceed with care. Do not be too direct or too passionate, for if they realize that they are being pursued, your advances are certain to be rebuffed. Should you succeed in cultivating a friendship and eventually in developing a more intimate relationship, remember that the Capricorn-born are people of few words. If they utter endearments or, finally, profess their love, take their words seriously, as they have been said only after careful deliberation. But do not expect Capricornians to reiterate their deep feelings frequently: they are basically strong, silent types. Once they commit themselves, you will be able to feel secure in the partnership, for they are extremely faithful.

To catch your Capricornian, it is essential to realize that there are two distinct types governed by the sign, although they have many characteristics in common: a dry sense of humour, high standards of behaviour, a tendency to remoteness. One type is lively and ambitious, and is symbolized by the mountain goat who nimbly and steadily advances from crag to crag; the other is gloomy and tends to complain constantly about responsibilities, and is generally described as a domestic goat who is chained to a stake in a particular spot.

If you find a dark, sultry-looking Capricornian appealing, but discover that he or she is the whining, self-pitying type, accept the fact that you are facing a challenge and devise ways to lift this Capricornian out of the rut. When you ask for a date, be prepared to hear excuses. But do not be dismayed: there are several possible courses of action you can follow. Arrive with a delicious, ready-cooked meal and take the situation into your own hands. Undoubtedly, the unconventionality of the situation will shock the Capricornian, but pay no attention and start laying the table carefully. After dinner, avoid making any passionate advances for Capricornians generally are not highly sexed or too eager to commit themselves sexually or emotionally in the early stages of a relationship. Tact and decorum, however boring, are the ways to the Capricorn heart.

Most individuals born under the tenth sign of the Zodiac are extremely musical and will have very definite tastes. You would do well to find out the preferences of your Capricornian and then take some favourite records along with you. But if you feel that the response to this plan will not be positive, remember that Capricornians tend to be social climbers and place great importance on externals. Snobbery is not uncommon among them. Consider inviting the Capricorn-born to a formal dinner party with a few other carefully chosen guests, including at least one mutual acquaintance. Those born under the sign of the Goat are rather shy and will feel more comfortable when familiar faces are present.

As for the menu, economy plus expertise and innovation should be the rule. Omit anything elaborate, and when serving wines, choose dry ones for Capricorn guests, perhaps a Muscadet. Mushroom soup or stuffed eggs, followed by lamb cutlets marinated in a tasty sauce, and a simple but slightly exotic dessert of pineapple in kirsch should satisfy the most discriminating Capricornian. In addition, they will be delighted that the meal was not costly yet tasty and elegant.

There is yet another route to the Capricorn heart: tickets for a modern jazz or Beethoven concert would be certain to please, for the majority of them love to read and listen to music. Of course, their taste may not be the same as yours, but Capricorn knowledge and enthusiasm, plus your attentive ear, can bring many rewarding and fascinating experiences. Capricornians will always be ready to explain techniques and complex scores.

If you are wondering what types of gifts the Capricorn-born would enjoy receiving, do not forget their fondness for anything which is antique. The women of the sign usually have lovely complexions and would certainly appreciate any rich moisturizers or skin tonics. Books on geology, general history or any which contain photographs of mountain scenery are bound to be welcomed, as Capricornians are avid readers.

The Aquarius Woman

January 20th – February 18th

Ruling Planet: Uranus
Triplicity: Air
Keywords: Intellectual ✳ Communicative
Jewel: Amethyst
Flower: Orchid
Trees: Fruit Trees
Cities: Hamburg ✳ Stockholm ✳ Leningrad ✳ Moscow ✳ Salzburg

The Aquarius Woman in Love...

Although Aquarian women have a strong romantic streak, it is frequently an aspect of their personalities that most of them try to deny. Consequently, if the Aquarian woman suspects that she is in love, she is likely to push any romantic thoughts about a deep emotional commitment to the back of her mind and concentrate on its more practical implications. The Aquarian woman will give considerable thought to her free and unconventional life-style, which she will be most reluctant to change, even for the man she loves. This will be a definite source of conflict. She treasures her independence to such an extent that she could well decide to get involved only in a series of sexual liaisons or in relationships based purely on friendship. The Aquarian woman must recognize her tendency to be stubborn and guard against becoming too inflexible.

Once she agrees to a permanent relationship, however, she makes an excellent and faithful partner. She views a commitment more seriously than many other zodiacal types. Friendship, above all, should highlight her marriage. An air of personal detachment will always form an integral part of her personality; this can be both an advantage and a disadvantage. Although it will help her view any problem objectively, it can, unfortunately, make her too self-sufficient and remote. If this happens, her partner's problems will have virtually no emotional impact or effect on her. The man who loves her must recognize and respect her highly individual needs, and curb any feelings of possessiveness for she cannot tolerate any sign of it.

While the Aquarian woman is extremely kind and friendly, always willing to lend a helping hand, she never seems to be emotionally involved in any of her humanitarian or charitable acts.

The Aquarian attitude towards love is also logical. The position of Venus will influence her capacity for love and affection. If she has Venus in Aquarius with the Sun, she will probably have many admirers, for the position of that planet will bestow a "distant glamour" on her. But the woman born under the sign of the Water Carrier will inevitably erect psychological barriers that will warn those attracted to her to keep their distance, physically, psychologically and emotionally.

The Aquarian-born is an individualist; she is modern in outlook and enjoys sexual experimentation. She is well aware of her behaviour and does not care what others think of her and her opinions.

with Aries

The Arien man will probably be pleased to discover that his Aquarian girlfriend wants an affair without emotional ties and will happily accommodate her. An affair between these two should prove to be mutually rewarding in many respects. She will find him extremely passionate and emotional, in a fiery and enthusiastic manner. Fortunately, she should be able to cope with this kind of emotional expression. The Aquarian woman will not be able to resist her Arien partner's love of life and natural warmth. He is a freedom-loving, independent type, and, of course, she will sympathize with this aspect of his personality. When she first confronts his worst fault—selfishness—she is bound to be disillusioned, as the Aquarian woman is one of the most humanitarian types of the Zodiac. Perhaps she will be successful in helping him to overcome it, or at least be able to point out how it can damage their relationship. She will benefit most if he has Mars in an air sign.

with Taurus

It is essential for the Taurean man and the Aquarian woman to consider, as well as each partner's Sun sign, their respective rising signs, and any sign except Aquarius and Taurus that may have a definite influence on either individual. The Taurean man will certainly be generous and kind, but temperamentally, he will be very different from her. The Aquarian woman needs the freedom to live her life in her own way, but she will soon realize that her Taurean lover wants to possess her completely. He is basically conventional; she is modern in outlook. Intellectually, they will function at different speeds, but she will admire his patience. Although the Taurean man is passionate, he will not try to sweep her off her feet. Both are stubborn, and she could easily find that he can be as inflexible as she. In addition, he is likely to be a creature of habit and too materialistic for her taste. A joint interest is particularly important in this pairing. She should check the position of his Venus sign.

with Gemini

Excellent communication will highlight a relationship between an Aquarian woman and a Gemini man. Intellectually, they complement each other well. Virtually all their time together will be spent in long, fascinating discussions and arguments, attending lectures, visiting TV talk shows and seeing old movies. Consequently, the emotional side of their partnership may not develop for some time. In the sexual sphere they are likely to be well matched, and the Aquarian woman will be delighted to learn that her Gemini lover enjoys trying new techniques in his lovemaking. Should they eventually fall in love, they may well use hypothetical examples to illustrate what they are feeling. If they consider marriage, however, the Aquarian woman must remember that although she is naturally faithful, the Gemini man has an inherent duality and is adept at talking himself out of tricky situations. If he has a Gemini ascendant and/or Venus in Leo, he will be more affectionate.

The Aquarius Woman in Love ...

with Cancer

In astrological terms, Cancer has very little in common with Aquarius. Consequently, it is essential that the Cancerian man and the Aquarian woman carefully consider other signs in their respective birth charts. Perhaps they will find factors that are strong enough to mitigate some of the basically incompatible elements which will emerge. Undoubtedly, he will be strongly motivated towards marriage and is certain to work hard for his wife and family. So if the modern Aquarian woman is interested in a more settled existence than she has been living, she should seriously consider her Cancerian partner. He is emotional, very sensitive and easily hurt. In addition, he is as kind as she and will look after and protect her well. But the Aquarian woman will have to adopt a philosophical attitude towards his sudden changes of mood. He will probably keep talking sentimentally about the past, particularly if he has Venus in Cancer with the Sun, while she naturally looks to the future.

with Leo

There will be a natural sympathy between Aquarius and Leo as they were born under polar signs of the Zodiac. The Aquarian woman will easily adjust to the grand leonine life-style, although she may initially be shocked at his extravagance and at lavish arrangements for their evenings out. But her love of glamour will help her overcome such feelings. It will not take her long to realize that the Leo man can be quite pompous on occasion, particularly if Leo is his rising sign. He is the epitome of elegance, both in dress and in manner, and he will show her a great deal of warmth and affection, to which she will respond well. The Leo man has an excellent chance to melt the cool Aquarian heart, and try as she may to detach herself from her emotions and be logical, she must be prepared for her usual strong lines of defence to crumble. Although they are different in many ways and may be engaged in friendly rivalry, theirs can be a long-lasting, fulfilling partnership.

with Virgo

The Aquarian woman will appreciate the Virgoan man's analytical mind and will identify with the logical way in which it works. Psychologically, they are good for each other. She will also discover that he is an emotional lightweight, and perhaps sexually reticent. This knowledge should not distress her, for she herself is neither emotional nor passionate. It is important for her to realize that the Virgoan man will particularly enjoy the friendship stage of a relationship, so in that respect this couple should be in complete accord. Although he is dependable and more conventional than she, there is no reason why the partnership should not work out well, provided that due consideration is given to their different personality traits. Their affair will benefit tremendously if they can find an interest, perhaps in astrology, or a hobby to share. If he has Venus in Leo, he should be warmer and more affectionate towards his Aquarian lover, but if Virgo is his rising sign, she may find him too critical.

with Libra

This partnership should be easygoing and fun-filled. Although he is not sexually demanding, the Libran man is a pure romantic and will certainly see that his Aquarian lover enjoys herself. She can gain a great deal from a relationship with him, whether it is brief or long term. There is a distinct possibility that his interests and choice of friends will be different from hers, perhaps less intellectual, and, consequently, he could expose her to an exciting but less serious side of life. They are likely to share an interest in the arts, particularly music, and she may help him gain a fuller appreciation of them. The Aquarian woman will find her Libran partner very amiable, although he may try to give the impression that he does not consider some aspects of life as important as she does. Many Librans do not feel that they are fully integrated psychologically until they have settled into a permanent relationship. As a result, they are inclined to rush into marriage. She must be mindful of this tendency.

with Scorpio

It may be the Scorpio man's dark eyes and intense look that first captures the attention of the Aquarian woman. But she should think carefully before getting involved in an affair with him, for he is the most sexually demanding and deeply emotional of all the zodiacal types. Although she is neither of these, she could learn a lot from a Scorpio lover. Since both have strong characters and can be quite stubborn in their attitudes, it may not be too easy for them to reconcile their differences. Therefore, if they want their relationship to develop, they must carefully study the signs in their individual birth charts to see if any can have a moderating influence on their basic dissimilarities. If there are no mitigating factors, the Aquarian woman and her Scorpio partner will have tense moments together: while he will admire her freedom-loving spirit and the efficient way she deals with situations as they arise, he can become jealous of her independence and other interests.

with Sagittarius

Sexually, the Aquarian woman could find the Sagittarian man demanding and perhaps even too passionate, but a partnership between them has much to commend it. Both will understand and respect the other's need for independence, although their mutual desire for freedom, if misdirected, could weaken their relationship. Intellectually, they should be well matched; he has breadth of vision; she has advanced ideas. Sometimes, however, Sagittarian optimism can reach such illogical heights that a battle of wits may develop with his clear-thinking Aquarian woman. She will do well to challenge him on any topic that he is even vaguely interested in, and he will thrive on such treatment. It may take her a long time to realize how rigidly she upholds her opinions, for it is quite likely that she will have convinced herself that the Sagittarian man is too flexible and restless. If he has a Sagittarius ascendant, great warmth and affection will be lavished on the Aquarian woman.

with Capricorn

Aquarius and Capricorn are the exceptions to the general rule that neighbouring signs of the Zodiac are not naturally compatible. One fact stands out above all others when assessing the possibility for happiness between two people born under these signs, and that is the excellent chance that they will have to enjoy a long-lasting relationship, for both are extremely faithful. This will certainly not be a dull partnership. Overall, the Capricorn man tends to be formal, ambitious, materialistic and unemotional. But if he utters any words of affection, they will be deeply meant. His sincerity will strongly appeal to her. But the affair could develop along unromantic lines, so it will probably be the Aquarian woman's responsibility to see that affection and warmth are not lacking in their love life. Undoubtedly, he will respond well to her initiative. They may possibly share the same Venus signs, which would be particularly advantageous to their affair.

with Aquarius

In general, when two people of the same sign meet, they find that they have several character traits in common. There is a strong possibility, however, that when two Aquarians are mutually attracted, they will soon discover that they are quite dissimilar. Individualism is one of the characteristics of the eleventh sign of the Zodiac. They should be compatible, unless one partner's rising sign upsets the balance. Inventiveness, a modern outlook and a sensible give-and-take attitude will probably strengthen their relationship; they are certain to learn a great deal from each other, as both are likely to have different thoughts and opinions on a variety of topics. One is bound to spark off the other intellectually. This is a pairing in which friendship will play an extremely important role; together they could produce some remarkable results if they have joint fields of interest. Chances for a lasting union are excellent if one of them has an Aquarius ascendant.

with Pisces

An Aquarian woman will learn a great deal from an affair with a Piscean lover, although she is likely to be puzzled by many of his reactions. Aquarius and Pisces are neighbouring signs in the Zodiac, which usually indicates that individuals born under these signs are not well matched either temperamentally or psychologically. He is illogical, irrational, intuitive, emotional; she is just the reverse. But there may be mitigating influences in their individual birth charts which could help the relationship. Should they share Venus signs, for example, several factors could work in their favour to bring them together. Since the Piscean lover is sensual and often emotionally demanding, a liaison between them cannot be taken lightly. They will have to work hard for it to succeed, but both will be pleased to find that they share several interests in common—acting, dancing, photography, for example. The couple will benefit most if he has Pisces as his rising sign.

Making the Most of Aquarius

In recent years so much has been written about the coming of the Age of Aquarius, a time of great scientific expansion and of humanitarian deeds, that some Aquarians tend to think that they are the greatest and most inspired of the astrological types. They are not. The Age of Aquarius is an astronomical phenomenon, which is related to complexities in the earth's motion. When it does arrive, it will have an effect on every zodiacal member, not solely on Aquarians.

Since Aquarius is the most forward-looking and individualistic of all the astrological signs, it is not surprising to learn that the Aquarian-born function best in an up-to-the-minute setting. This is reflected in their style of dress and in the interior décor of their homes. They are extremely original and frequently dictate fashion rather than slavishly follow it. Aquarians might well be echoing the words of Oscar Wilde on this subject: "Fashion is what one wears oneself—what is unfashionable is what other people wear."

Sometimes, however, those born under the sign of the Water Carrier find a new image so exciting and appealing that they stick to it for too long; eventually, it begins to look decidedly old-fashioned. They must remember that an outdated, perhaps too youthful, image can achieve an effect contrary to what is desired. If they have worn the same hairstyle for years, for example, and have strongly resisted any changes, they may well look much older than they actually are or want to appear.

In general, Aquarians can be stubborn for they have a tendency to remain fixed in their views. They will listen to the opinions of others, but they are not easily persuaded to alter theirs. At times this is unfortunate, as those born under the eleventh sign have the potential to express themselves freely.

In their schemes of interior decoration, they often use a marvellously off-beat kind of lighting to emphasize the contrast between light and shadow. The sources of light will be unobtrusive and functional; they will probably blend in with the choice of furniture, which is likely to be modern. In addition, there are usually several mirrors placed in strategic spots throughout their rooms to give the illusion of space, as well as to show off the Aquarian-born to their best advantage.

The majority of Aquarians tend to prefer winter; they seem to thrive in cold weather. They enjoy mountain scenery, skiing and most winter sports. In terms of health, they are prone to diseases arising from poor circulation, which can be aggravated by chilly conditions. Plenty of fresh air is essential to their well-being, but they must also keep themselves warm, particularly their feet and legs.

Aquarians, symbolized by the Water Carrier, are known for their kindnesses and the good turns that they do for their friends and families. They seem to be at their happiest when they can offer advice or assistance. They willingly put aside personal aims or considerations. But they are frequently not aware of the extent to which they perform humanitarian acts. Whenever modest, unassuming Aquarians lend a helping hand, it seems an obvious course of action to them. Consequently, when others try to do something in return to thank them, the Aquarian-born may seem distant.

The Aquarian-born are even-tempered, relatively free from prejudice and extremely adaptable, but their greatest pitfall is their tendency to put too much faith in human nature. As a result, they can easily be taken advantage of and sometimes not fully appreciated. They must learn to be more discriminating in their choice of friends.

When it is a question of love, the psychological distance at which Aquarians put themselves is often noticeable. They cherish their independence to such a degree that it is possible for them to alienate themselves from some relationships, which, if they were allowed to develop, might not be as overdemanding or emotionally cloying as they had feared. Therefore, it is necessary for the Aquarian-born to meet prospective partners at least halfway. Consequently, it is not surprising that they often marry late in life. Once they do, however, they are most generous and tender to their loved ones.

The Aquarius Man
January 20th – February 18th

Ruling Planet: Uranus
Quadruplicity: Fixed
Keyword: Resistant to change
Metal: Uranium
Countries: Russia * Sweden * Ethiopia * Turkey
Animals: Large Birds
Colours: Turquoise * Electric Blue

The Aquarius Man in Love...

The Aquarian man will probably have to come to terms with several inner conflicts when he first realizes he is in love. He has such a demanding need for independence that he frequently erects psychological barriers between himself and prospective partners and may well sacrifice many love affairs for it. He usually prefers relationships without emotional attachments, but when he eventually feels that he has found the right woman, he will be an extremely faithful partner. Moreover, he will then do everything in his power to

gratify her. He views a commitment as a very serious matter.

A long-lasting as well as a constantly enriching friendship will be vitally important to the Aquarian man within a permanent relationship. When considering marriage, he should always ask himself whether the woman concerned will be his friend as well as his lover. Undoubtedly, he will be most interested in their intellectual and social compatibility.

Originality of approach is natural to him in all spheres of his life.

Sexually, he may well have advanced ideas and enjoy experimentation; as a consequence, his partner must be receptive and understanding of his particular needs. In addition, his moral attitudes may be unconventional, so it is important that his loved one does not inhibit his individualistic style and attitude in sexual matters.

Although the Aquarian-born have modern and advanced opinions, they can occasionally get caught up in an atmosphere of romantic nostalgia. When in love, they should try to

give this area of their personalities free rein, for it will add a touch of colour and sheer fun to their lives. He should consider, for example, sending his girlfriend an orchid, his flower, even if he feels somewhat self-conscious making such a conventional gesture.

Since the Aquarian man was born under an extremely musical sign, he is likely to take a date either to a Stockhausen or pop music concert. But whatever his choice of entertainment, his date can definitely assume it will be avant-garde.

with Aries

An affair with an Arien woman should prove to be a lively and exciting experience for an Aquarian man. He will find her extremely passionate and probably quite eager to develop the sexual side of their relationship long before he is ready. Fortunately, she is as independent and freedom-loving as he. This should help forge a strong bond between them, and make it easier to surmount any difficulties which may arise. The Aquarian lover will certainly enjoy an affair with her, for she is warm-hearted and enthusiastic. In addition, he should be in sympathy with her pioneering spirit. Basically the Arien woman will be more conventional than her forward-looking partner despite her need for independence. The Aquarian man would do well to consider the position of Mars, her ruling planet; he will profit most if it falls in an air sign. Should Aries be her rising sign, her energetic straightforward nature is likely to overshadow her major flaw—selfishness.

with Taurus

If the Aquarian man is attracted to the Taurean woman, he should make a point of consulting her birth chart to find out the position of her rising sign, as well as the positions of the planets at the time of her birth. This is of particular importance since it is likely that she has many character traits that could prove basically incompatible with his. Although the Taurean woman is likely to be extremely attractive and charming, she has a possessive and conventional attitude towards life and love. It is perhaps her tendency to possessiveness that could cause the independent Aquarian the most difficulty; he will have to come to terms with this without upsetting her too much. Both can be quite stubborn at times, and deadlocks may occur. If she wants a deep emotional involvement and he does not, then as soon as possible, he must make her understand his position. Should she have Venus in Gemini, there is a chance that she will take the relationship less seriously.

with Gemini

Both the Aquarius man and the Gemini woman were born under signs of the air triplicity, and both have a rational and intellectual approach towards life. The Gemini woman often keeps her relationships with men on a light-hearted basis. Conversations with her will always be interesting and challenging for the Aquarian man, for she is prone to change her opinion frequently, merely for the sake of argument. Sexually, she is usually a lively partner and may well have advanced ideas on the subject. The Aquarian man will be pleased to learn that she is not extremely passionate and that she prefers ties of friendship with the opposite sex. If they decide to make their relationship permanent, communication and compatibility should highlight their life together. If she has Venus in Cancer, a fair measure of old-fashioned sentimentality will bring the couple even closer together. If Gemini is her rising sign, similarities between them should be even more obvious.

with Cancer

This is a pairing in which the two concerned must look carefully at the other signs involved in their respective birth charts, for, in general, there is not a great deal of natural rapport between an Aquarian man and a Cancerian woman. In terms of mutual interests, however, they should find it relatively easy to cement a friendship. The deep past usually holds a particular fascination for her; history and archaeology frequently absorb his attention. The Aquarian man must remember that she is extremely emotional and sensitive and does not have a progressive outlook on life. In many cases a Cancerian woman will consider every man she dates as a potential husband and father of her children, so unless he is seriously thinking of settling down, the Aquarian man must make his feelings perfectly clear to her. There may be fewer problems to resolve if Cancer is her rising sign. Should she have Venus in Gemini, she may be more light-hearted.

The Aquarius Man in Love ...

with Leo

The Aquarian man may well find that his Leo partner has a tendency to dominate, but if he can learn to relax in a relationship with her, he is bound to enjoy every minute of it. She should be able to bring out his latent romantic streak: he will find it difficult to resist her warmth and enthusiasm. They share a mutual love for ballet, cinema and the theatre, which will undoubtedly help to cement their partnership. There is an excellent chance that the Aquarian man's unconventionality can keep the Leo woman's somewhat pompous nature in check. It will not take the Aquarian man long to realize that she is more conventional in her outlook and in her opinions than he. In addition, they share a tendency to be stubborn, which could cause some rivalry between them. If Leo is her rising sign, she may be more expansive in her display of feelings. She may also be more dogmatic. Should she have Venus in Gemini, the Leo woman is likely to have a less emotional attitude.

with Virgo

The Aquarian man's considerate and friendly nature will serve him in good stead when he becomes involved with a Virgoan woman. Her genuine shyness and modesty often presents problems in her sexual relationships, but fortunately he seems to prefer ties of friendship to deep emotional attachments. It is a good idea for them to share common interests or hobbies. More than likely, the Aquarian man will admire his Virgoan partner's analytical and critical mind as well as her logical opinions; he will discover, however, that she has a similarly clinical attitude towards sex. Although he is not particularly passionate, he may be frustrated at times by the slow progress of their affair. In terms of intellectual rapport and friendship, theirs should be a good partnership; emotional problems should not be insurmountable. But they have different psychological motivations, so some clashes appear to be inevitable. Both the rising signs and the position of Venus should be considered.

with Libra

If the Aquarian man is experiencing a trying time, perhaps in his studies or at work, one of the best things he can do is to visit his Libran girlfriend. Then he will be assured of a relaxed evening. Undoubtedly, she will be her usual easygoing, relaxed self and should succeed in making him forget his problems. If the Aquarian man is not in the mood for sex, he can rely on her to be an understanding partner. He need never make excuses or feign passionate feelings. Romance is frequently more important to the Libran woman than sex, and the Aquarian man will enjoy and understand that aspect of her personality. Basically this is an excellent partnership, although he may find her opinions and conversation somewhat trivial at times. As the relationship matures, the Aquarian man is likely to assume responsibility for the decision-making. Should she have a Libra ascendant, her affectionate nature will be emphasized. He would do well to study the position of her Venus, as it is her ruling planet.

with Scorpio

The Aquarian man will find his Scorpio partner sexually knowledgeable, passionate and intense, but at the same time he could be rather disturbed by her high emotional level, by her jealousy and by her otherwise demanding nature. Consequently, some friction is inevitable between these two vastly different personalities. There is a strong possibility that the Scorpio woman may be more concerned with the sexual side of their relationship than with the intellectual side. If this is the case, the Aquarian man may well be displeased. In addition, she is probably highly intuitive and perhaps instinctive in her actions, which is in direct contradiction to his clear-cut logical approach. This can be a partnership worth developing if allowances are made for their respective emotional levels, and if some of their opposing character traits can be harmonized. Since both were born under fixed signs, they are liable to resist change. They should cultivate a joint interest or hobby.

with Sagittarius

It is not unusual for an Aquarian man to become involved with a Sagittarian woman. More than likely, her intelligence and her need for freedom will particularly appeal to him. Although he will find her sexually enthusiastic and emotionally warm, she does not always take her relationships seriously, and may have more than one lover at a time. These two may encounter difficulties should they decide to make their relationship permanent, for her duality could clash with his intuitive faithfulness. On other levels they make an excellent combination; they should be stimulated by each other's ideas, opinions and outlook. The Aquarian man is forward-looking, but the conventional Sagittarian woman has considerable breadth of vision; both often are united through mutual understanding and respect. If she has Sagittarius as her rising sign, she is likely to be idealistic. Should her Venus fall near his Sun in Aquarius, prospects for a mutually fulfilling life together are very high.

with Capricorn

Although this seems to be a rather chilly combination of types, a relationship between them could work out well. The Aquarian man will find his Capricorn woman either extremely interested in helping him advance in his career, as well as in their life together, or she will complain about her responsibilities and her difficult lot in life. Emotionally, they should be quite compatible, although their sexual needs will be influenced to a great extent by the positions of Venus and Mars in their individual birth charts. Of all the zodiacal signs, Capricorn is perhaps the most practical and conventional; the Aquarian man will appreciate her practicality, but will have to reconcile himself to her conventionality if he wants the liaison to deepen. In addition, he is not likely to care for her formality, which is a strong Capricornian characteristic. Complications may occur, however, if she has a Capricorn ascendant, for then she may be too protective towards him.

154

with Aquarius

Since Aquarius is the most individualistic sign of the Zodiac, it is probable that when two Aquarians are mutually attracted, they will discover that they have few characteristics in common. Both will, however, be independent, and want to live their lives without interference from anyone. Consequently, they will respect each other's life-style, but one of the partners may have to make some sacrifices for the relationship to mature. A great deal will depend on other factors in their respective birth charts. If, for example, either had Venus in Pisces, they would be in the best position to make their partnership permanent. In any case, the Aquarian man will find that his girlfriend has a similar outlook on life; both are unbiased, open-minded and strongly inclined to ignore tradition and authority. Mutual interests should be easily cultivated, as most people born under the sign of the Water Carrier enjoy astronomy, astrology and archaeology.

with Pisces

This will probably be an interesting and very different pairing for the Aquarian man and the Piscean woman. He is basically logical, rational and clinical; she is intuitive, irrational and emotional. But the Piscean woman's idealism should please him, and they will probably find that they have a similar attitude towards humanitarian interests. In fact, both may be involved in charitable work. Common interests are likely to be an integral part of their relationship, and if she is creative, as are most Pisceans, he will be fascinated by her work. Sexually, she is sensuous and fairly demanding; if she was not shown much affection as a child, she may rely rather heavily on her Aquarian partner for emotional support. The Piscean woman responds well to encouragement and security, and she will probably be stronger if she has a Pisces ascendant. Should they share Venus signs, they will have an excellent chance to harmonize their contrasting character traits.

The Way to the Aquarius Heart

There is a glamorous quality about most Aquarians that attracts many people to them. Those born under the sign of the Water Carrier, however, are usually not aware of their magnetic charm. In any event, they will kindly, but firmly, keep people at a distance. Should the Aquarian-born not want a deep emotional entanglement, this will be made abundantly clear to their partners in the early stages of an affair. As a rule, Aquarians do not fall in love easily or often; they willingly give a great deal of themselves in a humanitarian sense, but not in terms of intimate affection. Theirs is usually a universal rather than a personal love.

Surprisingly, Aquarians do seem to be able to involve themselves in sexual relationships without forming emotional attachments. Perhaps the ease with which they do this is related to their basic outlook on life or the personal detachment which is an integral part of their personality.

It is difficult to reach the heart of the Aquarian-born by using a direct approach. Consequently, other routes need to be considered. But whatever course you decide to take, proceed with caution and avoid any seductive advances. These are bound to fail. As is the case with those individuals born under Leo—the opposite sign across the Zodiac—Aquarians are usually very fond of the theatre and will respond well to an invitation to a play. Any form of live entertainment, particularly a pop music concert, will appeal to them. In addition, they have a somewhat vain streak and tend to admire themselves when passing mirrors or store windows. So a little flattery, judiciously applied, will do no harm.

If you decide to invite the Aquarian-born to dinner, you would do well to ask a few other friends along the first time. Do not serve anything that is too heavy or too rich, but they will certainly appreciate food that is not in their everyday diet. Chilled watercress soup would make a rather unusual starter. Follow this either with chicken cooked in a light sauce or *veau à la marsala*.

Lemon souffle will provide a perfect ending to the meal.

Aquarian hobbies and pastimes are another avenue to explore. Fortunately, they are extremely varied and frequently incorporate their interest in the past and in the future. Astrology, astronomy and archaeology are favourites. Aquarians also seem to prefer light sports to heavy team games. Many of them spend their leisure hours gliding, flying or playing tennis.

If you are thinking about appealing to their intellectual side and hoping to stimulate interesting discussion and argument, be advised that it will be a challenge to make those born under the sign of the Water Carrier change their minds. Since Aquarius is a fixed sign, they are likely to be extremely stubborn. While they will listen to opposing viewpoints, they are not easily persuaded to alter their opinions.

If one of these approaches has proven successful and the relationship is developing satisfactorily, you will soon discover that Aquarians have a modern outlook and are generally enthusiastic about sexual experimentation in their lovemaking.

So if you are rather conventional, you will have to readjust your thinking and try to meet their individual needs, should you want the liaison to deepen.

In general, presents for Aquarians should be related to their love of skiing and other sports, perhaps a suitable item of clothing or a piece of equipment. Those born under the eleventh sign also like anything that focuses on the unusual. An ornament or a piece of·jewellery that has an abstract design would be well received by the female Aquarians. A transistor radio or a small telescope would suit the males.

If the Aquarian-born begins seriously to contemplate either marriage or a single long-lasting relationship, you must recognize and accept that friendship will be of the utmost importance. Furthermore, Aquarians must be allowed a certain degree of independence, for they will not tolerate possessiveness. Although you must be very understanding of their individual needs, this will not be a one-sided partnership. Those born under the sign of the Water Carrier are loyal and generous; they will never quibble over petty matters.

The Pisces Woman

February 19th – March 20th

Ruling Planet: *Neptune*
Triplicity: *Water*
Keywords : *Emotional ✳ Intuitive*
Jewels: *Moonstone ✳ Bloodstone*
Flowers : *Water Lily ✳ White Poppy*
Tree: *Willow*
Cities: *Alexandria ✳ Seville ✳ Worms ✳ Compostela*

The Pisces Woman in Love ...

It is very easy for the Piscean woman to fall in love; in fact, her heart will probably be broken many times. This is not too surprising, since she is the most emotional of all the zodiacal members and is inclined to lack logic and consistency. The Piscean woman is so honest that she usually accepts with confidence whatever she has been told. She may meet someone who is going through a difficult period of his life, for example, and at once her sympathies will be aroused. She will offer to help in any way possible and gradually will become so involved that she is likely to deplete herself. She is generous to a fault and gives of herself both wisely and foolishly. The Piscean-born is not a particularly strong type, however, and her unselfish nature can easily be appealed to and often taken advantage of.

The woman born under the twelfth sign of the Zodiac frequently finds herself in an unhappy, confused state, unless she is able to channel her feelings positively. She will live with conflicts like the symbol of her sign—two fishes swimming in opposite directions. It would not be unusual for her to become the mistress of a married man who has a demanding family. More than likely, she will cling desperately to the affair, knowing all the time that her lover will not give up his wife for her. In the meantime, she is missing out on opportunities to develop more positive and meaningful relationships.

On the brighter side, if the Piscean woman in love suddenly finds herself working particularly well, perhaps in some artistic or creative activity such as painting or dancing, she can probably rest easy in the knowledge that she has finally met a partner who will be good for her. His gentle influence will help her make the most of her excellent potential. He will give shape and direction to her life; otherwise she will remain her naturally disorganized self, working long hours without achieving any worthwhile results. In turn, her loved one will find that she has a romantic nature and will not be reluctant to express her deep feelings to him. Furthermore, the Piscean-born is good natured, broadminded and undemanding.

It is important for the Piscean woman to recognize and understand that she needs someone who is stronger and more practical than she. Although she may be living a fully liberated, independent life, if her relationships are unstable or she tends to drift rather aimlessly from one man to another, her life could revolve around suffering in various forms. In this respect, the kindness, charity and love which are the main characteristics of the Piscean-born can drive her into impossible situations. While it will be extremely difficult for her, she must try to be as objective as possible about this sphere of her life. It is important that she does not exaggerate her worries or become anxious about trivial matters.

with Aries

Although the Piscean woman and the Arien man have very different character traits, they can learn a great deal from each other. She will admire his lively, pioneering spirit and uncomplicated outlook on life; he will learn to appreciate the quieter, more artistic aspects of life. Since the Piscean woman is sensitive and highly emotional, he will have to use a tender and understanding approach rather than his usual passionate, direct one. Venus often plays an important role in this pairing, for the couple may well have the planet of love in the same sign. If this happens, they are likely to be more responsive to each other's needs. The Arien man's tendency to selfishness will distress her, but she may be able to help him become more considerate. In the sexual sphere, the Arien lover may prove too energetic for her; intellectually, however, there should be great rapport between them. Theirs will not be an easygoing relationship, but it can be a fulfilling one.

with Taurus

Although the Piscean woman may find her Taurean man too conventional and possessive, there is a great deal to be said in favour of a relationship between these two. He should be able to give her the psychological and material stability that she needs, for his pace of life is slow but steady, and his general outlook is practical and laden with common sense. In addition, the Taurean man will be ready to encourage her to make the most of her potential talents. She must make an effort, however, to control her usual vagueness, as it is likely to annoy him. Sexually, they should be extremely compatible: the Taurean lover is passionate, but will be considerate of her feelings. Pisces and Taurus are close to each other in the Zodiac and, consequently, they may share Venus in the same sign or find it is in their respective Sun signs. Since it is the Taurean man's ruling planet, the position of Venus will strongly influence his capacity for love and affection.

with Gemini

There is an inherent duality in both the Piscean woman and the Gemini man, but each will express it differently: while the Gemini man always does more than one thing at a time, the Piscean woman tends to be swayed by opposing forces, wanting one thing, but often choosing another. She is not well organized and finds it difficult to gain a clear perspective on life. Although she may be living with one man, for example, she may actually be emotionally involved with someone else. A relationship between the two will never be relaxing unless they both make a conscious effort to overcome their restlessness. For the affair to deepen, the rational, logical Gemini man will have to accept his Piscean partner's illogical and intuitive nature. The fact that he is considerably less emotional than she, however, could cause occasional strain between them, as she is easily upset. The Piscean woman will be in a better position to enjoy the affair if she has Gemini rising.

The Pisces Woman in Love...

with Cancer

Since the Piscean woman and the Cancerian man share the same element—water—it will not take them long to realize that they are similar in certain respects. Both are intuitive, highly emotional and sensitive, although she will find that her Cancerian partner has a strong protective urge. Psychologically, they are often on the same wavelength and sexually, they are well suited. The Piscean woman will be delighted by his romantic, sentimental streak. But one word of warning: the Cancerian man is usually eager to marry and start a family. As a consequence, he may be somewhat clinging. So if the Piscean woman is not yet ready to make a permanent commitment, she should make him aware of her feelings at the outset of their liaison. If he has Cancer rising, however, there may be some problems because he will want to look after her and is prone to sentimentality. Should he have Venus in Leo, he may have a tendency to be domineering.

with Leo

The Piscean woman and the Leo man have a different approach to life, but otherwise they have a great deal in common. Both are creative, emotional and appreciative of the beautiful, worthwhile elements in life. The Piscean emotion, however, is related to her element, water: it is illogical and intuitive. Leo's is connected to his element, fire: it is enthusiastic and passionate. Since the Piscean woman is extremely sensitive, he would be wise to let their liaison develop slowly and concentrate on encouraging her to develop herself fully, as well as increasing her self-confidence. The Piscean woman should listen to his suggestions, which will usually be sound. She is likely to find him somewhat pompous at times, but she should be able to persuade him not to be too conventional or bossy. If he has Venus in Cancer, he will be more demonstrative and strongly motivated to protect her. Should Leo be his ascendant, he will appreciate her unconventionality.

with Virgo

These two were born under polar signs of the Zodiac, so there will be a natural rapport between them despite their considerable temperamental differences. The Piscean woman must try to develop the relationship gradually and carefully. Undoubtedly, she will discover that her Virgoan partner is less emotional than she, and is sometimes sexually inhibited. In general, she will find him clinical, logical and rational in his approach to life. The Piscean woman can benefit immeasurably from his practical ability, for she tends to be somewhat disorganized. The Virgoan man should guard against a tendency to be critical, however, as his Piscean partner is easily upset. She must get him to relax, or she will be in danger of becoming restless and nervous herself. If these two can blend their contrasting characteristics, they could share a mutually rewarding life together. Their chances will be better if he has Virgo rising, or if she has Pisces as her rising sign.

with Libra

An affair between a Piscean woman and a Libran man would appear to be set on a splendidly romantic course. More than likely, it will take some time before either partner comes to a definite decision about the other; the Piscean woman is not known for straightforward, logical thinking, and the Libran man will put off making up his mind for as long as possible. She will certainly enjoy herself with him, but he may leave her to cope with too many practical responsibilities. If this happens, their lives could become chaotic. Although the Piscean woman will respond well to Libran kindness, she knows that in a permanent relationship she needs a strong partner who will give her life a sense of purpose. He could easily find her problems too taxing for his quiet, relaxed nature. The position of Mars at the time of his birth will be of particular importance in this respect. If Venus was in Virgo in his birth chart, he will be more critical of her.

with Scorpio

If the Piscean woman is attracted to a Scorpio man, she must expect to be swept off her feet and caught up in a passionate affair. She should respond well to him and will find that she can readily identify with his high emotional level. Should these two quarrel, for example, their feelings will be expressed in an explosive manner. Fortunately, he is a strong personality who can be a source of great strength to her. Decision-making will undoubtedly become his responsibility. Since both partners were born under water signs, there will be a certain degree of sympathy and understanding between them, but their relationship will never be a calm, easygoing one. In fact, it may possibly be too high-powered to last. But if the Piscean woman can come to terms with her demanding lover, her life will be richer and more fulfilled. She will soon discover that a minor incident or statement can frequently trigger off the Scorpio man's jealousy. She will benefit most if he has Scorpio rising.

with Sagittarius

There is a definite affinity between the Piscean woman and the Sagittarian man. Camaraderie and conversation usually characterize their friendship. In a more intimate relationship, however, their individual faults could, if unchecked, destroy any chance they have of happiness. Both have a tendency to daydream about future possibilities and may neglect the factors which will ensure a successful union. They are inclined to drift along and make so many changes in direction that it will be almost impossible for them to fully realize their individual potential. Although the Sagittarian man is basically an enthusiast and is often very energetic, he may be influenced by his Piscean partner's less determined attitude and outlook. There is no doubt that they will enjoy each other's company, but he is a freedom-loving type. Should their liaison deepen, the Piscean woman must accept his inherent duality. If he has Sagittarius rising, she will find him more loving.

with Capricorn

The Capricorn man is ambitious and conventional, has a low emotional level and tends to be a loner. Not one of these traits is applicable to the Piscean woman, so if she finds herself attracted to a man born under the sign of the Goat, she must ask herself if she admires these qualities. Although they are very different types, they can learn a great deal from each other. The Capricorn man is essentially practical and should be able to provide his Piscean partner with encouragement and support whenever necessary. They are not likely to agree on the priorities of life: the Capricorn man, in his desire to progress, may become a social climber. If this is the case, he will be eager to impress people and will attempt to persuade her to help him. There is a good chance that this will not appeal to her easygoing nature, and she must then make her feelings known immediately. He, in turn, could find her too casual. If Capricorn is his rising sign, however, he will be loyal.

with Aquarius

The basic temperamental characteristics attributed to the Piscean woman and the Aquarian man could not be more dissimilar. She was born under a water sign, which denotes a high emotional level; he was born under an air sign, which signifies a rational, intellectual outlook on life. But they are both humanitarians and readily perform any charitable act. The Aquarian man is friendly, although unconventional and independent. Once he has chosen a particular life-style, he is not likely to change it. He can be surprisingly inflexible for a man with modern, forward-looking opinions. The Piscean woman will probably find that he is more interested in developing a friendship than a deep emotional relationship. These zodiacal neighbours should be able to meet on common ground, perhaps through a hobby or an interest in some art form. Venus may fall in the same sign for them both or in their respective Sun signs. Should this occur, their future bodes well.

with Pisces

The respective rising signs should be carefully considered in this partnership to learn how these two Pisceans differ. Hopefully, there will be some contrasting characteristics that will have a positive influence on their lives together. Undoubtedly, the relationship will be romantic and sensuous, but it is possible that it will lack direction and shape. Their natural adaptability could prove a disadvantage at times. Neither partner is likely to want the responsibility for decision-making, even when faced with such mundane matters as choosing which movie or television programme to watch. Their emotional needs will probably be considerable, but in this respect, as well as sexually, they should be extremely compatible. A happy, carefree attitude will characterize their relationship, but both must make a deliberate effort to develop a practical outlook on life. If not, they are bound to live in a state of chaos. They would do well to encourage each other's creative efforts.

Making the Most of Pisces

In general, Pisceans rely on their natural charm and flair to make the most of themselves. The women of the sign look fantastic whether they are wearing second-hand or *haute couture* clothes. Neither spends a great deal of time fussing about his or her appearance; it is best not to examine the clothing of the Piscean-born too closely. For example, that lovely floating evening gown worn by the Piscean woman, who has probably inherited it from her grandmother, may actually be held together by temporary fastenings. She is likely to be wearing old sandals.

Piscean women often make their own clothes and choose flattering designs. Most of them prefer soft wool in winter and fine Indian cotton in warmer weather. The influence of Neptune, the ruling planet of the sign, can been seen in their tendency to favour various shades of green.

The Piscean woman, however, does not seem to take the time factor into consideration when she is sewing. Consequently, she may have to rush to finish her latest project, which could well spoil the overall effect. Pins may still be left in the seams of a dress, or a hem may not be finished when she wears it for the first time.

Most of the time, the Piscean man is quite content to wear his oldest jeans. But in an effort to develop a romantic image, he may choose a beautiful velvet jacket and a shirt with a small patterned design. If you were to look at his feet, you would probably notice that he is not wearing any socks. In fact, both men and women born under the sign of the Two Fishes prefer to go barefoot whenever possible. They should be careful, however, as Pisces rules the feet, and they are, therefore, more likely to suffer from infections or ailments to that part of the body than other zodiacal members.

Creativity is a word constantly used in connection with the Piscean-born. Whatever career they may be following, their inclinations are basically artistic. Unfortunately, many Pisceans tend to underestimate themselves. They forget, for example, the poems they wrote for their school newspaper or magazine, or the pottery dishes and vases they used to make in their leisure time. This is an area in which loved ones and practical, stronger friends can be most helpful; they should give the necessary encouragement and moral support so that the Piscean creative potential can be developed. They will also discover that reminders and compliments about earlier achievements can work wonders on Pisceans.

Those born under the twelfth sign of the Zodiac need to be persuaded to realize their latent talents. It is not laziness that prevents effort, but rather a lack of self-confidence. They can easily convince themselves that they are not what others think they are. Sometimes, however, those who are closest to the Piscean-born are least likely to be believed when they try to help. A casual remark from a comparative stranger may have a greater effect and provide the necessary stimulus.

Although Pisceans have a high emotional level, it is not always well directed. It needs positive expression, perhaps through a creative outlet such as craft work—flower arranging or model-making. In fact, anything that has a beautiful end product should appeal to their aesthetic sense. Should they be successful in channelling their emotions in constructive ways, other fine qualities, notably charity and humility, will surface.

Concentration and persistence of effort may not come easily or naturally to the Piscean-born, so it is best for them not to start on any project which is too ambitious. They usually lack organizational ability and a practical approach. In addition, they are inclined to worry, and if anything does not proceed as they anticipated, they will probably give up when a project is only half completed. Psychologically, this would be unsatisfactory, as it will reinforce their lack of self-esteem.

Cinderella is a fictional character who represents the quintessential Piscean. She was marvellous to all her ghastly relatives—long-suffering, kind and always helpful. But once she met her Prince Charming, she was able to develop herself fully. Pisceans might well learn a lesson from this childhood tale.

The Pisces Man

February 19th – March 20th

Ruling Planet: Neptune
Quadruplicity: Mutable
Keyword: Adaptable
Metal: Tin
Countries: Portugal * Scandinavia
Animals: Fish * Marine Mammals
Colour: Pale Green

The Pisces Man in Love...

When the Piscean man realizes he is in love, he is frequently afraid to make a move. He underestimates his charm and is afraid of being rebuffed. As a consequence, his approach is likely to be cautious and somewhat oblique until he feels that his feelings are reciprocated.

The Piscean man is a romantic lover, and if he is creative, this side of his personality will flourish. He will enjoy, for example, sending a constant stream of poems or paintings to his loved one. He will bring her presents of perfumes and flowers, and he will take her to the theatre as well as to dinners at intimate restaurants. The Piscean man is an attentive escort and will see to it that his loved one enjoys herself fully.

The man born under the twelfth sign of the Zodiac must pay more attention to organizing his life. There is a definite tendency in the Piscean-born to be chaotic and forgetful; he is likely to forget to turn up for a date or else he will arrive late. Of course, he will feel remorseful afterwards, and his suffering may even be disproportionate to the oversight, so he would do well to see that such situations do not arise.

The Piscean man can benefit most in a psychological sense from a good permanent relationship, because his life frequently lacks direction. In addition, there is always a certain tendency for him to take the easy way out of a problem. But when he has a loved one to encourage him, he will no longer lack a sense of purpose. Although the Piscean man is easygoing, he can infuriate stronger types by his lack of self-confidence

and possible pessimism; he needs a strong partner who is willing to give him the necessary support to make the most of his excellent potentialities. In a permanent commitment, he must guard against his natural tendency to take the line of least resistance when difficulties occur. He may find it hard to come straight to the point. But if he does not do so, some of the weaker areas of his personality will be exposed.

Boiseloup by Pablo Picasso
© *S.P.A.D.E.M., Paris, 1974*

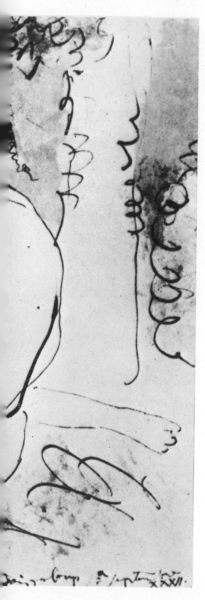

with Aries

There are some striking differences between these two types. The Piscean man could find his Arien partner too brash and extroverted for his taste. Her tendency to think of herself first in most situations will be difficult for the charitable Piscean to accept. Although he will meet the challenge of her sexuality, an affair with her may prove exhausting for him in all respects. He will certainly admire her strength of character and pioneering spirit; she will be able to provide him with the encouragement he so sorely needs, as her outlook on life is positive, surprisingly uncomplicated and straightforward. In addition, there is frequently an intellectual rapport between them. If they can blend their contrasting characteristics, this partnership can be truly rewarding. Should Venus fall in Aries at the time of his birth, and in Pisces at the time of hers, they will have a positive link that will significantly affect the relationship. Their respective rising signs should be carefully considered.

with Taurus

This relationship has excellent potential, and the Piscean man may find a great deal of sexual and psychological satisfaction in an affair with a Taurean woman. Her steady, dependable nature will make him feel secure, but he will quickly discover that she has a possessive streak. It may not disturb him if he is thinking in terms of a serious commitment, but he may find this trait difficult to cope with if he is used to being involved in more than one affair at a time. Furthermore, she will probably be more conventional than he, and is likely to be a creature of habit. Although these aspects of her personality may not appeal to him initially, long-term they could benefit him tremendously. There is a natural sympathy between these two zodiacal types, and provided there is a reasonable amount of compatibility between their other prominent signs, the partnership should be excellent. Venus, her ruling planet, may be in the same sign for both of them.

with Gemini

The Piscean man may possibly lack direction, and, unfortunately for him, his Gemini partner may also feel at times that she has no sense of purpose. Although he is usually highly emotional, she is more logical and analytical, especially when it is a question of her feelings. It is difficult for her to accept that she is in love, so her Piscean partner must be prepared to endure a barrage of questions as well as endless discussion. He will find it difficult to persuade her to relax and simply to accept the delights of a love affair. The Gemini woman's duality expresses itself in her desire to be involved with more than one lover at a time; she does not take her love life seriously. They should both be on their guard against restlessness. The Piscean man is bound to enjoy his liaison with her, particularly if Gemini is her rising sign. Should her Venus be in Taurus or Cancer, the Gemini woman will be strongly motivated to look after him and also to lavish affection on him.

with Cancer

The Piscean man will soon discover that his Cancerian partner can be delightful, charming and sensitive, but it may take him longer to realize that she has more inner strength than he has been led to believe. He will marvel at the way in which she can defend herself under adverse conditions as well as the speed at which she can revert to her kind, gentle self. She is a pure romantic—sensual, loving and highly emotional. Sexually, they should be compatible partners. Both have vivid imaginations, which could add considerable interest to their romance. The Piscean man should remember that the Cancerian woman is usually eager to marry and start a family, so if he is only interested in an affair with no strings attached, he would do well to make his feelings known at the beginning. If she is hurt through a misunderstanding, she may effectively torment the Piscean man. Theirs can be a mutually rewarding relationship, particularly if Cancer is his rising sign.

The Pisces Man in Love...

with Leo

A Piscean man would certainly benefit from an involvement with a Leo woman. He must make an effort, however, to be firm with her, as she tends to be domineering. Admittedly, the Piscean man often prefers to have other people organize his activities for him, but in this pairing it may not be wise. He should listen to what his Leo partner says, for she generally puts her lovers on a pedestal, and this could encourage the Piscean man to make the most of his potentialities. Both are emotional but express their feelings in opposite ways. He is illogical and deep: she is enthusiastic and passionate. Moreover, he will enjoy her natural sense of drama, as well as her ability to make every date an occasion. Psychologically, the basic differences between them are considerable, but both types are essentially creative and should be able to cultivate common interests easily. He will find her tender and more protective towards him if she has Venus in Cancer.

with Virgo

This is a partnership between polar signs of the Zodiac, and thus there will be a certain rapport between these very different types. The Piscean man should use a cautious and subtle approach, for the Virgoan woman is usually shy when first approached. In addition, he will benefit most if he concentrates his efforts on developing a strong tie of friendship between them, for she has a low emotional level. The Virgoan woman likes to keep busy and enjoys helping others, particularly with practical matters. So if the Piscean man lives alone, she is likely to offer to cook a meal for him, tidy his room, or type any work he needs done. He, in turn, must help her relax. Sexually and emotionally, she will probably not be too demanding, although a great deal will depend on the positions of the planets and her rising sign. If they can [resolve] their varied character[istics, it] can be a long-lasting [one, especial]ly if she has Virgo as

with Libra

An affair between these two may be slow to develop because of the Piscean man's possible hesitancy and the Libran woman's indecisiveness. Eventually, if the relationship deepens, they are likely to bemoan the fact that they waited so long. The Piscean man should therefore take the initiative and encourage his Libran partner not to keep him waiting too long for a decision. Both are easygoing and are certain to derive a great deal of pleasure and happiness from each other's company and conversation. A mutual love of music and poetry could bring these two closer. The Piscean man may find that she is more eager for romance than for sex. Frequently she is in love with the idea of love, but the Libran woman may not be able to resist his natural charm for long. Prominent signs should be studied in their respective birth charts, for the relationship could lack force and direction. If she has a Libra ascendant, for example, she may be more assertive.

with Scorpio

In an affair between a Piscean man and a Scorpio woman, both partners are likely to make considerable demands, so that life together could prove exhausting. If a calmer and more placid element can be injected into their relationship, there is a lot to commend it. Since both were born under water signs, there will be a certain affinity and understanding between them. The Scorpio woman, however, probably has a sense of purpose, while her Piscean partner's life may lack direction. If this is true, she can be relied upon to lend him moral support, but she must control her tendency to push him into action. In marriage, they are bound to go through some very stormy periods because of their high emotional levels. Extremes of passion, happiness and dissatisfaction will not be unknown to them. If she has Scorpio rising, she will be in a better position to give her Piscean lover stability and security. He should also check the position of Mars at the time of her birth.

with Sagittarius

There is a deep-rooted affinity between the Piscean man and the Sagittarian woman; in general, they seem to get along well together. He will find that his Sagittarian partner has a warm personality and straightforward, honest approach to life. She needs to feel free in her emotional relationships, however, and could be too optimistic and enthusiastic for him at times. Both have high ideals which they may be able to express though joint humanitarian activities. The Sagittarian woman is the stronger of the two, and should be able to exert a restraining influence on her partner if he tends to take the easy way out of a problem. They will enjoy their love affair and will share considerable happiness, but it is the psychological differences that need to be accepted and resolved. For this couple, it may be a question of blending a thoroughly optimistic outlook with a more apprehensive and perhaps pessimistic one. Fortunately, the Sagittarian woman and the Piscean man are adaptable types.

with Capricorn

The Capricorn woman can influence and encourage the Piscean man as well as provide the common-sense approach to problems that he desperately lacks. But a long-term relationship between them could have its complications, particularly if the Capricorn woman becomes so involved in helping him make the grade and get to the top of his profession that she does not respond as warmly and affectionately as she should. She may spend too much time arranging dinner parties so that he can entertain his boss or other business colleagues. Social climbing is an important activity for the Capricorn woman. Although her emotional level is basically low, she is a faithful partner. In love, she finds it difficult to express her deep feelings, but whatever she does say is sincerely meant. A mutual interest in music will help strengthen this partnership. The outlook is most favourable for this couple if Capricorn is her rising sign, or if she has Venus in Pisces.

with Aquarius

Although the temperamental differences between the Piscean man and the Aquarian woman are vast, they are likely to have certain things in common. Both are humanitarians and will eagerly offer to help those in need. Psychologically, however, the Aquarian woman is extremely rational and unemotional, although the friendliest member of the Zodiac. The Piscean man is intuitive and highly emotional. He will soon discover that she is unconventional and completely independent. In general, she prefers ties of friendship to emotional entanglements. Consequently, the Piscean man must proceed with care; he must not allow himself to get too upset if the affair progresses slowly. Since these two are zodiacal neighbours, Venus may be in Aquarius in his birth chart and in Pisces in hers. Should this occur, the Piscean man and the Aquarian woman will have the most promising factors working in their favour to develop a loving and affectionate relationship.

with Pisces

Since the Piscean-born are not basically strong personalities, they would do well to check the prominent signs in their respective birth charts, for these will add other dimensions to their character and contribute to their individuality. There will certainly be considerable psychological sympathy between two Pisceans, and they are quite likely to share common interests. A carefree atmosphere will characterize their liaison, and their physical relationship should also progress well. They must make a conscious effort to adopt a practical outlook on matters of daily concern, otherwise chaos will reign supreme. They will instinctively know what the other is thinking; this could prove unfortunate if one of them is worried or tense. Venus could fall in the same sign for both partners, which would not necessarily be an advantage since both are highly emotional. If this planet was in Aries at the time when either was born, however, the partnership would definitely be strengthened.

The Way to the Pisces Heart

Friends and relatives will have no difficulty recognizing when the Piscean-born fall in love, for tears of joy are never far away. They are the most emotional members of the Zodiac.

One way to the Piscean heart involves appealing to their romantic nature. Suggest going to the theatre or to the ballet, especially if *Giselle* or *Les Sylphides* is on the bill. Consider asking them to see an old-time film starring Errol Flynn or Greta Garbo; they are bound to accept the invitation. Do not forget that there is a strong element of humour in most Pisceans, so they are also likely to appreciate a good comedy.

In general, those born under the twelfth sign of the Zodiac need exercise. Although most do not have vast appetites, they seem to gain weight far too easily. Since crash diets do not work for them, you would do well to encourage joint visits to a nearby swimming pool, ice-skating rink or gymnasium.

It sometimes seems that Pisceans are determined not to give themselves a fair chance in life. In the company of loved ones, they often apologize unnecessarily for themselves, as they are inclined to underestimate their charms. You will probably find this extremely tedious if it happens frequently. Do not hesitate to express your disapproval of this Piscean tendency.

Those born under the sign of the Two Fishes are usually complicated characters; they are not always straightforward. Since they are so enthusiastic and highly emotional, they are capable of self-deception, whether they are in a jubilant or pessimistic frame of mind. Moreover, Pisceans rarely hold steadfastly to an idea and have a tendency to go back on their word. Hopefully, you will be successful in helping them overcome their inherent weaknesses by offering impartial advice. But if not, you will simply have to accept these ... tionship to mature.

... vivid imaginations, ... et if channelled ... ion, such as ... g. Un-

fortunately, many of their ideas will be totally impractical. You must try to point out possible flaws to them before it is too late. The Piscean-born are blessed with excellent memories, and you will be amply rewarded for any help or kindness you give them.

Selecting presents for Pisceans should not be too much of a chore, as they are not difficult to please. The women of the sign love cologne and perfume with a fairly light scent as well as silvery jewellery. Since the men are generally interested in fishing, a suitable item of sports equipment or clothing should be well received. Both sexes would welcome slippers or sandals, as they have a definite fondness for shoes. Remember that the feet are ruled by Pisces. In addition, most Piscean-born have an instinctive love of animals. You would be wise to check with the Piscean in question, however, before arranging delivery of any pet or tropical fish. Incidentally, an unusual present is likely to appeal to individuals born under the sign of the Two Fishes. The women would be delighted with a lovely flowing sari.

When it is a question of entertaining Pisceans at dinner, do not take them to one of the most expensive places in your area. A pleasant, quiet bistro would be better. Neptune is the ruling planet of the sign, and its influence can be seen in their choice of food. If it is possible to plan a day in the country, make a reservation at a secluded inn that is known for its seafood. Pisceans love sole, trout, lobster or crab.

If you are cooking at home for the Piscean-born, concentrate on rich, tasty food. Either French onion soup or seafood cocktail will make a good starter. As a main course, serve *coq-au-vin* or salmon poached in white wine. Water ice will make a perfect ending to this meal.

Piscean guests will appreciate a romantic atmosphere. They favour pale green; if possible, set your table with napkins or a tablecloth of that colour. They will admire a well-laid table, for if they live alone they tend to be lax about such matters.

If you are successful in reaching the Piscean heart, and begin thinking in terms of a permanent commitment, be advised that they can be critical about trivial matters. Immediately afterwards, however, they are likely to regret their carping tone.

The Charts of Love

Interpreting Your Ascendant

Your Sun sign depends only on your day of birth. Your rising sign, or ascendant, depends on the time and the place of your birth. If you know these, you can discover your rising sign by looking at the tables on pages 172–185. Then, reading about the characteristics of that sign will add another dimension to all that astrology can tell you about yourself.

The rising sign works in a different dimension from the Sun sign. It reveals the real you—the you known only to yourself and to those closest to you. The Sun sign, on the other hand, describes your image, the you that is presented to the world.

In the sections of this book about love relationships, the rising sign is often mentioned. Here the theme is further extended, and another element has been taken into consideration, too. While you are basically the kind of person described by your rising sign, your reaction in emotional relationships is shown by the opposite sign across the Zodiac. If, for example, your rising sign is Sagittarius, your reaction to your partner will reflect the qualities of Gemini.

The unique ascendancy tables on pages 172–185 are published here for the first time in a book for the layman. They make it possible for you to find your rising sign quickly and simply and, with the help of the character descriptions given here, to discover things about yourself which cannot fail to help you in every area of your life—and particularly in love.

Aries Rising

Those who have Aries rising are forthright, uncomplicated and straightforward. They are adventurous and probably pioneering in a chosen area. They are prone to headaches, minor cuts and burns. Their worst fault is selfishness and being self-centred. There is a strong romantic element in their attitude to love, and a tendency to rush into relationships. Those born with this sign rising must be careful that they do not rush into relationships or become too involved too quickly.

Taurus Rising

Patience, conventionality, kindness and the ability to express affection are characteristics of those who were born with Taurus rising. It is possible that money may be over-important to them, and they should keep this in mind. People born under this sign are generally good-looking, but they have a tendency to like too much sweet food and to gain weight easily. They are vulnerable to throat infections. Possessiveness is the worst fault of those who have a Taurus ascendant. They do, however, express intensity and deep emotion in permanent relationships.

Gemini Rising

Those who have Gemini rising are usually quick-witted and quick-thinking. They are lively and there is never a dull moment when they are around. They do have a tendency to lung infections and to chesty coughs, and are susceptible to broken arms and wrists, as well as to nervous tension and restlessness. Their worst faults are superficiality and inconsistency. Although duality is expressed in all spheres of their life, it is most pronounced in love, and they require freedom of expression.

Cancer Rising

Hypersensitive and kind, those people who have Cancer rising have a strong psychological need to protect and take care of those they love. Cancerians are extremely changeable, and their worst fault is moodiness. In love they are romantic but over-clinging. A hard side of their personality is often expressed towards a partner, and needs conscious control. Those with Cancer rising are, however, wonderful homemakers and parents. Breasts are vulnerable, and worry can injure the health.

Leo Rising

Magnanimous and generous, those who have Leo rising do things in a big, dramatic way, Their worst faults are dogmatism and a need to dominate. In relationships, Leo needs a partner who is in some way extraordinary, but Leo may try, nevertheless, to rule single-handed. Leos must go out of their way to develop a partnership. A woman who has Leo rising must try to become "the power behind the throne", rather than always trying to be in the limelight herself.

Virgo Rising

Clinical, matter-of-fact, hardworking, those with Virgo rising are often shy and rather self-effacing. They are the sort who live on their nerves and are always full of restless nervous energy. They are usually interested in health and vegetarianism. Their worst fault is being too fussy and over-critical. Often they are very easygoing and kind to a partner. Worry can lead to stomach upsets. They tend to have a very low emotional level and may have to fight to free themselves of sexual inhibitions.

Libra Rising

Romantic, kind, generous, charming, those people who have Libra rising are good company and have a great ability to relax and make others do the same. They do have a romantic attitude which may lead to premature marriage. In marriage a selfish element may be expressed towards the partner. Their worst fault is resentfulness. Their kidneys are vulnerable, and it is common for them to have headaches. They must try very hard to make decisions, for this is a major difficulty.

Scorpio Rising

Those who were born with Scorpio rising are hardworking, have a great sense of purpose and an extremely high and intense emotional level which must have a positive and satisfying sexual outlet, as well as a career outlet. Their sexual organs are most vulnerable. The person who has Scorpio rising makes a marvellous if very demanding partner. While kindness and generosity will be fully expressed, possessiveness may colour the relationship, and every attempt must be made to try not to demand too much from the partner.

Sagittarius Rising

Those who have Sagittarius rising have broad vision and are optimistic. They like challenge—and they like it all the time. They have a tendency to think the grass is greener over the hedge. Their worst faults are blind optimism and restlessness. Their hips and thighs are vulnerable and in these areas they will put on weight. Too much rich food may be disastrous for the liver. They have a light-hearted and enthusiastic attitude to love. They may have dual relationships and needs. They hate any inhibiting or claustrophobic situation, be it psychological or physical.

Capricorn Rising

Ambitious, sometimes rather a "loner", the person who has Capricorn rising has an offbeat sense of humour, and is unemotional, cool, perhaps distant. He or she will either get right to the top or stay right at the bottom and make no progress in life at all. The worst fault of those with a Capricorn ascendant is their constant complaining about life. While they can carry a lot of responsibility, they also have a tendency to spread money about to impress others. They have vulnerable knees, shins, skin, teeth and bones. They make good and faithful partners.

Aquarius Rising

Those who have Aquarius rising are independent to a fault. They are very friendly and humanitarian, but difficult to get close to, emotionally. They are very kind, and will try to do the impossible for others. They have vulnerable ankles and, perhaps, some difficulty with circulation. They are very faithful and romantic once they have settled into a relationship, and then a surprising warmth and

emotional colour will gradually develop. While those with an Aquarian ascendant are forward-looking, their worst fault is their unpredictability.

Pisces Rising

Kind, extremely considerate, sensitive, very emotional, lacking in self-confidence—generally describe those who have Pisces rising. They need a lot of encouragement and are often pessimistic. They are surprisingly critical of their partner, and sometimes carping. Their worst faults are diffuseness and deceptiveness. Their feet are the most vulnerable parts of their body. Although they are usually creative, those with a Pisces ascendant will constantly try to justify themselves and make excuses for not using their potential to the full.

The tables on the following pages provide a way by which you can find your rising sign without having to calculate it as an astrologer would. Simply place a ruler across the page from the date of your birth (in the left-hand column) to the time of your birth (in the right-hand column), and read off the rising sign where the ruler crosses the central line.

There are certain factors to remember. First, daylight-saving time may have been in operation when you were born, in which case you must adjust the time so that it shows "true" time—GMT in England, or Eastern Standard Time in America, for example. (Someone born in New York in May 1942 at 6 pm, when the clocks in the city were showing Eastern War Time—an hour in advance of normal time—would have to deduct one hour, making the "true" birth time 5 pm.) Make sure of your correct time of birth. Your local library, or Town Hall, should be able to make the check, if you are in any doubt.

Second, because it would be impracticable to print these tables for more than a limited number of places, we have chosen some major cities of the world to serve as points

of reference for places near them. Look in a good atlas and note the *latitude* of your birthplace; then turn to the table printed for the city nearest to that latitude. For example, the table printed for New York (40° North) will serve also for Madrid, Peking, Denver, Salt Lake City and Pittsburgh.

If you do not know the time of your birth, you will not be able to discover your rising sign, nor could the most competent astrologer tell you for certain, although he might make an intelligent guess.

Finally, these tables cannot be totally accurate for every person and every location on earth. There is a possibility that in some cases the rising sign they show will not be the right one. Check this by reading the interpretation of your rising sign. If this seems to be inaccurate, then read the interpretation of the sign before, and the one after; one of these should fit you exactly—and you can assume it to be your rising sign. Someone born in London, for example, at 4.30 am on April 20 is shown to have Aries as his rising sign. This may not fit him, so he reads the interpretations for Pisces (before) and Taurus (after), and decides which fits him best.

London 51° 32′ N

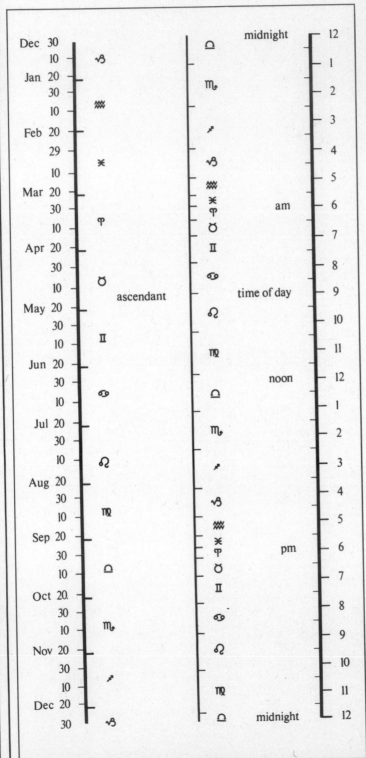

The following are some of the principal cities to which this ascendancy chart can be applied:

Amsterdam 52°23′N
Antwerp 51°13′N
Berlin 52°32′N
Birmingham, England 52°30′N
Bristol, England 51°26′N
Calgary 51°2′N
Cardiff 51°28′N
Dortmund 51°32′N
Leipzig 51°20′N
Warsaw 52°13′N

♈ Aries	♎ Libra
♉ Taurus	♏ Scorpio
♊ Gemini	♐ Sagittarius
♋ Cancer	♑ Capricorn
♌ Leo	♒ Aquarius
♍ Virgo	♓ Pisces

Paris 48° 50′ N

The following are some of the principal cities to which this ascendancy chart can be applied:

Budapest 47°29′N
Kiev 50°24′N
Munich 48°8′N
Seattle 47°45′N
Stuttgart 48°46′N
Vancouver 49°14′N
Vienna 48°12′N
Winnipeg 49°55′N

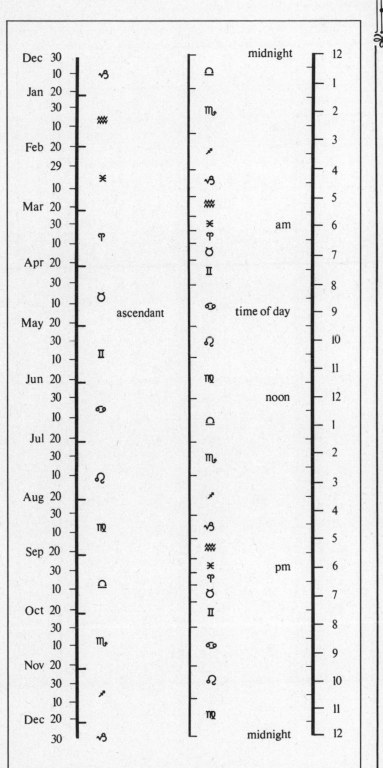

Toronto 43° 40' N

The following are some of the principal cities to which this ascendancy chart can be applied:

Belgrade 44°50′N
Bilbao 43°16′N
Boise 43°38′N
Bordeaux 44°50′N
Bucharest 44°27′N
Halifax, Canada 44°45′N
Marseilles 43°18′N
Milwaukee 43°9′N
Toulouse 43°37′N
Vladivostok 42°58′N

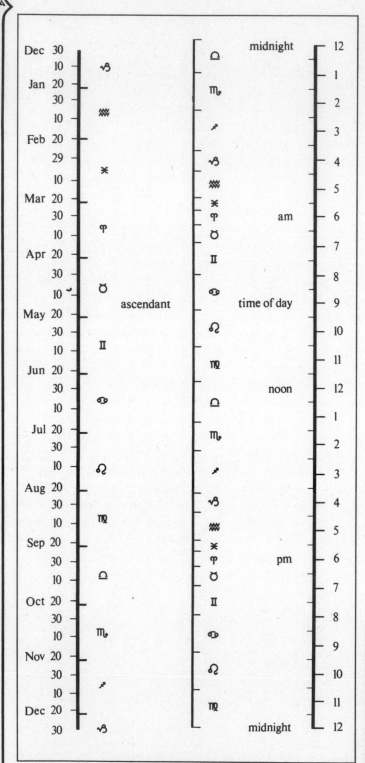

♈ Aries	♎ Libra
♉ Taurus	♏ Scorpio
♊ Gemini	♐ Sagittarius
♋ Cancer	♑ Capricorn
♌ Leo	♒ Aquarius
♍ Virgo	♓ Pisces

Rome 41° 54′ N

The following are some of the principal cities to which this ascendancy chart can be applied:

Barcelona 41°21′N
Boston, Mass. 42°18′N
Chicago 41°50′N
Detroit 42°22′N
Dubrovnik 42°39′N
Mukden 41°50′N
Oporto 41°8′N
Saragossa 41°39′N
Tashkent 41°7′N

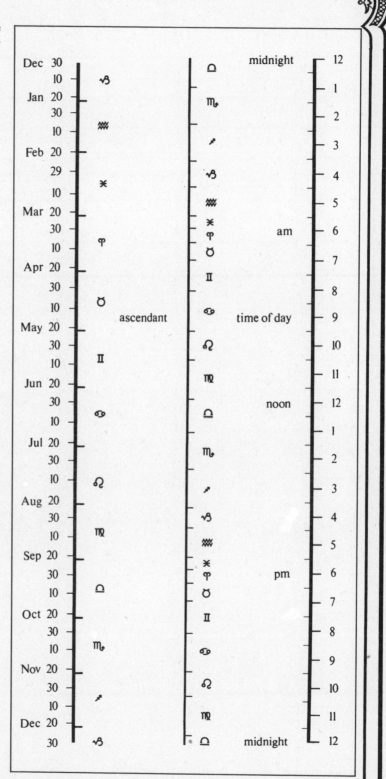

New York 40° 45' N

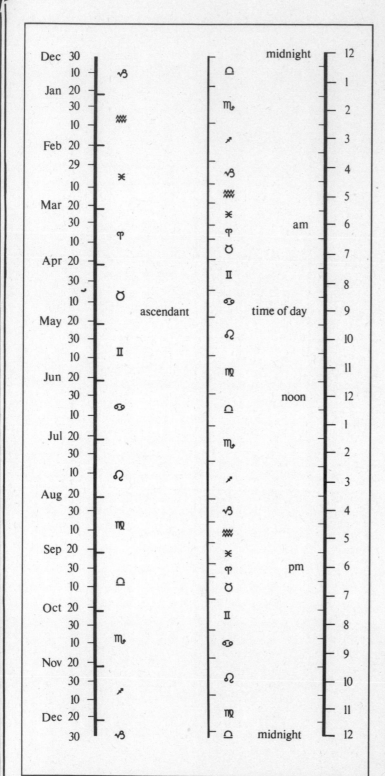

The following are some of the principal cities to which this ascendancy chart can be applied:

Ankara 39°58'N
Baku 40°27'N
Denver 39°50'N
Madrid 40°27'N
Peking 39°49'N
Pittsburgh 40°30'N
Reno 39°32'N
Salt Lake City 40°45'N
Valencia 39°27'N

♈ Aries	♎ Libra
♉ Taurus	♏ Scorpio
♊ Gemini	♐ Sagittarius
♋ Cancer	♑ Capricorn
♌ Leo	♒ Aquarius
♍ Virgo	♓ Pisces

San Francisco 37° 47' N

The following are some of the principal cities to which this ascendancy chart can be applied:

Athens 37°59′N
Dodge City 37°42′N
Lisbon 38°43′N
Norfolk, Va. 36°52′N
St. Louis 38°40′N
Washington, D.C. 38°58′N

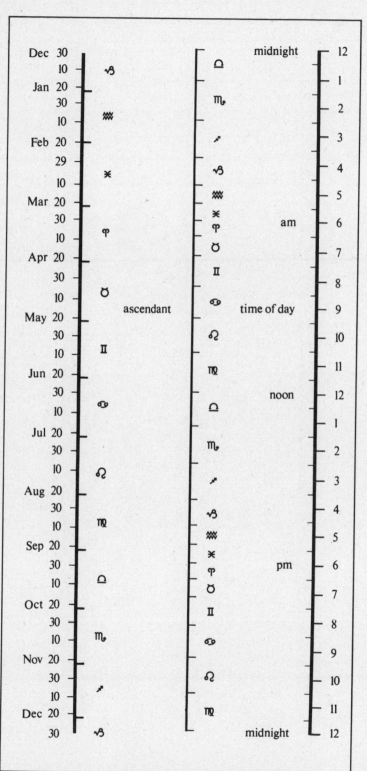

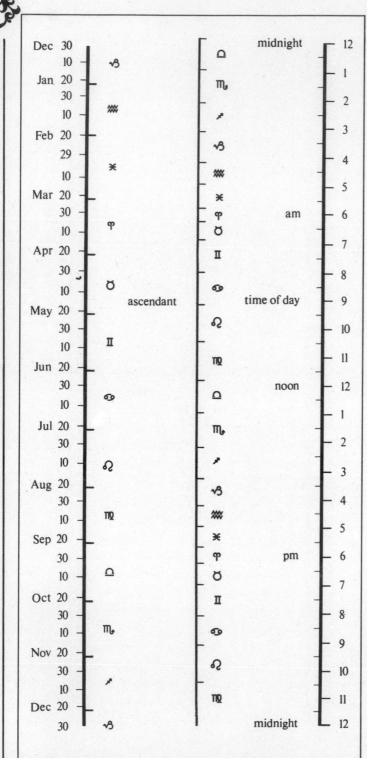

Tokyo 35° 41' N

The following are some of the principal cities to which this ascendancy chart can be applied:

Albuquerque 35°5'N
Chattanooga 25°2'N
Kyoto 35°0'N
Los Angeles 34°0'N
Memphis, Tenn. 35°7'N
Oklahoma City 35°25'N
Oran 35°37'N
Pasadena 34°5'N
Tangier 35°50'N
Teheran 35°44'N

♈	Aries	♎	Libra
♉	Taurus	♏	Scorpio
♊	Gemini	♐	Sagittarius
♋	Cancer	♑	Capricorn
♌	Leo	♒	Aquarius
♍	Virgo	♓	Pisces

New Orleans 29° 57' N

The following are some of the principal cities to which this ascendancy chart can be applied:

Cairo 30°1′N
Delhi 28°42′N
Houston, Tex. 29°45′N
Jacksonville, Fla. 30°15′N
Marrakesh 31°40′N
Shanghai 31°15′N

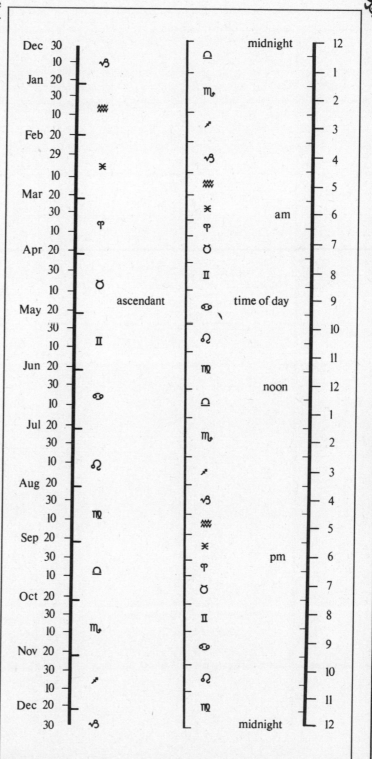

Mexico City 19° 26' N

The following are some of the principal cities to which this ascendancy chart can be applied:

Guadalajara 20°40'N
Haiphong 20°55'N
Mecca 21°30'N
Pachuca 20°10'N
Puebla, Mex. 19°0'N

ascendant		time of day	
Dec 30	♑	midnight	12
10		♎	1
Jan 20		♏	2
30	♒	♐	3
10		♑	4
Feb 20		♒	5
29	♓	♓ am	6
10		♈	
Mar 20		♉	7
30	♈	♊	8
10		♋	9
Apr 20	♉	♌	10
30			11
10		♍	
May 20	♊	♎ noon	12
30		♏	1
10	♋	♐	2
Jun 20		♑	3
30	♌	♒	4
10		♓ pm	5
Jul 20	♍	♈	6
30		♉	7
Aug 20	♎	♊	8
30		♋	9
Sep 20	♏	♌	10
30		♍	11
Oct 20	♐	midnight	12

Legend
♈ Aries, ♎ Libra, ♉ Taurus, ♏ Scorpio, ♊ Gemini, ♐ Sagittarius, ♋ Cancer, ♑ Capricorn, ♌ Leo, ♒ Aquarius, ♍ Virgo, ♓ Pisces

180

Bombay 18° 55' N

The following are some of the principal cities to which this ascendancy chart can be applied:

Asmara 15°19'N
Bangkok 13°45'N
Dakar 14°34'N
Guatemala City 14°40'N
Khartoum 15°31'N
Madras 13°8'N

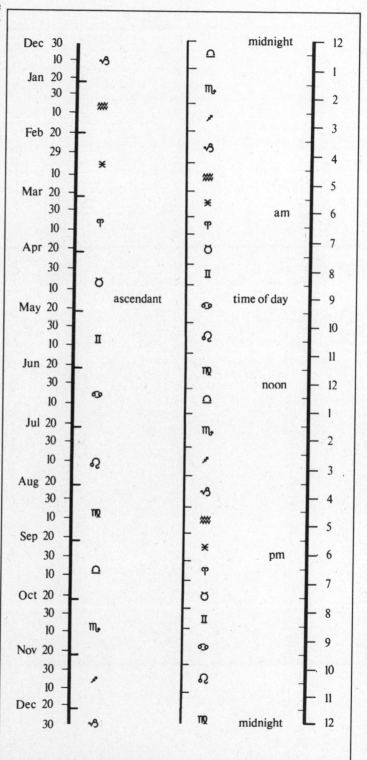

Rio de Janeiro 22° 54′ S

The following are some of the principal cities to which this ascendancy chart can be applied:

Alice Springs 23°36′S
Antofagasta 23°50′S
Concepción, Paraguay 23°30′S
Rockhampton, Australia 23°32′S
Sao Paulo, Brazil 23°40′S

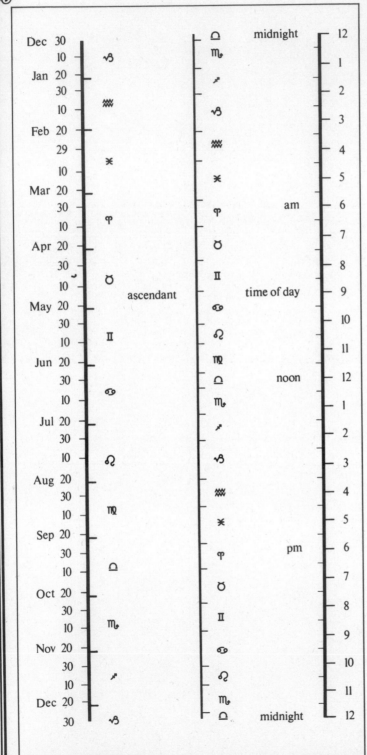

♈ Aries		♎ Libra
♉ Taurus		♏ Scorpio
♊ Gemini		♐ Sagittarius
♋ Cancer		♑ Capricorn
♌ Leo		♒ Aquarius
♍ Virgo		♓ Pisces

Johannesburg 26° 12′ S

The following are some of the principal cities to which this ascendancy chart can be applied:

Asunción 25°25′S
Brisbane 27°25′S
Lourenço Marques 25°58′S
Mafeking 25°50′S
Pretoria 25°44′S
Tucumán 26°50′S

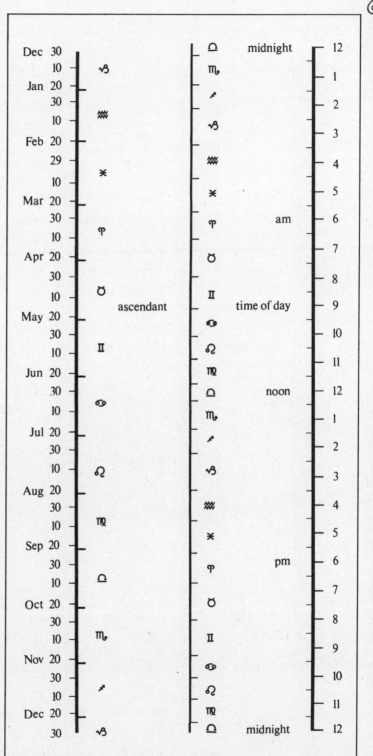

The following are some of the principal cities to which this ascendancy chart can be applied:

Adelaide 34°55'S
Buenos Aires 34°40'S
Cape Town 33°59'S
Cordoba, Argentina 31°22'S
Perth 31°57'S
Port Elizabeth 33°58'S
Santiago, Chile 33°24'S
Valparaiso 33°5'S

	ascendant		time of day	
Dec 30		midnight	♑	12
10	♑		♏	1
Jan 20			♐	2
30	♒		♑	3
10			♒	4
Feb 20			♓	5
29	♓			
10		am	♈	6
Mar 20				
30	♈		♉	7
10				8
Apr 20				
30	♉		♊	9
10		time of day		
May 20			♋	10
30	♊		♌	11
10			♍	
Jun 20			♎	noon 12
30	♋		♏	1
10			♐	2
Jul 20				
30	♌		♑	3
10			♒	4
Aug 20	♍		♓	5
30				
10			♈	pm 6
Sep 20	♎			7
30			♉	8
Oct 20			♊	9
30	♏		♋	10
10			♌	11
Nov 20	♐		♍	
30			♎	midnight 12
Dec 20 ♑				

♈	Aries	♎	Libra
♉	Taurus	♏	Scorpio
♊	Gemini	♐	Sagittarius
♋	Cancer	♑	Capricorn
♌	Leo	♒	Aquarius
♍	Virgo	♓	Pisces

Wellington N.Z. 41° 18′ S

The following are some of the principal cities to which this ascendancy chart can be applied:

Auckland 36°52′S
Bahía Blanca 38°35′S
Canberra 35°15′S
Christchurch 43°33′S
Melbourne 37°40′S
Valdivia 39°50′S

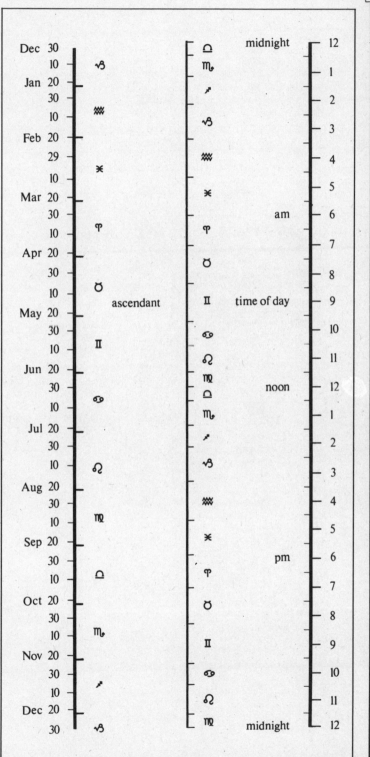

Where's Your Venus ?

Venus influences the capacity for love and affection; its effects are strongest when it is in Taurus or in Libra. If your Venus is in the same sign as your Sun, what you read about your love life under your zodiacal sign should be accurate; if Venus falls in a different sign, this gives another dimension to the expression of your love.

In order to find out where your own or your partner's Venus is, look at the astrological table on the next page. First find your year of birth on the top line of the table and then your month of birth at the left-hand side of the chart (1=January, 2=February, etc.). The table shows in which sign of the Zodiac Venus was on the first of each month and also any date during that month on which it moved to another sign. If you look at the table, for example, you will see that in January 1947 Venus was in Scorpio on the first of the month and moved into Sagittarius on the sixth of the month.

Venus in Aries

This denotes a warm and affectionate man or woman who probably express their emotion in a fiery, positive manner. Their character is best summed up as ardent and true, although it is necessary to watch out for selfishness, especially if the Sun sign is Aries. There will be kindness, but there may also be self-seeking tendencies. There is a readiness to apologize when in error.

Venus in Taurus

Here is someone who will lavish affection on a partner and will contribute a great deal to the development of a relationship. Possessiveness is bound to be present, and the loved one will almost inevitably be thought of as "mine", in much the same way as any other treasured possession is considered.

Venus in Gemini

Those who have Venus in this sign will enjoy their relationships and perhaps take them lightly. There is a strong possibility that they will have "more than one string to their bow", and they can find themselves in love with two people at the same time. Inconstancy, however, may spoil their liaisons.

Venus in Cancer

This placing contributes much tenderness and a strong tendency to look after the loved one. A certain claustrophobic atmosphere may be in evidence, because the person is so cherishing or sentimental. He or she may also dwell in the past too much. A high emotional level is likely as well as abrupt changes of mood.

Venus in Leo

Love, affection and loyalty will be expressed in a grand and probably expensive way, especially if the Sun sign is Leo or Libra. There may be a tendency to dominate or rule the partner, and dramatic scenes are possible. Loved ones are frequently praised and birthdays or anniversaries will always be remembered.

Venus in Virgo

This placing tends to contribute overcritical, clinical or chaste tendencies, inhibiting a full, satisfactory expression of love. Conflict can occur, especially if the Sun sign is loving, romantic Libra. The need for a perfect partner may be the primary cause of difficulty in developing emotional relationships.

Venus in Libra

This placing indicates a wholehearted romantic who is not a fully integrated person until he or she is enjoying a permanent relationship. If the Sun sign is Virgo, this will warm the matter-of-fact, practical Virgoan heart. Happiness, and affectionate feelings characterize these easygoing, generous individuals.

Venus in Scorpio

Considerable intensity, emotion and intuition will be quite evident in the expression of affection and feelings. Jealousy and possessiveness may mar relationships, and a black-and-white attitude towards love is likely. These tendencies are modified if the Sun sign is either Libra or Sagittarius. These individuals are secretive about their motives.

Venus in Sagittarius

This is definitely a lively position for Venus, and the overall attitude towards love and relationships may not be too serious. More than one liaison at a time is common; there is an idealistic facet to love. Great warmth, affection and enthusiasm will be expressed, but there is a definite need for intellectual rapport with a partner.

Venus in Capricorn

The influence of Venus in this sign is chilly, but once the barriers are broken one finds an extremely loyal, faithful and dependable person. There will be few words of affection, but what is said is meant, especially if the Sun sign is Capricorn rather than Sagittarius. The attitude towards love is extremely conventional and cool.

Venus in Aquarius

This placing nearly always contributes a sort of film-star glamour. If the Sun sign is Capricorn, it may be difficult for these individuals to become emotionally or physically involved with others. There is often a marked tendency towards platonic rather than romantic relationships. Freedom of expression is of the utmost importance.

Venus in Pisces

Here are kind, loving and willing slaves who cannot do enough for their loved ones. Life could become blissfully romantic in a disorganized way. Escapism is common for these individuals who are totally ruled by their emotions. Consequently, much pain and pleasure is experienced in their love life.

Venus Chart

The chart shows, for each year 1913–1960, twelve numbered rows. Each row gives a day number (or two) and the zodiac sign symbol(s) for Venus's position.

1913–1928

#	1913	1914	1915	1916	1917	1918	1919	1920	1921	1922	1923	1924	1925	1926	1927	1928
1	1 8 ≈ ♓	1 26 ♑ ≈	1 ♐	1 21 ≈ ♓	1 16 ♐ ♑	1 ≈	1 10 ♑ ≈	1 5 30 ♏ ♐ ♑	1 7 ≈ ♓	1 25 ♏ ♐	1 3 ♏ ♐	1 20 ♐ ♑	1 16 ♑ ≈	1 ♐	1 10 ♐ ♑	1 3 30 ♐ ♑ ≈
2	1 3 ♓ ♈	1 18 ≈ ♓	1 7 ♑ ♈	1 14 ♓ ♈	1 9 ♑ ♈	1 ≈	1 3 28 ≈ ♓	1 24 ♑ ≈	1 3 ≈ ♓	1 18 ♏ ♐	1 7 ♏ ♐	1 14 ♓ ♈	1 8 ♑ ≈	1 ♐	1 ≈ ♓ ♈	1 23 ♓ ♈
3	1 7 ♈ ♉	1 14 ♓ ♈	1 7 ♈ ♉	1 10 ♈ ♉	1 5 29 ≈ ♓ ♈	1 ≈	1 24 ♈ ♉	1 19 ≈ ♓	1 8 ♈ ♉	1 14 ≈ ♓	1 10 ♈ ♉	1 4 29 ♓ ♈	1 ≈ ♓ ♈	1 ♈	1 23 ♈ ♉	1 19 ♓ ♈
4	1 ♉	1 8 ♈	1 2 28 ♈ ♉	1 6 ♉	1 22 ♈ ♉	1 6 ≈ ♓	1 18 ♈ ♉	1 13 ♈ ♉	1 26 ♉ ♈	1 7 ♈ ♉	1 2 27 ♈ ♉	1 6 ♉	1 22 ♈ ♉	1 7 ≈ ♓	1 17 ♈ ♉	1 12 ♈ ♉
5	1 3 ♉ ♈	1 2 27 ♉ ♊	1 23 ♉ ♈	1 6 ♊ ♋	1 17 ♈ ♉	1 17 ♓ ♈	1 13 ♊ ♋	1 7 ♈ ♉	1 ♉	1 26 ♉ ♈	1 22 ♉ ♈	1 6 ♊ ♋	1 16 ♈ ♉	1 7 ♓ ♈	1 13 ♊ ♋	1 6 31 ♈ ♉ ♊
6	1 ♉	1 21 ♉ ♊	1 16 ♈ ♉	1 ♋	1 10 ♊ ♋	1 4 29 ♈ ♉ ♊	1 9 ♋	1 25 ♊ ♋	1 3 ♉ ♊	1 20 ♊ ♋	1 16 ♈ ♉	1 ♋	1 10 ♊ ♋	1 3 29 ♈ ♉ ♊	1 9 ♋	1 24 ♊ ♋
7	1 9 ♉ ♊	1 16 ♊ ♋	1 11 ♊ ♋	1 ♋	1 5 29 ♋ ♌ ♍	1 25 ♊ ♋	1 8 ♋ ♌	1 19 ♊ ♋	1 8 ♋ ♊	1 16 ♊ ♋	1 11 ♊ ♋	1 2 ♋ ♌	1 4 29 ♋ ♌ ♍	1 25 ♊ ♋	1 8 ♋ ♌	1 19 ♊ ♋
8	1 6 ♊ ♋	1 11 ♋ ♌	1 5 29 ♋ ♌ ♍	1 ♋	1 23 ♋ ♌	1 19 ♋ ♌	1 ♍	1 13 ♋ ♌	1 6 31 ♊ ♋ ♌	1 11 ♋ ♌	1 4 28 ♋ ♌ ♍	1 ♋	1 22 ♋ ♌	1 19 ♋ ♌	1 20 ♌ ♍	1 12 ♋ ♌
9	1 2 27 ♋ ♌ ♍	1 8 ♌ ♍	1 22 ♍ ♎	1 9 ♋ ♌	1 17 ♌ ♍	1 13 ♌ ♍	1 2 ♍ ♏	1 6 30 ♌ ♍ ♎	1 27 ♍ ♏	1 8 ♌ ♍	1 22 ♍ ♎	1 9 ♋ ♌	1 16 ♌ ♍	1 12 ♌ ♍	1 ♍	1 5 30 ♌ ♍ ♎
10	1 22 ♍ ♎	1 11 ♎ ♏	1 16 ♎ ♏	1 8 ♌ ♍	1 12 ♍ ♎	1 7 31 ♎ ♏	1 ♍	1 25 ♎ ♏	1 21 ♎ ♏	1 11 ♎ ♏	1 8 ♍ ♎	1 12 ♍ ♎	1 6 30 ♎ ♏	1 ♍	1 24 ♎ ♏
11	1 15 ♎ ♏	1 ♐	1 9 ♏ ♐	1 4 29 ♎ ♏ ♐	1 8 ♏ ♐	1 24 ♏ ♐	1 10 ♎ ♏	1 18 ♏ ♐	1 14 ♎ ♏	1 29 ♏ ♐	1 ♐	1 3 28 ♎ ♏ ♐	1 7 ♎ ♏	1 23 ♏ ♐	1 10 ♎ ♏	1 18 ♏ ♐
12	1 9 ♏ ♐	1 7 31 ♐ ♑ ≈	1 3 27 ♐ ♑ ≈	1 23 ♏ ♐	1 6 ♐ ♑	1 18 ♐ ♑	1 10 ♏ ♐	1 13 ♐ ♑	1 8 31 ♏ ♐ ♑	1 ♐	1 3 27 ♐ ♑ ≈	1 22 ♐ ♑	1 6 ♐ ♑	1 17 ♐ ♑	1 9 ♏ ♐	1 13 ♐ ♑

1929–1944

#	1929	1930	1931	1932	1933	1934	1935	1936	1937	1938	1939	1940	1941	1942	1943	1944
1	1 7 ≈ ♓	1 24 ♑ ≈	1 4 ♏ ♐	1 20 ≈ ♓	1 15 ♐ ♑	1 ≈	1 9 ♑ ≈	1 4 28 ♏ ♐ ♑	1 7 ≈ ♓	1 24 ♏ ♐	1 5 ♏ ♐	1 19 ♐ ♑	1 14 ♑ ≈	1 ♐	1 9 ♐ ♑	1 4 29 ♐ ♑ ≈
2	1 3 ♓ ♈	1 17 ≈ ♓	1 7 ♏ ♐	1 13 ♓ ♈	1 8 ♑ ♈	1 ≈	1 2 26 ≈ ♓	1 23 ♑ ≈	1 2 ≈ ♓	1 17 ♏ ♐	1 7 ♏ ♐	1 13 ♓ ♈	1 7 ♑ ≈	1 ♐	1 2 26 ≈ ♓	1 22 ♓ ♈
3	1 9 ♈ ♉	1 13 ♓ ♈	1 6 31 ♈ ♉ ♊	1 10 ♈ ♉	1 4 28 ≈ ♓ ♈	1 ♈	1 23 ♈ ♉	1 18 ≈ ♓	1 ♈	1 13 ≈ ♓	1 6 ♈ ♉	1 9 ♓ ♈	1 3 28 ♓ ♈	1 ♈	1 22 ♈ ♉	1 18 ♓ ♈
4	1 21 ♉ ♈	1 7 30 ♈ ♉ ♊	1 27 ♉ ♈	1 5 ♉	1 21 ♈ ♉	1 7 ♈ ♉	1 17 ♈ ♉	1 12 ♈ ♉	1 15 ♉ ♈	1 6 30 ♈ ♉ ♊	1 26 ♉ ♈	1 5 ♉	1 21 ♈ ♉	1 7 ♈ ♉	1 16 ♈ ♉	1 11 ♈ ♉
5	1 ♈	1 26 ♉ ♊	1 22 ♉ ♈	1 7 ♊ ♋	1 16 ♈ ♉	1 7 ♓ ♈	1 12 ♊ ♋	1 6 30 ♈ ♉ ♊	1 ♉	1 25 ♉ ♈	1 21 ♉ ♈	1 7 ♊ ♋	1 15 ♈ ♉	1 7 ♓ ♈	1 12 ♊ ♋	1 5 30 ♈ ♉ ♊
6	1 4 ♉ ♊	1 20 ♉ ♊	1 16 ♈ ♉	1 ♋	1 9 ♊ ♋	1 3 29 ♈ ♉ ♊	1 8 ♋	1 23 ♊ ♋	1 5 ♉ ♊	1 19 ♊ ♋	1 15 ♈ ♉	1 ♋	1 9 ♊ ♋	1 3 28 ♈ ♉ ♊	1 8 ♋	1 23 ♊ ♋
7	1 9 ♉ ♊	1 15 ♊ ♋	1 10 ♊ ♋	1 14 21 ♋ ♌ ♍	1 3 28 ♋ ♌ ♍	1 24 ♊ ♋	1 8 ♋ ♌	1 18 ♊ ♋	1 9 ♋ ♊	1 15 ♊ ♋	1 10 ♊ ♋	1 6 ♋ ♌	1 3 28 ♋ ♌ ♍	1 24 ♊ ♋	1 8 ♋ ♌	1 ♋
8	1 6 31 ♊ ♋ ♌	1 11 ♋ ♌	1 4 28 ♋ ♌ ♍	1 ♋	1 22 ♋ ♌	1 18 ♋ ♌	1 ♍	1 12 ♋ ♌	1 4 31 ♋ ♌ ♍	1 10 ♋ ♌	1 3 28 ♋ ♌ ♍	1 2 ♋ ♌	1 22 ♋ ♌	1 18 ♋ ♌	1 ♍	1 11 ♋ ♌
9	1 26 ♌ ♍	1 8 ♌ ♍	1 21 ♍ ♎	1 9 ♋ ♌	1 16 ♌ ♍	1 12 ♌ ♍	1 ♍	1 5 29 ♌ ♍ ♎	1 26 ♍ ♏	1 8 ♌ ♍	1 21 ♍ ♎	1 9 ♋ ♌	1 16 ♌ ♍	1 11 ♌ ♍	1 ♍	1 4 29 ♌ ♍ ♎
10	1 21 ♍ ♎	1 13 ♎ ♏	1 15 ♎ ♏	1 8 ♌ ♍	1 12 ♍ ♎	1 6 30 ♎ ♏ ♐	1 ♍	1 24 ♎ ♏	1 20 ♎ ♏	1 14 ♎ ♏	1 15 ♎ ♏	1 7 ♍ ♎	1 11 ♍ ♎	1 6 29 ♎ ♏	1 ♍	1 23 ♎ ♏
11	1 14 ♎ ♏	1 23 ♏ ♐	1 8 ♏ ♐	1 3 27 ♎ ♏ ♐	1 7 ♏ ♐	1 23 ♏ ♐	1 10 ♎ ♏	1 17 ♏ ♐	1 13 ♎ ♏	1 16 ♏ ♐	1 8 ♍ ♎	1 2 27 ♎ ♏ ♐	1 7 ♎ ♏	1 22 ♏ ♐	1 10 ♎ ♏	1 17 ♏ ♐
12	1 8 31 ♏ ♐ ♑	1 ♐	1 2 26 ♐ ♑ ≈	1 22 ♏ ♐	1 5 ♐ ♑	1 17 ♐ ♑	1 9 ♏ ♐	1 12 ♐ ♑	1 7 31 ♏ ♐ ♑	1 ♐	1 2 26 ♐ ♑ ≈	1 21 ♐ ♑	1 6 ♐ ♑	1 16 ♐ ♑	1 9 ♏ ♐	1 12 ♐ ♑

1945–1960

#	1945	1946	1947	1948	1949	1950	1951	1952	1953	1954	1955	1956	1957	1958	1959	1960
1	1 6 ≈ ♓	1 23 ♑ ≈	1 6 ♏ ♐	1 19 ≈ ♓	1 14 ♐ ♑	1 ≈	1 8 ♑ ≈	1 3 28 ♏ ♐ ♑	1 6 ≈ ♓	1 23 ♏ ♐	1 7 ♏ ♐	1 18 ♐ ♑	1 13 ♑ ≈	1 ≈	1 8 ♐ ♑	1 3 28 ♐ ♑ ≈
2	1 3 ♓ ♈	1 16 ≈ ♓	1 7 ♏ ♐	1 11 12 ♓ ♈	1 7 ♑ ♈	1 ≈	1 25 ≈ ♓	1 22 ♑ ≈	1 3 ≈ ♓	1 16 ♏ ♐	1 7 ♏ ♐	1 11 ♓ ♈	1 6 ♑ ≈	1 ♐	1 25 ≈ ♓	1 21 ♓ ♈
3	1 12 ♈ ♉	1 12 ♓ ♈	1 6 31 ♑ ≈ ♓	1 9 ♈ ♉	1 2 3 27 ≈ ♓ ♈	1 ♈	1 22 ♈ ♉	1 17 ≈ ♓	1 15 ♈ ♉	1 12 ♈ ♉	1 5 31 ≈ ♓ ♈	1 2 26 ♓ ♈	1 ♈	1 21 ♈ ♉	1 17 ♓ ♈
4	1 8 ♈ ♉	1 6 30 ♈ ♉ ♊	1 26 ♉ ♈	1 5 ♉	1 20 ♈ ♉	1 7 ♓ ♈	1 16 ♈ ♉	1 10 ♈ ♉	1 ♉	1 5 29 ♈ ♉ ♊	1 25 ♉ ♈	1 5 ♉	1 20 ♈ ♉	1 7 ♓ ♈	1 15 ♈ ♉	1 10 ♈ ♉
5	1 ♈	1 25 ♉ ♊	1 21 ♉ ♈	1 8 ♊ ♋	1 15 ♈ ♉	1 6 ♓ ♈	1 12 ♊ ♋	1 5 29 ♈ ♉ ♊	1 ♉	1 24 ♉ ♈	1 20 ♉ ♈	1 9 ♊ ♋	1 14 ♈ ♉	1 6 ♓ ♈	1 11 ♊ ♋	1 4 29 ♈ ♉ ♊
6	1 6 ♉ ♊	1 19 ♉ ♊	1 14 ♈ ♉	1 30 ♊ ♋	1 9 ♊ ♋	1 2 28 ♈ ♉ ♊	1 8 ♋	1 23 ♊ ♋	1 6 ♉ ♊	1 18 ♊ ♋	1 14 ♈ ♉	1 24 ♊ ♋	1 7 ♊ ♋	1 2 27 ♈ ♉ ♊	1 7 ♋	1 22 ♊ ♋
7	1 8 ♉ ♊	1 14 ♊ ♋	1 8 9 ♊ ♋	1 ♋	1 2 27 ♋ ♌ ♍	1 23 ♊ ♋	1 9 ♋ ♌	1 17 ♊ ♋	1 8 ♋ ♊	1 14 ♊ ♋	1 ♋	1 2 27 ♋ ♌ ♍	1 23 ♊ ♋	1 9 ♋ ♌	1 ♋	1 10 ♊ ♋
8	1 5 30 ♊ ♋ ♌	1 10 ♋ ♌	1 3 27 ♋ ♌ ♍	1 4 ♋	1 21 ♋ ♌	1 17 ♋ ♌	1 ♍	1 5 10 31 ♋ ♌ ♍	1 5 31 ♋ ♌ ♍	1 10 ♋ ♌	1 2 26 ♋ ♌ ♍	1 5 ♋	1 21 ♋ ♌	1 17 ♋ ♌	1 ♍	1 10 ♋ ♌
9	1 25 ♌ ♍	1 7 ♌ ♍	1 20 ♍ ♎	1 9 ♋ ♌	1 15 ♌ ♍	1 11 ♌ ♍	1 ♍	1 4 28 ♌ ♍ ♎	1 25 ♍ ♏	1 7 ♌ ♍	1 19 ♍ ♎	1 9 ♋ ♌	1 15 ♌ ♍	1 10 ♌ ♍	1 21 26 ♍ ♎	1 3 28 ♌ ♍ ♎
10	1 20 ♍ ♎	1 17 ♎ ♏	1 14 ♎ ♏	1 7 ♌ ♍	1 11 ♍ ♎	1 5 29 ♎ ♏ ♐	1 ♍	1 23 ♎ ♏	1 19 ♎ ♏	1 24 28 ♎ ♏	1 14 ♎ ♏	1 7 ♍ ♎	1 10 ♍ ♎	1 4 28 ♎ ♏	1 ♍	1 22 ♎ ♏
11	1 13 ♎ ♏	1 9 ♏ ♐	1 7 ♏ ♐	1 2 27 ♎ ♏ ♐	1 7 ♏ ♐	1 22 ♏ ♐	1 10 ♎ ♏	1 16 ♏ ♐	1 12 ♎ ♏	1 ♏	1 7 30 ♏ ♐ ♑	1 26 ♏ ♐	1 6 ♎ ♏	1 21 ♏ ♐	1 10 ♎ ♏	1 16 ♏ ♐
12	1 7 31 ♏ ♐ ♑	1 ♐	1 25 ♐ ♑	1 21 ♏ ♐	1 7 ♐ ♑	1 15 ♐ ♑	1 9 ♏ ♐	1 11 ♐ ♑	1 6 30 ♏ ♐ ♑	1 ♐	1 25 ♐ ♑ ≈	1 20 ♐ ♑	1 7 ♐ ♑	1 15 ♐ ♑	1 8 ♏ ♐	1 11 ♐ ♑

Where's Your Mars?

Mars influences a man's or a woman's sexual response; its effects are strongest when it is in Aries or in Scorpio. In order to find out where Mars was on your partner's birth date and on yours, study the astrological chart on the following page. First find your year of birth on the top line of the table and then your month of birth at the left-hand side of the chart (1=January, 2=February, etc.). The table shows in which sign of the Zodiac Mars was on the first of each month and also any date during that month on which it moved to another sign. If you look at the table, for example, you will see that in January 1947 Mars was in Capricorn on the first of the month and moved into Aquarius on the twenty-sixth of the month.

Mars in Aries

Mars in Aries will contribute highly sexed and passionate tendencies. But if your partner does not respond quickly to advances, an impatient attitude will surface. The person with this placing will be demanding but straightforward, good company. There will be no lack of enthusiasm and warmth; a general feeling that life is to be enjoyed will be evident.

Mars in Taurus

This placing indicates passionate and highly sexed individuals. Feelings are usually slow to be roused, but once they are, sexual desire is strong. Jealousy and possessiveness can often creep into relationships. People with Mars in Taurus are extremely sensual, sexually demanding and extravagant. Although tolerant of others, their anger can be violent if unreasonably provoked.

Mars in Gemini

Here we have someone who may not want to become too deeply or emotionally involved with any partner. A strong sexual desire is unusual, but there is great liking for innovation and variety in lovemaking.

Although there are likely to be many lovers, affairs are generally on a superficial level. Restlessness and a tendency to fritter away energy can occur.

Mars in Cancer

Highly sexed individuals who intensely dislike roughness and boisterousness are found in this placing. They require a gentle and sensitive approach as strong feelings, emotions and intuitions are always present, and there is a tendency to cling to a relationship. In Cancer, Mars often increases fertility.

Mars in Leo

Mars in Leo appreciates comfort and luxurious, aesthetically pleasing surroundings for sexual activities. There should undoubtedly be lively responses to advances, but there may be a trace of condescension at times. Generosity, affection and a genuine dislike of pettiness are usual. The temper is quick, but easily appeased.

Mars in Virgo

Virgo is purity personified, but Mars exemplifies energy and sex. Desire is certainly present, but the expression of it in a straightforward way may not be too easy. Psychological difficulties as a result of conflict can cause repression or self-criticism, and deviation is possible. There is a definite need to follow one's instincts.

Mars in Libra

A languid attitude towards sex is very likely in those with Mars in Libra, and excuses may be made to put off the over-ardent lover. Basically, their sex egos are weak, but once aroused a highly sensual nature will be evident. Sex has to be idealistic and beautiful rather than earthy. He is usually attracted to smart, cultivated women, she to sophisticated men of the world.

Mars in Scorpio

Mars in Scorpio, more than in any other sign, will make the individual very highly sexed. Unfortunately, jealousy and resentfulness can frequently blight relationships. Possibly the best way to combat this is to cultivate demanding interests, so that the excess of energy and emotion is positively directed.

Mars in Sagittarius

A lively, unserious attitude towards sex is common. The man or woman with Mars in Sagittarius will enjoy relationships, but will make and break them easily, for freedom is highly prized. Although passionate, there is an inherent duality that will not permit possessiveness. Energy and enthusiasm go hand in hand.

Mars in Capricorn

If those with Mars in Capricorn, caught up in the essential business of getting ahead in their professional lives, can find the time to indulge in sexual relationships, they will undoubtedly be passionate one moment and chilly the next. They will, however, admire and identify with faithfulness and constancy. Emotions will always be under control.

Mars in Aquarius

Those with Mars in Aquarius will probably be undemonstrative in their physical relationships. They accept the fact that desires must be satisfied, but they are not passionate individuals. The emotional side of Mars is not conducive to Aquarian rationality or detachment, and some emotional discord, which can lead to tension, is likely.

Mars in Pisces

Passion must always be combined with a colourful romanticism for those with Mars in Pisces. The emotional level is extremely high, but simple earthy pleasures may not fully satisfy some highly individual escapist tendencies. A strong uncomplicated partner will have a beneficial steadying influence and provide much-needed assurance.

Mars Chart

The Mars Chart consists of three stacked blocks of year-columns, each column divided into two sub-columns (day-of-month and zodiac signs), with rows numbered 1–12 for the months. Values give the day the planet changes sign; zodiac symbols indicate the sign(s).

Block 1 — 1913–1928

Mo	1913		1914		1915		1916		1917		1918		1919		1920		1921		1922		1923		1924		1925		1926		1927		1928	
1	1 11	♐♑	1	♋	1 31	♑♒	1	♌	1 10	♑♒	1 12	♊♎	1 28	♒♓	1	♎	1 6	♒♓	1	♏	1 22	♓♈	1 20	♐	1	♈	1	♐	1	♉	1 20	♐♑
2	1 20	♑♒	1	♋	1	♒	1	♌	1 17	♒♓	1 26	♎♏	1	♓	1	♏	1 14	♓♈	1	♏	1	♈	1	♐♈	1 6	♈♉	1 10	♐♑	1 22	♉♊	1 29	♑♒
3	1 31	♒♓	1	♋	1 10	♒♓	1	♌	1 27	♓♈	1	♏	1 7	♓♈	1	♏	1 26	♈♉	1	♐	1 4	♈♉	1 7	♐♑	1 25	♉♊	1 24	♑♒	1	♊	1	
4	1	♓	1	♋	1 17	♓♈	1	♌	1	♈	1	♏	1 16	♈♉	1 24	♏	1	♉	1	♐	1 17	♉	1 25	♑	1	♊	1	♒	1 17	♊♋	1 8	♒♓
5	1 9	♓♈	1 2	♋♌	1 27	♈♉	1 29	♌♏	1 5	♈♉	1	♏	1 27	♉♊	1	♏	1 7	♉♊	1	♐	1 31	♊♋	1	♒	1 10	♊♋	1 4	♒♓	1	♊	1 17	♓♈
6	1 17	♈♉	1 27	♌♏	1	♉	1	♏	1 15	♉♊	1 24	♎♏	1	♊	1	♐	1 19	♊♋	1	♐	1	♒♓	1 25	♒♓	1 27	♋	1 16	♓♈	1 7	♊♋	1 27	♈♉
7	1 30	♉♊	1	♏	1 7	♉♊	1 24	♏♎	1 29	♊♋	1	♎	1 9	♊♋	1 11	♎♋	1	♐	1	♐	1 17	♋♌	1	♓	1	♋	1	♈	1 26	♋♏	1	♉
8	1	♊	1 15	♏♎	1 20	♊♋	1	♏	1	♋	1 18	♋♎	1 24	♋♋	1	♎	1 4	♐♈	1	♐	1 25	♌♏	1 13	♓♈	1 2	♋♌	1	♈	1 10	♏	1	♉♊
9	1 16	♊♋	1	♏	1	♋	1 9	♎♏	1 13	♋♎	1	♋	1	♋	1 5	♋♑	1 21	♈♑	1 14	♐♑	1 2	♏	1	♈	1	♌♎	1	♉	1 11	♏	1	♊
10	1	♋	1 8	♎♏	1 23	♋♌	1	♏♐	1	♏	1 2	♋♌	1 11	♋♌	1 19	♏♑	1	♋	1 31	♑♒	1 19	♏	1 20	♈	1	♌	1	♉	1 26	♏♐	1 4	♊♋
11	1	♋	1 12	♏♐	1	♌	1	♏♐	1 3	♏	1 12	♌♎	1 30	♌♎	1 28	♑	1 7	♋	1	♒	1	♏	1	♓	1 14	♌	1	♏♏	1	♉	1	♋
12	1	♋	1 23	♐♑	1	♌	1	♐	1	♏♐	1 21	♎♏	1	♎	1	♒	1 27	♒♓	1 12	♒	1 5	♏♐	1 21	♓♈	1 28	♌	1	♏	1 9	♉	1 21	♋♊

Block 2 — 1929–1944

Mo	1929		1930		1931		1932		1933		1934		1935		1936		1937		1938		1939		1940		1941		1942		1943		1944	
1	1	♊	1	♑	1	♌	1 18	♑♒	1	♏	1	♒	1	♎	1	♒	1 6	♎♏	1	♓	1 30	♏♐	1 4	♈♈	1 5	♏♐	1 12	♐♉	1 27	♐♑	1	♊
2	1	♊	1 7	♑♒	1 17	♌	1 26	♒♓	1	♏	1 5	♒♓	1	♎	1 23	♓	1	♏	1	♐	1	♐	1 18	♉♈	1 18	♐♑	1	♐	1	♑	1	♊
3	1 12	♈♋	1 18	♒♓	1 31	♌♌	1	♓	1	♏	1 15	♓♈	1	♎	1	♈	1 14	♏♐	1 13	♐	1 22	♐♑	1	♉	1	♑	1 8	♐♑	1 9	♑♒	1 29	♊
4	1	♋	1 25	♓♈	1	♌	1 4	♈	1	♏	1 23	♈♉	1	♎	1	♈	1	♐	1 24	♐	1	♑	1 2	♉♊	1 3	♑♒	1 27	♑	1 19	♒	1	♋
5	1 14	♋♌	1	♈	1	♌	1	♈♉	1 13	♎♏	1	♈	1	♎	1 13	♈♉	1 15	♐♑	1	♊	1 26	♑♒	1 18	♊♋	1 17	♒♓	1	♑	1 28	♒♓	1 23	♋
6	1	♌	1 4	♈♉	1 11	♌	1 23	♉♊	1	♏	1 3	♈♉	1	♎	1 26	♉♊	1	♐	1 8	♊	1	♒	1	♋	1 15	♓	1	♑	1	♓	1	♋
7	1 5	♌♏	1 15	♉♊	1	♌	1	♊	1 7	♏♎	1 16	♉♊	1 30	♎	1	♊	1	♏	1 23	♊♋	1 22	♒♓	1 4	♋	1 3	♓♈	1	♑	1 8	♓♈	1 13	♋♌
8	1 22	♏♌	1 29	♊♊	1 2	♌	1 5	♊	1 26	♎♏	1 31	♊	1	♎	1 10	♊♋	1 9	♏♐	1	♋	1	♒	1 20	♋	1	♈	1 2	♑	1 24	♈♉	1 29	♌♎
9	1	♌	1	♊	1 18	♌	1 21	♊♋	1	♏	1	♊	1 17	♎♏	1 27	♋♌	1	♐	1 8	♋♌	1 25	♓	1	♋	1	♈	1 18	♑	1	♉	1	♎
10	1 7	♌♏	1 21	♊♋	1 31	♌♌	1	♋	1 10	♏♐	1	♋	1 29	♏♐	1	♋	1	♐	1 26	♌♏	1	♓	1 6	♋	1	♈	1	♑	1	♉	1 14	♎♏
11	1 19	♏♑	1	♋	1	♌	1 14	♋♌	1 20	♐♑	1	♌	1	♏	1 15	♋♌	1 12	♐♑	1	♎	1 20	♓♈	1 21	♋	1	♈	1 2	♑	1	♉	1 26	♏♐
12	1 30	♐♑	1	♊	1	♌	1 29	♌♑	1	♎♏	1 12	♌♒	1 8	♐♑	1	♌	1 12	♑♒	1 12	♎	1	♈♏	1 16	♋	1	♈	1 16	♑	1	♉	1	♐

Block 3 — 1945–1960

Mo	1945		1946		1947		1948		1949		1950		1951		1952		1953		1954		1955		1956		1957		1958		1959		1960	
1	1 6	♐♑	1	♋	1 26	♑♒	1	♏	1 5	♑♒	1	♎	1 23	♒♓	1 21	♎♏	1	♓	1	♏	1 16	♓♈	1 15	♐	1 29	♐♉	1	♐	1	♉	1 15	♐♑
2	1 15	♑♒	1	♋	1	♒	1 13	♏	1 12	♒♓	1	♎	1	♒	1	♏	1 9	♓♈	1 10	♏	1 27	♈	1 29	♐♈	1	♉	1 4	♐	1 11	♉♊	1 24	♑♒
3	1 26	♒♓	1	♋	1 5	♒♓	1	♏	1 22	♓♈	1 29	♎♏	1 2	♓♈	1	♏	1 21	♈♉	1	♐	1	♈	1	♐♈	1 18	♉♊	1 18	♑♒	1	♊	1	♒
4	1	♓	1 23	♓♈	1 12	♓♈	1	♏	1 30	♈♉	1	♏	1 11	♈♉	1	♏	1 13	♉♊	1 11	♐	1 15	♈♉	1	♓	1 28	♊♋	1 11	♒♓	1	♊	1 3	♒♓
5	1 3	♓♈	1	♈	1 22	♈♉	1 19	♏♎	1	♈	1 3	♏	1 22	♉♊	1	♏	1	♊	1	♑	1 27	♉♊	1 5	♓♈	1	♋	1	♒♓	1	♊	1 12	♓♈
6	1 12	♈♉	1 21	♈♉	1	♉	1	♏	1 11	♉♊	1	♎	1	♊	1	♏	1 15	♊♋	1	♑	1 4	♊♋	1 23	♈♈	1 8	♋	1	♒♓	1 21	♊♋	1	♈♉
7	1 24	♉♊	1	♏	1	♉	1 18	♏♎	1 24	♊♋	1	♎	1 4	♊♋	1	♏	1 30	♋♋	1	♑	1 12	♋♌	1	♈	1	♋	1 22	♈♉	1 21	♋♏	1	♉
8	1	♊	1 10	♏♎	1 14	♉♊	1	♏	1	♋	1 11	♎♏	1 18	♋♌	1 28	♏	1	♋	1 25	♑♒	1 28	♌♏	1 9	♈♉	1	♋	1	♈	1	♏	1 3	♉♊
9	1 8	♊♋	1 25	♎♏	1	♊	1 4	♏♐	1 8	♋♋	1 26	♏♐	1	♋	1 5	♏♏	1 15	♋♑	1	♑	1	♌	1 25	♉♊	1 21	♋♋	1 22	♈♉	1 6	♏♐	1 22	♊♋
10	1	♋	1	♏	1 2	♋♌	1 18	♏♐	1 27	♋♌	1	♏♐	1 5	♋♌	1	♏♐	1	♑	1 22	♑♒	1	♌	1	♉	1	♊	1 22	♉	1	♏♐	1	♋
11	1 12	♋♌	1 7	♏♐	1	♌	1 27	♐♑	1	♌	1 6	♌♏	1 25	♌♏	1 22	♐♑	1 2	♑♒	1	♒	1 30	♏	1	♉	1 9	♊♋	1	♏♐	1	♉♊	1	♋
12	1 27	♋♌	1 18	♏♐	1	♌	1	♐♑	1 27	♎♏	1 16	♏♐	1	♌	1 31	♐♑	1 21	♒♏	1 4	♏	1 7	♏♐	1	♉	1 24	♊♋	1	♏	1 4	♊♋	1	♋

Where's Your Uranus?

The first of the three modern planets, Uranus, was discovered in 1781 by William Herschel. During the period covered in the planetary tables in this book, Uranus has travelled through seven signs of the Zodiac. It is so far from the Sun that it takes eighty-four years to make a complete journey through all the signs of the Zodiac.

Uranus is associated with dynamic attraction; its position can add an important dimension to your knowledge and understanding in love relationships. If, for example, your Uranus falls in the same sign as your partner's Venus, love at first sight would not be unusual. But should your partner's Mars fall in the opposite sign to your Uranus, both of you must take care that tension does not mar your liaison. And if your partner's Uranus shares your rising sign or Sun sign, life will be extremely lively and dynamic. When Uranus is in the same sign as your partner's Sun sign, ascendant, Venus or Mars, or their opposites across the Zodiac, the affair may be a fleeting one.

Unless there is a considerable difference in age between you and your partner, Uranus will probably be in the same sign for both of you. As a result, its influence will be general; it will only have a personal effect if Aquarius is a rising sign or a Sun sign for either of you.

Uranus in Aquarius

Uranus is at its strongest in Aquarius. Those born with the planet in this sign will have an independent streak, an enthusiasm for science and an ingenuous and original approach to life. They have considerable power to attract others.

Uranus in Pisces

Uranus in Pisces can add idealism to originality, as well as a touch of vision and pure romanticism. If Pisces is the Sun sign or rising sign, there may be a conflict between the emotions and the Uranian rationality. Uranus was in Pisces during most of the 1920s.

Uranus in Aries

Those individuals who have Uranus in Aries are known for their originality, dynamism and tendency to act quickly. There is a romantic streak associated with Uranus, but it is somewhat submerged in Aries; its influence will be directed towards a lively sexuality.

Uranus in Taurus

The smouldering intensity of Taurus will probably not blend well with the sudden, unexpected outbursts of Uranus. Stubbornness, passion and a tendency to suppress new ideas or originality will be common to the particular generation most strongly affected by this placing.

Uranus in Gemini

Uranus is well placed in this sign. Originality will enhance the Gemini's intellectual characteristics, and if the planet is joined by Venus in Gemini or in its opposite sign, Sagittarius, there will be a strong element of friendship in most relationships.

Uranus in Cancer

A tendency to eccentricity is sometimes shown by those with Uranus in this sign; this possibility is greatly increased if Cancer is the rising sign or Sun sign. Moreover, they are likely to change their minds often. Its influence on a generation manifests itself in unpredictability and indecision about objectives.

Uranus in Leo

In theory, Uranus should be poorly placed in Leo—the sign of its detriment—but the creativity and fiery enthusiasm of Leo is not unsympathetic to the originality of Uranus. Uranus is chilly, however, and Leo is warm, so there is bound to be a certain amount of conflict.

Uranus Chart *

	Mar 31–Nov 4	♈	1936–1940	♉	1949
	Nov 5–Dec 31	♓			Jan 1–Jun 9 ♊
1913–1918 ♒			1941		Jun 10–Dec 31 ♋
	1928		Jan 1–Aug 6 ♉		
1919	Jan 1–Jan 12	♓	Aug 7–Oct 4 ♊		1950–1954 ♋
Jan 1–Mar 31 ♒	Jan 13–Dec 31	♈	Oct 5–Dec 31 ♉		
Apr 1–Aug 16 ♓					1955
Aug 17–Dec 31 ♒	1929–1933	♈	1942		Jan 1–Aug 23 ♋
			Jan 1–May 14 ♉		Aug 24–Dec 31 ♌
1920	1934		May 15–Dec 31 ♊		
Jan 1–Jan 21 ♒	Jan 1–Jun 5	♈			1956
Jan 22–Dec 31 ♓	Jun 6–Oct 9	♉	1943–1947 ♊		Jan 1–Jan 27 ♌
	Oct 10–Dec 31	♈			Jan 28–Jun 9 ♋
1921–1926 ♓			1948		Jun 10–Dec 31 ♌
	1935		Jan 1–Aug 29 ♊		
1927	Jan 1–Mar 27	♈	Aug 30–Nov 12 ♋		1957–1960 ♌
Jan 1–Mar 30 ♓	Mar 28–Dec 31	♉	Nov 13–Dec 31 ♊		

*Uranus moves occasionally in retrograde (backwards). This accounts for the periodic shifting back and forth between signs.

Where's Your Neptune?

The French astronomer Le Verrier discovered the planet Neptune in 1846. It stays in one sign for about fourteen years, and its influence is usually on generations rather than on individuals. Since Neptune rules Pisces, however, it will have a strong effect on those who have Pisces as a Sun sign or rising sign. Neptune is associated with sentimentality, idealism and romance. The Piscean-born often tend towards escapism or the line of least resistance when faced with problems. At its worst, this planet prompts deception; at its best it fosters spiritual power, enlightenment and creative work.

Unless there is a great age difference between you and your partner, or you were both born at a time when Neptune was changing signs, you will have this planet in the same sign. Undoubtedly, you will have a similar attitude towards love. Should your Neptune fall in the same sign as your partner's Venus, your love life should be a happy one—as long as you are not too easily carried away by your emotions. The relationship could have its pitfalls if Mars falls in the opposite sign to Neptune for either you or your loved one.

Neptune in Cancer

Neptune was in Cancer from 1902 until 1915. Its influence on that generation emerged in the disruption and uncertainty many of them felt as children when their fathers were fighting in the First World War, and later when they themselves were caught up in the confusion and misery of the Second World War. Those with Neptune in Cancer in their birth charts have a romantic attitude, a gentleness and genuine shyness in their approach to love and a tenderness in its expression. The accent is on pure love.

Neptune in Leo

Neptune is exalted in Leo; it travelled through this sign between 1915 and 1929. The generation influence relates to the full development of the motion picture industry and its attendant glamour. Those with Neptune in Leo often have creative flair, which they can be relied upon to develop fully. They are extremely romantic and express their love in a grand and passionate manner. Those with Leo as their rising sign or Sun sign are less likely to be domineering than most other individuals born under the sign of the Lion.

Neptune in Virgo

Neptune was in Virgo from 1928/9 until 1942/3. It seems that this was the first generation to doubt accepted standards, especially those related to religion. Neptune in Virgo is in its detriment—in the sign opposite the sign it rules—and the more romantic side of life is sceptically treated. There may be a clinical attitude towards sex. Critical acumen and rationality dominate over escapism. Virgoans with Neptune in their signs are often blessed with excellent, vivid imaginations.

Neptune in Libra

Neptune was in Libra between 1942/3 and 1956/7. The flower children and the hippy generation, attracted to a less energetic and a less materialistic way of life, were born under this placing. Romanticism, love, affection and partnership are emphasized as well as escapism through drugs. Librans with Neptune in this sign must make a concentrated effort to use their energy positively. The position of Mars and the Sun will be important in this respect.

Neptune in Scorpio

Neptune was in Scorpio from 1956/7 until 1970/1. This placing is a deeply passionate and intense one, but it is too soon to predict how people born during this time will use their powerful emotional forces. They will definitely have a special feeling for matters of world importance. Hopefully, they will be able to channel it in a positive direction, but they need to be on the defensive so that the negative side of the planet does not dominate, particularly when it is in a powerfully explosive sign such as Scorpio.

Neptune Chart *

Year	Sign	Year	Sign	Year	Sign	Year	Sign
		Jan 1–Mar 19	♌	1930–1941	♍	Jan 1–Dec 23	♎
		Mar 20–May 2	♋			Dec 24–Dec 31	♏
1913	♋	May 3–Dec 31	♌	1942			
				Jan 1–Oct 2	♍	1956	
1914		1917–1927	♌	Oct 3–Dec 31	♎	Jan 1–Mar 11	♏
Jan 1–Sept 22	♋					Mar 12–Oct 18	♎
Sept 23–Dec 14	♌	1928		1943		Oct 19–Dec 31	♏
Dec 15–Dec 31	♋	Jan 1–Sept 20	♌	Jan 1–Apr 17	♎		
		Sept 21–Dec 31	♍	Apr 18–Aug 1	♍	1957	
1915				Aug 2–Dec 31	♎	Jan 1–Jun 16	♏
Jan 1–Jul 18	♋	1929				Jun 17–Aug 4	♎
Jul 19–Dec 31	♌	Jan 1–Feb 19	♍	1944–1954	♎	Aug 5–Dec 31	♏
		Feb 20–Jul 23	♌				
1916		Jul 24–Dec 31	♍	1955		1958–1960	♏

*Neptune, like Uranus, moves in retrograde occasionally.

Acknowledgements

The Compleat Astrologer's **Love Signs** features work by the following artists and photographers: Wayne Anderson, Michael Busselle, Michael Embden, Ian Garrard, John Garrett, John Hedgecoe, Michael Holford, Elizabeth Klein, Ann Meisel, Aean Pinheiro, Josephine Rankin.

Other illustrations are reproduced by courtesy of: City of Manchester Art Galleries; Editions Graphique Ltd; Galerie F. Welz, Vienna; Guildhall Art Gallery, City of London; Mansell Collection; Österreichische Galerie, Vienna; The Prado; The Science Museum, London, Crown Copyright; S.P.A.D.E.M., Paris, 1974; The Tate Gallery, London; Trustees of the National Gallery, London; Trustees of the Wallace Collection, London.

Special thanks to John Filbey, DF Astrol S, who did the computations and research necessary to devise the unique and comprehensive ascendancy charts which are published for the first time in this book.

Typesetting: Trade Spools Ltd., Frome, England
                Colebrook Mono Services, London, England